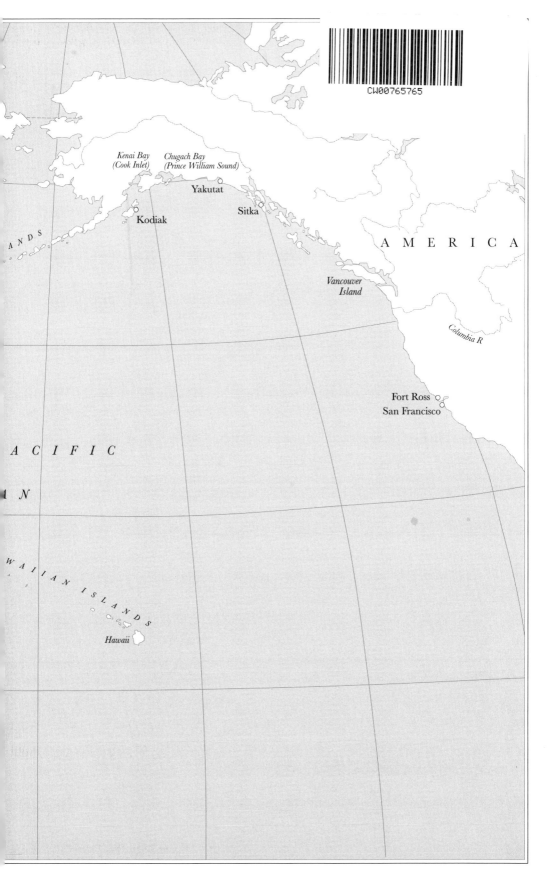

Kenai Bay
(Cook Inlet)

Chugach Bay
(Prince William Sound)

Yakutat

Sitka

Kodiak

ANDS

A M E R I C A

Vancouver
Island

Columbia R

Fort Ross
San Francisco

A C I F I C

N

W A I I A N   I S L A N D S

Hawaii

The Great Land

The Great Land

How Western America Nearly
Became a Russian Possession

Jeremy Atiyah

Pp

PARKER PRESS

OXFORD AND PORTLAND, OREGON, 2008

PUBLISHED BY PARKER PRESS

Parker Press is an Imprint of Hart Publishing dedicated to publishing
works of general interest in history, politics and current affairs.

Published in North America (US and Canada) by
Parker Press, c/o International Specialized Book Services
920 NE 58th Avenue, Suite 300
Portland, OR 97213-3786, USA
Tel: +1 503 287 3093 or toll-free: (1) 800 944 6190, Fax: +1 503 280 8832
E-mail: orders@isbs.com, Website: www.isbs.com

Published by Parker Press, an imprint of Hart Publishing,
16C Worcester Place, Oxford, OX1 2JW
Telephone: +44 (0)1865 517530 Fax: +44 (0)1865 510710
E-mail: mail@hartpub.co.uk
Website: http://www.hartpub.co.uk

British Library Cataloguing in Publication Data
Data Available

ISBN: 978-0-9558327-0-3

Typeset by Hope Services, Abingdon
Printed and bound in Great Britain by
TJ International Ltd, Padstow, Cornwall

FOREWORD

Jeremy Atiyah was an Oxford educated writer, fascinated by travel, especially to unusual and exotic places, who wrote many articles for newspapers and journals about his travels. He was mostly self-employed but spent a few years as Travel Editor of the *Independent on Sunday*. He was also an excellent linguist and learned to speak Italian, Russian, Chinese, Spanish and German, in each case with little if any formal instruction. He visited the Soviet Union several times, first in 1990 shortly after the Gorbachov reforms began, and was able to meet and talk privately with many ordinary Russians. He returned to Russia for many further visits after the break up of the Soviet Union and the collapse of communism. His imagination was fired when he discovered that in the depths of the winter it was in theory possible to walk across the frozen Bering Strait, the narrow strip of water separating the Western tip of Alaska from the most eastern part of Siberia. He hoped to undertake this walk, but was baulked by bureaucratic rather than physical obstacles. He did, however, visit many of the places referred to in his book, including Alaska and even Siberia, where he spent several winter weeks in Irkutsk in early 2001. His interest in the geographical connection between Siberia and Alaska dated from these visits and led to his researches into the history of that connection.

The Great Land was the product of that research. It was drawn from surviving correspondence from the archives of the Russian-American Company, as well as from contemporary journals, biographies and histories, published by the many witnesses and protagonists. The author intended this book for the general reader and not just for the world of scholarship, so he did not give individual footnote references to his sources, but the notes he took while doing his research, most of which are still extant on his computer, show that the many passages excerpted from the original sources are indeed authentic and accurate. He also compiled the bibliography which is published at the end of the book.

The author died suddenly in 2006 at the age of 43 before his book could be published. It has therefore fallen to me, his father, to edit the text for publication, and to verify, by reference to his notes, at least some of the quotations and references in the book. It was also necessary to flesh out a few incomplete passages in the last chapter by using his notes and other pieces he had written, such as a synopsis he had prepared to attract the interest of publishers. But these passages do not in total amount to more than a few hundred words, so this book is overwhelmingly the work of Jeremy Atiyah.

Professor Patrick Atiyah

But the very ice, which seems so awesome and so terrible,
Will offer us a path free of those fierce dangers . . .
Our dominion shall stretch into America.
Mikhail V Lomonosov, poet and scientist, St Petersburg, mid 1700s

They all drink an astonishing quantity, Governor Baranov not
excepted. I assure you it is no small tax on the health of a person trying
to do business with him.
Captain John Ebbets, fur trader from Boston, early 1800s

. . . with the advantages which so great a line of coast presents,
it would be in the power of Russia not only to open new sources of
commerce in that region of the world, but command a complete
monopoly of the commerce of those seas.
The Morning Chronicle, London, 1817

CONTENTS

PREFACE

For more than a hundred years after Europeans had begun populating the Atlantic shores of North America, the Pacific coast of that continent remained a blank on their maps and in their minds. When Russians from Siberia first sighted the mountains of Alaska in 1741, they called it the Great Land. In fact they were glimpsing part of a 4000-mile stretch of virgin coastline, reaching from western Alaska to Oregon to Southern California. As far as Spanish Mexico, all was uncharted and unknown. Its water, its salmon, its sea otters, its sunshine, its trees and its harbours remained the preserve of Native Americans, and were entirely free of international commerce.

But time was not standing still. In the second half of the eighteenth century, Europeans were aggressively taking their way of life to every corner of the globe. Northwest America could not remain exempt from this process. Who would be the first to settle the coast that was destined to become the cultural and economic powerhouse of the world? The answer to this question was not obvious. This book is the story of how western America very nearly came to be a possession of the Empire of Russia.

CHAPTER ONE

THE SALE OF ALASKA

Had Russian America always been Doomed
to End in this Way?

New Archangel in 1867 was not a hopeful town. It was usually raining. A line of wooden houses linked by planked sidewalks, straggled amid bracken on a dank shore above the ocean. The whole town clung to its harbour, under the backdrop of dark, menacing mountains that crowded around, bristling with thin black trees up to the snowline. And mountains were not the only threat: a stockade separated the main European population from an adjoining village of Tlingit Native Americans, upon which batteries of cannon were trained. On either side, the monochrome, gravel beach stretched away, strewn with boulders and trunks of driftwood.

This was one of North America's remotest towns. It belonged neither to Britain's Canadian territories, nor to the United States, but to the Empire of Russia. It lay so far up the sodden, dripping northwest coast of the continent that very few foreign travellers had ever been there. An American meteorologist, Henry M Bannister, surveying the area two years earlier, had complained of the 'detestable' climate, 'raining about all of the time'. Others had described the town's scant facilities as including a shipyard, a warehouse (stocked with furs and liquor) and a few places of prayer: the Orthodox cathedral, a church for Native Americans and a Lutheran chapel. Apart from a hospital and a handful of schools, that was it. There were no streetlights. On the long, wet winter nights men crept about with lanterns.

'The Greek church [is] the only building in the town having any claim to architectural beauty', wrote a haughty correspondent from New England, sent here in October 1867. Otherwise he was not impressed. 'A stream of moderate size flows through the town, on which is a sawmill', he noted disdainfully, 'yet there is less use of boards here than in any other civilised town I have visited'. In fact he saw only one street to speak of, which, in his words, had been 'for many years the fashionable promenade of both the aristocracy and the plebeians of New Archangel'.

And on a high rocky point overlooking all, squatted the yellow, two-floor house of the chief administrator of the Russian-American Company—that is to say, of the governor of Russia's colonies in the New World. In years still to come, the house would be nicknamed 'Baranov's castle', in honour of the melancholy, hard-drinking old man who had first settled this place in 1799. Readers of Washington Irving knew him as the 'hyperborean veteran . . . ensconced in a fort which crested the top of a high rock promontory'. The current structure was a replacement of his original house. But that crag beside the port was the very spot from which

Alexander Andreevich Baranov, half a century before, had so nearly claimed the whole of the American Pacific as a permanent possession for the tsars of Russia.

In fact, the territory governed by the current incumbent of that house was still vast, exceeding half a million square miles in extent. This was equivalent to a fifth of the land area of the whole of the United States. But in the context of expectations, it was a trifle. The Russian-American Company (the RAC) had once aimed to rule the Pacific and to seize half the trade and wealth of the world for St Petersburg. It had been established to make Russia the world's richest state. Oregon, California and Hawaii were to have counted among its outposts. Now that could never be. The fertile and gold-rich coasts to the south were already long gone, lost to the United States. And this—Russia's remaining American territory—was an empty wilderness, considered so valueless that it was about to be sold off, also to the United States. Of New Archangel's meagre population of 2500, just 400 were Russian.

What had gone wrong with Russian America in the fifty years since Baranov's departure? Nowadays it was almost impossible to conceive of the hardships that the grumpy old governor had endured on this hostile coast, running the Company for the best part of three decades. But where he had started out as a mere manager, he had ended up as a colonial ruler whose influence stretched from Siberia to Mexico. With little effective support he had endured shipwrecks, drunken employees, battles, frostbite, starvation and scurvy. In the words of the future Admiral AJ Kruzenshtern, writing in 1814, Baranov had made himself the 'boundless despot' over a country extending through sixty degrees of longitude. For the young *bon viveur*, GI Davydov, it had been the same. 'The fame of the name of Baranov resounds amongst all the savage peoples who live on the northwest coast of America', he had observed, 'even as far as the Strait of San Juan de Fuca'. The fact was, that where his successors would be navy stalwarts and aristocrats, Baranov had been a common manager, ruling by force of personality. And thanks to Baranov's work, back then, men in St Petersburg had been allowed to dream that the American Pacific could belong to Russia.

No longer. Now the chief manager's residence at New Archangel was no place for expansionist dreams of any kind. It had become a place of retreat. Like the town itself it too was surrounded by a wooden wall and guarded by cannon in case of native attack. And for the past three years, it had been the home of Baranov's latest and last successor, Prince Dmitrii

Petrovich Maksutov, an aristocrat marooned on a savage coast, in the twilight years of empire. To Maksutov and his wife, the fragrant Princess Maria, still only twenty-two years old, had fallen the unhappy job of presiding over the final act in the surrender of Imperial Russia's ambitions on this continent: the handover of New Archangel to the sovereignty of the United States of America.

Appearances were still being kept up. The governor's residence contained a ballroom, of sorts, and salons for musical and theatrical performances. The princess, 'greatly beloved by all who have the pleasure of her acquaintance', was spoken of as the loveliest hostess within a two-thousand-mile radius (not that this was saying much).

And travellers had long been commenting with surprise on the quality of 'society' at New Archangel. 'On Sunday', later recalled Sir Edward Belcher, the English navigator who had stopped there some years before, 'all the officers, civil and military, dine at the governor's'. By his account, this had permitted him to mingle with the 'female society' who, 'although self-taught, acquitted themselves with all the ease and elegance communicated by European instruction'. Sir George Simpson, governor-in-chief of the Hudson Bay Company, was another visitor who referred to eating good dinners at New Archangel 'in the French style'. And John Sutter, too, the man whose purchase had eventually put an end to Russian possessions in California, had enjoyed 'a pleasant month with the Russians' there, where he 'had the honour of dancing with the wife of the governor'.

But life for the residents had strict limits in New Archangel. Furs and shipping was the sum of it. And fur yields were paltry compared with what had been expected fifty years earlier. Sea otters were virtually extinct. And only very recently had the annual harvest of seal furs on the Pribilof Islands slightly risen again, due to new conservation measures. The cultural isolation, too, was formidable. The round-trip from St Petersburg by ship took one year, and the arrival of incoming vessels was anticipated not for letters or newspapers (which were never less than four months old), but for the replenishment of vodka and wine.

The Russian-American Company in the 1860s was better equipped than in years past, but had never managed to match the expectations set by men like Baranov. New Archangel had signally failed to become a Bombay or a Boston. Prince Maksutov could boast three large sailing ships, three barks, two brigs, one schooner, two screw steamers and two small harbour vessels; furs were still being taken to China and tea was still being shipped from there to St Petersburg; sometimes, too, ice or skins were traded in San Francisco. But everything now ran on government subsidies. Business was meagre.

In the context of Russia's status as a world power, in fact, New Archangel might have been described as a disgrace. The population of European Russia, at around 70 million, was still over double that of the United States. And yet while millions of dollars worth of gold and wool were now pouring out of America's Californian ports each year, the cold dead hand of St Petersburg had effectively smothered its last imperial possession on this continent. It did not seem to care a cent for the fabulous mineral resources that were one day destined to make Alaska rich. Nor did the calibre of workmen in the Russian colonies stand up to scrutiny, at least not in the view of visitors. These were no longer hard-headed pioneers like Alexander Baranov, risking all, to establish better lives in the New World. One American working on the Overland Telegraph in the 1860s, had written of the Russians in Alaska that they were 'nearly all convicts, transported from Siberia, and excessively indolent, great liars, cheats and in every way unreliable'. A travelling scientist, William H Dall, had said that the workmen of the Russian-American Company were convicts from Siberia, and 'men convicted of such crimes as theft, incorrigible drunkenness, burglary and even manslaughter'. He described the average Russian as being iron-willed, honourable and generous, not the type to bear a grudge 'for a black eye received in a drunken brawl'; but nevertheless 'a good deal of a brute'.

Even allowing for American prejudice in such reports, it seems no wonder that Baranov's hopes of controlling the whole of the west of America, from the Bering Strait, to California, to Hawaii, had long since vanished. The Russian state had not been an inspiring influence. The 'manifest destiny' of the United States of America to occupy the entire continent was working its inexorable course. And now even Alaska, Russia's last bastion in the New World, was to be abandoned, sold off for a contemptible dollar-sum. The date on which the Americans were due to take delivery of their new territory, with all due ceremony, was 18 October 1867.

Unlike in Russia, where the decision to *sell* Alaska had been closed after a cosy chat between the tsar and his brother the Grand Duke Constantine, the decision to *buy* Alaska would be argued over by Americans everywhere—long after the whole matter had been agreed by the respective governments.

Were the United States being conned by the administration of the hated President Andrew Johnson (who would shortly be facing impeachment) into wasting $7,200,000 on a lump of rock and ice, 'fit only for Eskimos'? Or were they, as the *New York World* declared on 1 April 1867, simply taking 'an advancing step in that manifest destiny' which was yet to grant them possession of the whole of the North American continent?

The hard-bitten secretary of state of the day, William H Seward, had wasted no time in negotiating the purchase with the Russian Ambassador to Washington, Eduard de Stockl. It had taken them just two weeks to agree a price and the main points of the deal. The tsar had then cabled his approval. But this had still only been the beginning: ratification in both Houses of Congress was now required.

Using his inimitable style to ram the purchase through Congress, Seward began wining and dining everyone in sight. With his 'beaked nose; shaggy eyebrows, unorderly hair and clothes; hoarse voice; offhand manner; free talk and perpetual cigar' (in the words of one contemporary observer), the secretary of state was an arrogant and perhaps brilliant man. But only after many a quip on the subject of 'Seward's ice-box' and 'Johnson's polar-bear garden' did senators begin to warm to his proposed purchase of Alaska.

There was much talk from Seward, no doubt, of the highly satisfactory consequences of previous enlargements: the 1803 Louisiana Purchase, for example, and the 1848 acquisition of California. He got so busy at one stage that his dinner table, according to one newspaper, was 'spread regularly with roast treaty, boiled treaty, treaty in bottles, treaty in decanters, treaty garnished with appointments to office, treaty in statistics, treaty in a military point of view, treaty in a territorial grandeur view, treaty clad in furs, ornamented with walrus teeth, fringed with timber and flopping with fish . . .'.

But it was the entirely serious three-hour speech from Charles Sumner, the Massachusetts senator and chairman of the Committee on Foreign Relations, in the Senate on 9 April , which seems to have swung the issue decisively. Sumner it was who first called the whole territory 'Alaska', appropriating the name from the native word meaning 'mainland'. In his speech he described the awesome physical environment of the region not as a burden, but as a wonder:

> . . . here are upwards of four thousand statute miles of coast, indented by capacious bays and commodious harbours without number, embracing the peninsula of Alaska, one of the most remarkable in the world, fifty miles in

breadth and three hundred miles in length; piled with mountains, many volcanic and some still smoking; penetrated by navigable rivers, one of which is among the largest in the world; studded with islands which stand like sentinels on the coast, and flanked by that narrow Aleutian range which, starting from Alaska stretches far away to Japan, as if America were extending a friendly hand to Asia.

Sumner went to on to cite an alleged British threat to seize Alaska, and to add it to her Canadian territories, if the United States did not take up the Russian offer quickly. He scoffed at a 'colonial ejaculation' recently published in a British newspaper of Vancouver Island, in which it had been stated that America 'must be' British. But most powerfully, Sumner evoked the traditional American distaste for kings. The British, the French and the Spanish he declared, had already been seen off. And by this treaty Americans would 'dismiss one more monarch from the continent'.

It may have been the clinching argument. The Senate ratified the treaty to buy Alaska for $7,200,000 that same day. The margin was 37 votes to 2. From one moment to the next, the territory of the United States of America had been extended to the Arctic and almost to the borders of Russia.

The world, briefly, was surprised, and in some parts furious. In British Columbia, Canadians were wondering why Alaska had not been purchased on *their* behalf instead. One newspaper referred to the 'imbecility, ignorance and neglect of British statesmen' which had 'allowed a glorious opportunity to pass unimproved', thus leaving the colony of British Columbia 'scarcely room left in which to draw a long breath'.

Not that this Senate vote was the end of the matter. The treaty still had a formidable obstacle to overcome: the question of the so-called 'appropriation of the funds'. It is possible that the autocratic Tsar Alexander II, far away in St Petersburg, never thoroughly understood what this meant. But while the Senate had agreed to acquire Alaska, the question of whether actually to *pay* for it remained in the hands of a sceptical House of Representatives—and might remain there for months to come. There was a simple reason for this. Many Americans were already furious at the notion of paying a single penny for the territory. From their point of view— contrary to common supposition—$7,200,000 was not such a trifling sum at the time. Could the federal government, in the immediate aftermath of a catastrophic civil war, afford it? At the same time as being asked to pay millions of dollars for Alaska, the House was fretting over sums as small as a few *thousand* dollars for important matters like the removal of obstructions to the navigation of the waters of the Mississippi and Ohio. The *New York Daily Tribune*, a couple of days after ratification of the treaty, remarked that 'we simply obtain by the treaty the nominal possession of impassable deserts of snow, vast tracts of dwarf timbers, frozen rivers, inaccessible mountain ranges . . .'. A year later the same paper had not dropped the issue: 'Taxes! Taxes! Taxes! Even more and heavier taxes! That is our part in the great acquisition'.

This question of payment, to the acute distress of the sensitive Russian Ambassador, Eduard de Stoeckl, would drag on long after the Russians had eventually departed from American soil. The treaty would not be submitted to the House of Representatives until 6 July 1867, and was not passed until May 1868, eight months after the territory had been handed over. By then, an increasingly panicky de Stoeckl had handed out as much as $200,000 on bribes for congressmen and lobbyists. Thus did Russia end up *paying* Americans to take Alaska off its hands.

In the meantime, tidings of the treaty seem to have reached last, those who they concerned most: the Russian residents of New Archangel. For Prince Maksutov and his wife, it must have been an unpleasant shock indeed. The governor would soon be out of a job. It had already been agreed that the transfer of sovereignty would take place on the joint arrival of commissioners from the two countries, with a number of US troops, at New Archangel—the town that would thenceforth be known as 'Sitka'.

So the countdown to the handover began. Meanwhile, the prince found himself in the disagreeable situation of having to close down Company affairs, terminate the contracts of employees and sell off stock. This was no small matter: his warehouses alone contained 80,000 seal furs and 30,000 gallons of liquor.

The first signs of visible change in New Archangel came slowly, over the summer. A trickle of newcomers started to affect the life of the town. In June, a British Columbia fur merchant named Leopold Boscowitz happened to ask Maksutov if any of the Company furs were for sale—only to be told that he could buy every single fur in the Company warehouse at the knockdown price of just forty cents each. Speculators, squatters, promoters, businessmen and plain crooks were soon on their way, in commercial vessels from the United States, to erect stores, to scout for minerals, to stake out city lots and to buy Company goods. A restaurant, two tenpin alleys and a row of saloons were soon under construction. And by the end of the summer, US navy vessels had begun joining them.

But not until 10 October, with the darkness and dampness of winter already in the air, did a chartered steamer finally chug into the harbour bringing one Brigadier General Jefferson Davis and two whole companies of US troops—far more than could conveniently be housed in New Archangel. Also on board that day was WS Dodge, set to become the first US customs officer in American Alaska. This opportunistic individual would turn out to be no friend to Prince Maksutov.

The last days of Russian rule had arrived. The US army men, one assumes, were itching to get ashore. But for a while longer, out of respect for protocol, they would find themselves obliged to wait in the rain-swept harbour, cooped up aboard ship. Not until the designated representatives of the two governments had arrived would it be politic for them to land. In fact they only had a week to wait, because on 18 October, from over the horizon, there appeared another steam ship, the USS *Ossippee*. On board was Brigadier General Lovell Rousseau, representing the government of the United States of America, Captain AA Peschurov representing the Tsar of Russia, and Captain FF Koskul, representing the Russian-American Company.

Nothing could stop the handover now. Instructions as to protocol, from Seward, were in General Rousseau's pocket. 'On arriving at Sitka, the principal town in the ceded territory', Seward had written, 'you will receive from the Russian Commissioner the formal transfer of that territory under mutual national salutes from artillery in which the United States will take the lead . . .'.

Problems were only likely to arise when it came to the small print. Seward's instructions went on to specify that the transfer would 'include all forts and military posts and public buildings such as the governor's house and those used for government purposes; dockyards, barracks, hospitals and schools; all public lands and all ungranted lots of ground at Sitka and Kodiak'. To be carefully distinguished from the above were all 'private dwellings and warehouses, blacksmiths, joiners, coopers, tanners, and other similar shops, ice houses, flour and saw mills . . . [which were] subject to the control of their owners and not to be included in the transfer to the United States'.

A last-minute exchange of letters between a brash Seward and a timorous de Stoeckl, immediately prior to the handover, betrays a collective rise in blood pressure. Seward urgently wanted information on how to accommodate American troops, given that the season would be 'too far advanced' to build homes for them this year. De Stoeckl anxiously pointed out the Russians had never seen the need to deploy large numbers of troops at New Archangel. 'The number of men we maintained there never exceeded two hundred, and latterly there were at Sitka only eighty men', he wrote, before conceding that the barracks would 'conveniently hold from a hundred to a hundred-and-twenty men'—if the Americans insisted on sending so many.

Provisions for the American troops, de Stoeckl then hinted, might be another problem. 'In the Sitka market, may be found fresh fish and wild goat meat in small quantity', he told Seward, somewhat dubiously. Otherwise, 'it would be well for the Federal Government to take measures for provisioning its troops with fresh or salt meat, coffee and other articles which are used in the United States Army . . .'. The Russian message seemed to be that they would prefer it if the Americans left their troops at home.

But it was too late now for sudden changes of plan. The transfer ceremony was to be held the very same afternoon on which the commissioners were arriving. According to General Rousseau, the weather over New Archangel that day was improbably 'bright and beautiful' despite the fact that he himself had been suffering from 'congestive chills' caught during the journey up here. It was at 3pm on the afternoon of 18 October 1867 that the Russian company, dressed in dark uniforms trimmed with red, and in flat glazed caps, assembled for the last time on the parapet in front of the governor's house. As they watched from the rise, about 250 American soldiers, in full uniform, with shining muskets, began landing in launches down below. Led by General Davis, these then marched up to the governor's house, and took up a position on the opposite side of the flagstaff from the Russians. The spectators around the hill numbered less than 300, including a bare handful of women. Of these none would have been more conspicuously glamorous than Princess Maria Maksutova, wife of the outgoing governor.

All was ready. At a signal from the bewhiskered Captain Peschurov, the Russian guard now prepared to lower their flag. And as the insignia of the Russian tsars began its descent down the pole, recalled General Rousseau later, 'the battery of the *Ossipee*, with large nine-inch guns, led off in the salute, peal after peal crashing and re-echoing in the gorges of the surrounding mountains . . .'. This was answered, in turn, by the firing of the Russian battery.

It was to be a twenty-one-gun salute, which should have left ample time to lower one flag and raise another. But now something seemed to go wrong. In front of General Rousseau's surprised eyes, 'the ceremony was interrupted, by the catching of the Russian flag in the ropes attached to the rope staff . . .'. Was old Baranov turning in his grave, in protest at the giving away of his beloved Alaska? It is hard to imagine that the watching Russian soldiers did not read some significance into the sight of the double-headed eagle, whipped round its ropes by the wind, stubbornly refusing to descend from the sky over Sitka. Nevertheless, several of them now jumped to attention and attempted shinning up the pole to grab it. But as General Rousseau later pointed out, this pole was a native pine perhaps 90 feet in height: and 'labouring hard, they soon became tired, and when half-way up scarcely moved at all, and finally came to a stand-still'. For a minute or two, hearts were in mouths. Then, 'in a moment' the matter was resolved. One more man was hauled up the pole on a rope, enabling him to cut free the flag. From the grass below, the Russian Captain Peschurov shouted up to him to 'bring it down' in a dignified manner. But not hearing the calls, the man simply dropped it. 'And in its descent' reported Rousseau, with an apparent shudder, 'it fell on the bayonets of the Russian soldiers'. At this ghastly sight (ran the rumour later), Princess Maksutova fainted clean away.

A minute later the Stars and Stripes was flying over Baranov's Castle. 'Democratic institutions now extend over an area hitherto the possession of a despotic government!' rejoiced one San Francisco correspondent. Into the silence left behind by the gun salutes, came the noise of three spontaneous cheers, from the hundred or so US citizens present—though Rousseau himself, as he recalled later, 'regretted' this display of patriotic ardour. He seems to have sensed the poignancy of the occasion. The Russians, one assumes, did not join in the cheering.

The following days, the first of American rule at Sitka, were as shabby and depressing for the Russians as could be expected. Authority had now passed from Prince Maksutov to the provisional military ruler, General Davis.

'The reputation of this place for raining, snowing and sleeting has been fully verified since our arrival', Davis was grumbling, within a week of the takeover, 'and the amount of work that can be accomplished per day in this climate is much less, probably, than in any other on the continent . . .'. In fact his discomfort should have come as no surprise. He had a lot of problems to sort out.

Disputes over property had started up almost from the very day of the handover. One of the first tasks that General Davis had undertaken had been to block off Russian access to the main warehouse of the Company. He had done it by the somewhat indelicate means of having a battery placed in the passageway, and placing sentries at either end of the building, under orders to prevent Russians from entering without permission. That had caused annoyance enough. What had caused even more distress had been his order to the Russian citizenry to give up their homes, without notice, to his soldiers. Incredibly, this was a point of controversy that had not been foreseen in advance by the assiduous de Stoeckl. The problem here was the doubtful legal status of these houses. Their occupants and their families, under Russian rule, had been entitled to stay in them for life—but, technically, had not owned them.

Those now being ordered out of their family homes in the rain immediately protested to Prince Maksutov. How could their properties be disposed of in this way? As the treaty stated, the transfer of ownership only covered 'the right of property in all public lots and squares, vacant lands, and all public buildings, fortifications, barracks, and other edifices which are not private individual property'. We have to imagine the embarrassment that the ex-governor must have felt during these first days of American rule. He was now impotent. He had also been at fault for not alerting his countrymen to the possibility that they were about to lose their homes. After reminding them, presumably, that he no longer exercised power in these parts, he was obliged to advise them to find new ones. The only 'homes' available, in fact, were rooms in ships in the harbour.

Bad feeling was soon rife. Gustave Niebaum, a long-term Russian resident in New Archangel, of Finnish birth, who had elected to take on American citizenship, reported Russians speaking very freely to him about 'the ill treatment received at the hands of the American authorities'. Captain Peschurov, too, complained that life was 'not very cheerful'. Accustomed to the niceties of life in the imperial capital St Petersburg, he was never going to feel comfortable in this rough, newly-Americanised town. But writing to de Stoeckl regarding the transfer, he had been unable to conceal his aristocratic contempt for 'Republican' forms of behaviour. 'As was anticipated', he snorted, 'the new American arrivals are behaving in a disorderly manner, particularly the soldiers, composed mostly of riff-raff. We have already had a number of brawls and thefts, and about thirty men of the comparatively small garrison are permanently under arrest . . .'.

On the subject of the forced evacuation of Russian citizens from their homes, he could only express resignation and bitterness:

> . . . such hasty clearance of the best houses caused much inconvenience to the chief administrator of the colony and to the people who were compelled to leave their homes during the rainy season here . . . nevertheless I asked Prince Maksutov to carry out this assignment as soon as possible, in order to avoid unpleasant conflicts with General Davis and his officers. Disregarding our frequent warnings that Sitka lacks available houses, the Americans sent over a great number of officials . . . to establish many separate chanceries and offices.

But the irritation of the haughty Peschurov was not solely directed towards General Davis and his military. Civil power, meanwhile, had rapidly been delegated, after a rowdy convention of the several hundred US citizens now in town: less than a month after the handover, Sitka had an elected mayor and a city charter. It was done without the help of lawyers, or indeed of law. 'Upon enquiry', one of the authors of the city charter later admitted, 'it was found that not a single copy of the Constitution of the United States, nor a single state, not a copy of any municipal charter or ordinance, not a law book, nor a statute of any kind, save one, which Murphy the tailor had—*Wharton's Criminal Practice*—was obtainable'.

Nevertheless, the new mayor was chosen, in the form of the customs officer, Mr WS Dodge, who was also given power to establish a 'mayor's court' (to be funded from what fines it could impose), and empanel juries. And despite its completely unconstitutional nature, its very first case was about to be heard. In a country with a fascinating record of courtroom drama, this must rank as one of the most improbable cases in American legal history. The defendant was a former clerk of the Russian-American Company, named Pavlov, who had rushed to take on US citizenship the moment sovereignty was transferred. Bringing the suit was none other than Prince Maksutov, former governor of the Russian colonies in the New World.

On paper, Maksutov's grievance looked valid. This Pavlov, in his duties as clerk of the Company, had been entrusted with certain pieces of property. He was now contractually required either to return them, or to submit reports on their disappearance. That he had done neither,

Maksutov could only assume was because he had embezzled them. In trying to wind up company business, it seems, the prince was ready to plead before an American jury.

But his choice of lawyer—the haughty Captain Peschurov—looked like a bad error of judgement from the start. For his own part, Pavlov had made a far more astute selection: Murphy the tailor. This honest American promptly roused the court with an impassioned lecture on the subject of Russian exploitation of the poor by the mighty, while Prince Maksutov and Captain Peschurov looked on with imperial distaste. Murphy's pleas would fall on fertile ground. This was the first American lawsuit ever heard in Alaska. The territory had only just been 'liberated' from imperialism. To the undoubted pleasure of Mr Dodge, his jury acquitted Pavlov without bothering to leave the room.

Prince Maksutov would rue the day that he had thus exposed himself to the prejudices of American law. Soon, he himself was in the dock facing various lawsuits, including demands from his own former employees that he pay for their passages back to Russia (in spite of the fact that many had already taken money *in lieu*).

But such freedoms as the right to sue their governor, it seems, were not enough to persuade most Russians to stay in the United States. Only 250 out of the 800 resident in Alaska at the time of the transfer would remain to become US citizens. Some clerks and officials had already gone within days of the handover; on 15 December 1867 the *Tsaritsa* then sailed for Russia via London, carrying 168 passengers; and a few weeks later the *Cyane* followed, direction Siberia, with 69 soldiers of the Russian garrison. More would follow.

The Maksutovs themselves, on the other hand, remained stubbornly in town. For a few more months they would even manage to maintain a semblance of social normalcy. One American later recalled the prince from these days as 'a businesslike, affable gentleman' and his wife as 'a lady of rare intelligence, speaking English with ease and singular accuracy'. In November 1867, another wrote of attending a 'very pleasant little party at the Princess' house in the evening. Fifteen *ladies* on the occasion. The entertainment was drinking and games'. Into 1868 the parties still lingered on. 'Society here is very agreeable and has really been cosmopolitan', we hear in another account. 'The weather has been remarkably pleasant, and parties numerous; indeed it has been one round of pleasure—first a party at the Prince de Maksoutoff's, then at General Davis', then at Mr Dodge's, the Collector of the Port'.

It was the last hurrah of Russian America. But it would not last for much longer. A gloom now overspread the social horizon, on the news that the Princess Maria, the elegant and accomplished wife of the former governor—'she who has been the centre of our joys and our pleasures'—was on the point of leaving. It was late in January 1868 that she boarded the USS *Resaca* with the family's five children and a nurse, sailing for Russia via San Francisco, Panama, New York and Europe.

For Prince Maksutov himself, however, the dreary task of winding up company affairs still had a year to run. Not until late December 1867 did he succeed in selling off the bulk of the trade goods, mostly in one lot. As a local newspaper reported, Maksutov sold the entire 'valuable but promiscuous stock: houses and lots; old steamboats, hulks and lighters, warehouses full of good merchandise; groceries, provisions, liquors and tobaccos; gew-gaws and jimcracks; old guns; anchors, chains, iron, copper, brass, junk and lots of other traps . . . the purchase money for all of which is about $15,000'.

Next, he was obliged to sail down to San Francisco to settle yet another law suit over non-payment for a ship that he had sold on behalf of the company. For once, the law would find in his favour. But it was during this Californian sojourn that he also found himself the target of a newspaper campaign, instigated by London furriers, angry at having lost their exclusive contracts with the Russian-American Company. Allegations began to appear of fraud, speculation and profiteering, in the winding up of the company. Prince Maksutov himself was accused of laying schemes 'to feather his nest at the expense of the Fur Company's stockholders'. Instead of disposing of company assets for the benefit of the stockholders, it was now claimed, he had done so for his own benefit, using 'a system of indiscriminate and general smuggling, selling the valuable peltry and other property of the company to any purchaser who offered'.

These were probably smears. A subsequent investigation by the House of Representatives uncovered a letter testifying that the writer of many of these attacks had fabricated them. But even so, it was a dismal end, not only to Maksutov's tenure of the governorship, but also to the whole story of Russian America. Around this same time, moreover, back in Washington, Congress was wondering whether it would deign to pay Russia for its newly acquired territories. Amid such bad news, the prince now took his final tour of duty, to pick up employees stranded by the handover, round the remote northern outposts of the company in Alaska.

On this last depressing journey, in the summer of 1868, he doubtless had time enough to reflect on the significance of the loss of Alaska as he steamed from port to port. There to the north were the rainy Pribilof Islands, with their famous seal rookeries, once destined to supply the fur needs of the world. To the west was Unalaska, stepping stone from Siberia, where Baranov had been shipwrecked on his very first visit to America, 77 years before. And here, tucked into the green southern shore of the peninsula, was Kodiak Island, site of northwest America's first European settlement, pioneered by the dauntless Grigori Ivanovich Shelikhov in 1784. On Kodiak had Baranov then first battled to build a habitable town from which the project to claim America could be launched.

It had only been one human lifetime ago. And if Maksutov, now, during this final visit to Kodiak, could have heard the arguments currently being aired in Congress regarding the purchase of these territories, his gaze might well have lingered on the dark, rich, mountains of the American mainland: 'I look forward to a time not far distant when the civilisation of the world will be transferred from the Atlantic to the Pacific Ocean!' he might have heard, booming out, from Representative Banks of Massachusetts. 'When that time comes, this purchase will enable us to occupy a geographical position which, if wisely improved, will enable us to control the commerce and the maritime affairs of that vast ocean highway . . .'.

A little later would have come the ringing, prophetic words of Representative Donelly of Minnesota: 'Beyond the present importance of this land, let its future consequence be recognised! The entire Pacific coast of the North American continent fronting Japan, China and India should belong to the nation whose capital is here, and whose destiny it is to grasp the commerce of the seas and sway the sceptre of the world . . .!'.

These sentiments, so warming to Americans, contained the seeds of Russia's worst nightmare. The truth was that St Petersburg was now abandoning its last toehold on this coast, just as its immense value was becoming obvious to the rest of the world. This would have been a bitter notion for any Russian. If Baranov had had his way, fifty years earlier, it could have been Russians, not Americans, now making speeches about grasping the commerce of the seas. It could have been a Russian destiny, not an American one, to control that fabulous Pacific trade via California and Hawaii.

But now, of course, that chance was long gone. It would not return. Six months later, on 6 January 1869, the last governor of Russia's colonies in the New World, would depart America forever, bound for the motherland. It is easy to imagine one question that would still have been bothering Prince Maksutov, as he watched the mountains of Alaska disappear into the drizzle forever.

Had Russian America *always* been doomed to end in this way?

CHAPTER TWO

Siberia was the Back Door to a Great Prize

Siberia, today, may not sound like a promising launching pad for the possible conquest of America. But in the last years of the eighteenth century, the idea was less absurd.

Alexander Andreevich Baranov did not look or sound like a man to attempt the conquest of America. He originated from the obscure Russian town of Kargopol. A friend described him as 'shorter than average, fair-haired, well-built with very prominent features, erased neither by his labours nor by his age'; but in contemporary drawings, he presents an almost comic appearance. We see him in a tatty uniform; a stocky, balding man, tired, visibly irritable, with drooping eyelids and the crotchety, pouting expression of a frog. It is a face that speaks of ill-tempered resignation to hardship; to rain; to drunken employees; to the hopelessly unrealistic demands of superiors.

'Baranov was not very talkative and seemed like a dry stick until you came to know him', was the view of the naval officer GI Davydov, who met him in 1802. 'But on the other hand he always explained matters with enthusiasm, especially when he knew his subject well . . .'. The fact is that Baranov was nothing but a trader. As a child, he had never been enrolled in any prestigious guard regiment or school for naval officers. He would play no part in the glorious victory over Napoleon, nor would Catherine the Great or any future tsar dream of inviting him to St Petersburg. In many ways he was a typical Russian who drank too much and whose business ventures could barely keep him afloat. None of this is to say that in the month of August, in the year 1790, he was not a satisfactory choice to be manager of a Siberian fur company.

His main drawback, in the eyes of the wealthy and powerful company boss, Grigori Ivanovich Shelikhov, was probably his age. Baranov was forty-five years old, two years older than Shelikhov himself. By the standards of the desperate Cossack fur-trappers who inhabited these remote parts of Siberia, he should already have been dead; and we can assume that he had got well beyond the stage of undertaking adventure for the fun of it. Indeed, the prospect of travelling by ship across the north Pacific to take up his post on America's mysterious northwest coast, was likely to have struck him as highly dangerous and unpleasant.

But this was to be expected. Life in parts of Siberia was grim enough anyway. Baranov may not have loved remote places, but his record suggested that he could certainly face them. As Shelikhov would have noted with approval, his most recent project had been to establish a trading post on a branch of the Anadyr River in Chukotka, the far northeastern corner of Siberia. There, in one of the coldest places on the planet, Baranov had attempted, in the company of his brother, to trade in walrus ivory and furs with the notoriously bellicose Chukchi people.

To live and work in so hostile an environment was to risk death every time you got out of bed. It was helpful that Baranov had got used to this: there were few riskier places to live in the 1790s than northwest America. As for the enterprise in Chukotka, it had ended in ignominy after less than two years. Chukchis had destroyed his fort, killed the employees and stolen the stores. It seems to have been this personal disaster, and the threat of imminent bankruptcy, that was now driving Baranov to accept Shelikhov's new job offer—a job that would require crossing the ocean to an unknown coast.

The Siberian Pacific port of Okhotsk was where the two men were now lodged, haggling over the contract of employment. It was a notoriously remote, squalid place, populated by drunken fur-hunters, ice-bound for half the year, chilly even in summer. But in the covetous eyes of a man like Shelikhov, Okhotsk was also the back door to a great prize. From here, by ship, the way was wide open to four thousand miles of American coastline: all virgin fur-hunting terrain. Shelikhov himself had been one of the great pioneers in exploring that coast. Six years earlier, at Three Saints Bay on Kodiak Island, off the coast of Alaska, he and his wife had established, in person, the first permanent European settlement in northwest America, for the purpose of collecting furs. Now he needed an obedient servant to run—and expand—his empire.

We know the kind of thing he was looking for, because before departing from Kodiak four years earlier, he had taken care to pen a letter, dated 4 May 1786, detailing his instructions on the running of the colony in his absence. Ostensibly, the letter had been for the benefit of the man he was leaving in charge at the time. It was also one for the public records. Shelikhov had been keen to enhance his image as a seafaring discoverer, and as a responsible and religious human being; in short, as a man fit to run a colony on behalf of the Empress of Russia.

From the contents of that letter, we can surmise the kinds of advice that Shelikhov must have been giving to Baranov right now, a mix of fantasy and self-glorification with a sprinkling of practical detail. He would have referred with pride to his colony's products (ranging from squirrel skin parkas to woollen rugs trimmed with sea otter and leather) as well as to the minerals he had 'heard about' in the region, including mica, crystal, dyes, ores and clays. Giving details of where his 163 men were to be stationed, he would then have told Baranov to 'add as many of the local pacified natives as possible, to strengthen the Russians. In this manner we move faster along the shore of the American mainland to the south toward California'.

Shelikhov then would have turned to his duties as a caring imperialist—of the eighteenth-century mould. 'Try, by giving them all possible favours, to bring into subjection to the Russian Imperial Throne the Kykhtat, Aliaksa, Kinai and Shugach people', he had written in his official instructions, adding that all native peoples had to be made to understand that the purpose of paying yasak (tribute), was to earn the protection of Her Imperial Majesty. 'You must see that the inhabitants who become subjugated do not lack food and clothing, as is apt to happen due to their laziness and negligence. . . . After they know what good housekeeping and order are, they will acquire a taste for a better life and will become ambitious and quit their licentious and willful ways. When they know a better way of living, they will understand and will take part in the work that enlightened people are doing . . .'.

As for the treatment of the local women, Shelikhov had warned against 'dissolute behaviour of any kind'. Women must be clothed and shod, and 'must not be insulted by our people, either by actions or words'. In an unexpected attack of political correctness, he had even demanded, 'native women employed by the company are not to sew or wash clothes for anybody except by your order'.

But beyond all else, there were feats of exploration that remained to be done, with the goal of expanding the Russian Empire, and bringing glory to himself. Alongside various items of wisdom on the subject of good food, cleanliness, health, ventilation and the upkeep of ships in winter, Shelikhov had left commands for the use of the two ships he was leaving behind. One was to be taken north, through the Aleutians, 'as far as the northern sea will permit'. And a second was to go south, 'in the open sea as far as 40 degrees latitude, and from there take its course toward the mainland nearly to California'. 'And when', he had asserted finally, 'to strengthen the Russians here, I send a ship or two more . . . the people from these ships should be accepted as employees of the company, and parties will be sent to pacify the Americans, to the glory of Russia, all over the above-mentioned American territories and California as far as 40 degrees'.

In light of the deep anger that was to characterise future relations between these two men, we can imagine the reaction of the bankrupt trader Baranov to such grandiose talk. He must have seen that Shelikhov was not a man to let facts come in the way of ideas. His wild assertions about colonising America as far as California must have sounded airy, at the very least, in the context of the leaky wooden shack in which they were probably sitting at the time. The travelling Englishman Martin Sauer, who had seen this town of Okhotsk in 1786, described it as being composed 'of sand, shingles and driftwood, the whole thrown up by the surf'. It contained '132 miserable wooden houses, a church and a belfry, several rotten storehouses and a double row of shops . . .'. From Okhotsk, the nearest hospital was 2200 miles away in Irkutsk, across virtually trackless territory. The point was that if Siberian Okhotsk was this bad, Alaskan Kodiak—more remote still—was likely to be worse.

There is no doubt that Shelikhov was very keen on recruiting Baranov. This was not the first time that he had offered him the job. One factor would have been the extreme shortage of good men hereabouts: Siberia was a place for exiles, criminals and misfits, not for honest workers. Baranov, with his experience in small business, had an eye for the accounts and fine details that tended to escape grander men such as Shelikhov himself. And the Kargopol trader had more on his side. Although born cautious, he was inquisitive, industrious and intrepid. He was a commoner, who had left his home town and come to Siberia to seek refuge from Russia's stifling class system. He had shown a capacity for working with indigenous peoples. Moreover, the acting commandant of Okhotsk, Ivan G Koch, seemed ready to give his official approval to the choice.

Knowing Shelikhov's talent for glossing over difficulties, we can be sure that he gave Baranov a seductive view of his colony at Three Saints Bay. When Shelikhov had left it four years earlier, it had already grown into a proper village of eight dwellings, a set of bunkhouses, a commissary, a counting house, barns, storage buildings, a smithy, a carpentry shop and a ropewalk. A dozen outlying stations had also been established. And what potential Kodiak offered! In his own self-promoting autobiography, soon to be published, Shelikhov's account of the agricultural possibilities would make reference to millet, peas, beans, pumpkins, carrots, mustard, beets, potatoes, radish and rhubarb. And as he wrote himself: 'everything grew well except for the millet'. He would also speak of the 'many meadows' ideal for hay and long grass, adding that in some places livestock could live without hay all winter. Then there was the natural abundance of the land, producing endless supplies of 'raspberries, blueberries, blackberries, cloudberries, red cowberries, cranberries and currants . . .'.

On a relatively warm August day, in the company of the visionary Shelikhov, no doubt over a vodka or two, storm-swept Kodiak might have sounded almost congenial.

And thus things were agreed. Baranov would take up the position of chief manager of Shelikhov's establishments in America, with a salary, and a right to company shares. He would be subject to orders from Shelikhov himself, and from officials of the Russian government only. Provision furthermore would be made for Baranov's wife and daughter, enabling them to be sent back to Kargopol in European Russia and cared for. The contract was signed on 15 August 1790. Just four days later, Baranov would board the galiot, the *Tri Sviatitelia* (Three Saints), and set sail for America.

But before his departure, there was one more matter to detain him. The local commandant, Ivan Koch, it seemed, also had things to say to Baranov—things pertaining not to the planting of carrots and potatoes, but to altogether more complex affairs. If Shelikhov's extravagant schemes could be dismissed as the insecure bluster of new money, the letters handed to him on the eve of his departure by a representative of Her Imperial Majesty had an altogether more serious intent.

Two of the letters were marked, 'most secret'. The first of them, as Baranov soon saw, concerned the location of 'plates' and 'Imperial Crests', to be buried in the soil of the American coast. If sailors from other nations should come by, trying to claim these lands, Koch had written, 'you may say sternly that the land, the islands, and all the trade, belong to the Russian Empire'. This was not all. 'I hope that you will do all in your power to carry out these instructions', the letter then went on, 'making it your goal to extend the boundaries of the Russian Empire east and southeast and to confirm our right of possession from former times . . .'.

And if this government-order sounded like an onerous responsibility for a man who thought he had been recruited to run a business, the second of the two secret letters must have given Baranov even more pause for thought. This told of an enemy ship, armed with fourteen cannons, captained by an Englishman and paid for by the King of Sweden, presently on its way to Russian America with the intention of 'plundering and destroying all Russian establishments'. Ominous instructions followed, on what to do in the event of being attacked while still at sea: on how to grapple with the foe at close-quarters, and how to 'vanquish' the enemy by 'superior numbers and Russian bravery'. Koch had finally added: 'I advise you to take precautions against all foreign ships, and to beware of a surprise attack . . . and have everything in readiness for an emergency'. Russia's rivals, it seemed, were reaching the Pacific at the same time as Baranov. Anxiety, if not outright fear, must been on his mind as he bade farewell to Russia and boarded the dilapidated, over-crowded *Tri Sviatitelia*, bound for America.

As yet, tiny numbers of Russians or other Europeans had ever seen those mysterious islands and harbours and valleys and rivers and mountains, stretching from the Aleutian Islands in the far northwest, down towards Spanish Mexico in the south. Russians only supposed that it was a coast populated by savages, and located (even) further from St Petersburg than the bleak and remote end of eastern Siberia.

From the *Atlantic* side, moreover, northwest America was even less accessible. The land route from the eastern side of the American continent, after all, had not yet been discovered. Lewis and Clark had not yet blazed their trail. The Rockies remained virtually unexplored. The Wild West was unimagined, the gold-panning, gun-toting, railway-building immigrants of the mid-nineteenth-century were unborn, and San Francisco's first independent settler would not raise his tent for another fifty years. The destiny of the fledgling United States to occupy the whole continent of North America was far from manifest.

Only in recent years, had travellers' reports from that remote land started reaching the outside world. They told of an unclaimed coast, thousands of miles in length, stretching from the Arctic to Spanish Mexico, blessed by '. . . an abundance of wild animals, fish, birds, fine meadows, rich soil, and the amount of forest . . . that is suitable for shipbuilding'. To those paying attention, one loud message had been coming through: that the northwestern parts of America, caressed by mild winds and ocean currents, were quite another world from the grim, frost-stricken shores of eastern Siberia. This was news of colossal significance. Even in Baranov's own lifetime, the very existence of this American coast had been scarcely known in Europe. Only forty years had passed since the respected father of Siberian studies, Gerhard-Friedrich Müller, compiling ethnographic data, had reported finding a strange man in Kamchatka, eastern Siberia. This man had told Müller that he was not a native of Siberia, but had come 'from a country to the east [across the Pacific] where there were larger cedars which bore bigger nuts than those of Kamchatka; that his country was situated to the east of Kamchatka; that there were found in it great rivers where he lived, which discharged themselves westward into the Kamchatkan sea . . .'. He was, of course, a Native American.

For years to come, in St Petersburg and Moscow, knowledge of this 'Great Land', as the Russians were calling it, had barely got beyond the level of mythology and rumour. 'There are . . . said to be people in that country who have tails like dogs, speak their own language, are often at war among themselves and are without religion . . .'. Müller had subsequently written. 'Another nation there, is said to have feet like ravens, covered with the same kind of skin as theirs. They never wear shoes or stockings . . .'.

It was fair to say that, by 1790, many uncertainties still remained about the Great Land. Not all Russians were even convinced that Asia and America were separated by ocean at all. What knowledge there was comprised largely the garbled reports of displaced natives or Cossack fur hunters, fresh from desperate journeys on leaky, self-built vessels across the north Pacific from Siberia.

Would this semi-mythical region ever be anything except a wilderness for explorers and adventurers? Would anyone ever farm California? Might thriving cities, harbours and highways someday fill that gap between Mexico and the Arctic? To judge by his urgency to settle in it, Grigori Shelikhov would have answered 'yes' to all of these questions, as would the beloved Russian poet and scholar, Mikhail Vasilyevich Lomonosov. 'Our dominion shall stretch into America!' he had thundered. But ideas regarding future Russian empires in the Pacific were rarely more than material for romantic poems. In contrast to the great *European* missions of the Empress Catherine—building a Black Sea fleet; colonising the Crimea; establishing hegemony over Constantinople—Shelikhov's colonial projects in western America would have been viewed by most as trifling and exceedingly speculative.

This is not to say that Russians did not consider that they had a legitimate claim to this coast. They did. By all accounts, Alaska lay virtually in Russia's back garden, right across the water from Siberia. Nearly five decades had now passed since the tragic destruction of the granddaddy of all Russian state-sponsored voyages to the Great Land, that of Vitus Bering. But during the course of that superhuman, if doomed, expedition, the Russian naval officer Aleksei Ilyich Chirikov had become the first white man to glimpse the Alaskan coast, and just days afterwards, on Kayak Island, in the shadow of Mount Elias, Georg-Wilhelm Stellar, Bering's frustrated naturalist, had finally won permission to step ashore. On a July day back in 1741 he had then had six hours in which to make the first scientific study of northwest America from a European perspective. He had done it in the service of the Empire of Russia.

That Alaska was Russian, then, by right of first discovery, was beyond dispute. Exactly how much of the coast was Russian remained harder to say. The most modest position was to declare that the coast north of the point spotted by Chirikov—around latitude 55°—was

Russian. Bolder men, such as Shelikhov, held that the Russian claim should extend at least as far as Spanish California. Anyway, it was accepted that the best way for Russia to claim possession of any coast, was to begin exploiting it.

In fact, reports from Russian traders in the Aleutian Islands, dotting the sea between Siberia and Alaska like a primitive necklace had, for upwards of twenty years, conveyed reassuring evidence to Catherine's court that these places were being exploited. The fashionable and respectable way to publicise one's activities in remote lands, was to submit ethnographic reports. One Fedor Afanasevich Kulkov had sent just such a report to St Petersburg as early as 1764, concerning the residents of the Attu island group. Without referring to the vile treatment meted out to these people by Russian traders (including murder and kidnapping), Kulkov had described them as healthy and happy, simple and guileless, going barefoot and wearing thin, hooded apparel 'sewn from sea-lion intestines or fish-bladders'. He spoke of the women painting their faces red, but being very 'clean and comely' as well as 'merry, frivolous and quite inclined to infinitely improprietous behaviour with the men'. They did not live in yurts or huts, but sought 'shelter in burrows and clefts in the mountains' and used 'reeds or sedge for bedding'. Not all reports were equally scientific. The Cossack Ivan Kobelev, scouting in the Bering Strait region for information on the Great Land, had—as recently as 1779—brought back sombre reports of two-faced men, including 'one in the back of the head', and 'both provided with speaking mouths, though only one was adapted to taking nourishment . . .'.

But in late eighteenth-century Russia, few could dispute such allegations. The remoteness of the northwest coast of America when Baranov first set sail for Kodiak Island cannot be over-stated. In 1790, Atlantic travellers from Europe and the United States alike faced a choice of two routes to this coast. Both were hazardous and lengthy in the extreme. One way took ships round southern Africa, across the Indian Ocean to Java, and then over the vast Pacific. The other involved doubling the Horn: the dreaded Cape Horn, the storm-buffeted and treacherous southern tip of South America. The journey down to the Horn and up the other side of America to Alaska was one of over 20,000 miles; return journeys would last a good three years, as long as projected twenty-first century missions to Mars. For sailors from Atlantic ports, the result was that northwest America lay as far as, if not further than, that strange new land of the South Seas, by the name of Australia, which the great Englishman,

Captain James Cook, had recently claimed for the kingdom of Great Britain.

By tradition, the one country able to launch ships directly into the Pacific had been Spain, from its imperial possessions in Peru and Mexico. But what Spain had had in opportunity, it seemed to lack in motive. Spanish settlers were disinclined to make the arduous journey north from Mexico, beyond the arid deserts of Baja (Lower) California. The region they referred to as Alta (Upper) California, had always been perceived as an infertile wilderness, populated only by savages. No gold-rich Aztec or Inca kingdom of the north awaited plunder there. In recent years, the Spanish had sent a couple of ships as far north as Alaska, and had relocated perhaps three hundred soldiers and missionaries to Upper California. But in the immensity of North America, so thin a sprinkling of men might as well have disappeared into the sands.

Only recently had citizens of a second country begun to launch ships straight into the north Pacific. Over the past century, they had been building their own Pacific ports on the Siberian coast of Asia. Geographically, the territory of this country lay almost within sight of America. By 1790, its fur traders had already erected the first European settlements in Alaska and its government was sending expeditions to investigate its potential. This country was Russia.

Who, at that time, could speak of the 'manifest destiny' of the United States to dominate north America? Who could yet predict the fabulous future that lay in store for the unclaimed regions of that continent? Not even conceited Grigori Shelikhov could pretend to answer these questions. But whatever mechanism had given Peru to Spain, Brazil to Portugal, and Australia to Britain, now seemed ready to bestow northwest America upon another suitable claimant. And in 1790, the strange truth was that few were in a better position to stake that claim for their country than Shelikhov's new manager, Alexander Baranov.

Siberia today may not sound like a promising launching pad for the possible conquest of America. But in the last years of the eighteenth century, the idea was less absurd. Its proximity to Alaska has already been mentioned. And unlike northwest America, Siberia had already been suffused with some of the benefits of European civilisation. Even travellers from Western Europe could enjoy it. 'Throughout the whole of Siberia, hospitality prevails in the extreme', Martin Sauer had written, en route to Irktusk, in 1786. 'A traveller is perfectly secure on the road, and certain of a hearty welcome wherever he puts up . . .'. Captain Cook's old assistant, the Connecticut marine John Ledyard, also encountered great hospitality while walking the length of Siberia in the early 1790s, with practically no money in his pocket. 'In Russia I am treated as an American with politeness and respect', he later wrote, 'and on my account the healths of Dr Franklin and General Washington have been drunk'. Ledyard's enjoyment of Siberia, it should be added, was later tempered by his arrest and expulsion for suspected espionage.

As for the Scotsman Samuel Bentham, touring Siberia in 1782—he had depicted the countryside in summertime as a kind of Russian Arcadia. Floating down the Angara River between Yeniseisk and Irkutsk, he described seeing 'delightful meadow grounds, with clumps of birch trees, bounded by thick deep green wood. A straggling village with a white church, that has a gilded cross on it, not a cloud to be seen, and to complete the whole, a peasant on the shore, while his cattle are drinking at the river, sits on a willow stump and entertains us as we pass with a charming lively pastoral air on a Scotch bagpipe. I regret the swiftness with which we glide along out of hearing of these pastoral notes . . .'.

And many travellers remarked on the bizarre experience of travelling the 4000 arduous miles east from St Petersburg, only to arrive in a handsome, flourishing city like Irkutsk. Even the sniffy German naturalist Dr Georg Heinrich von Langsdorff described it as 'very far from the horrible abode which is generally supposed'. This remote Siberian outpost had quietly been growing rich for years, ever since the opening up of the land trade with China in 1728. Any Siberian (then as now) who could spot a niche in that colossal Chinese market to the south, would soon be able to build a wooden house with ornamental carved window frames, buy a piano for the salon, get his sons commissions in officer schools in St Petersburg, marry his daughters to aristocrats, and still have change to sponsor a local theatre or an orchestra or two. In an age when many of the best European fabrics originated in China, ladies in Irkutsk, and in the nearby border town of Kiakhta, were said to be more modishly dressed than in Paris.

The town of Kiakhta had only been founded, on Chinese insistence, as a border trading station; it had been assigned to a zone 200 miles to the southeast of Irkutsk. Otherwise, the best thing one could say for its location was that it lay somewhere on the road between St Petersburg and Peking. It was, and still is, a cold, windy place miles from anywhere, stuck on the edge of the Mongolian steppe. Nearly a hundred years after its foundation, the walking Scotsman John Cochrane was complaining about the soil of Kiakhta being 'so poor that even common vegetables are with difficulty raised'. Today Kiakhta's churches and arcades stand marooned and almost forgotten, by-passed since the arrival of the railways. But in the eighteenth century this unlikely town in the middle of nowhere was the one through which China insisted on funnelling its Russian trade. To the frustration and despair of Irkutsk merchants, Russians were forbidden—by strict treaty—from trading with China anywhere else.

This absurdity, of having to collect furs in Alaska, transport them 1500 miles by sea to Okhotsk, then another 2000 miles inland to Kiakhta, in order to sell them to the Chinese on the edge of the Gobi Desert, went on for years. Big fur traders like Shelikhov could very well calculate the possible savings to be made by transporting the goods directly, by ship, from Alaska to Canton on the Chinese coast. But Peking was stubborn on issues like this one. 'The mutual trade at Kiakhta did not really benefit China', ran an official Chinese statement, presented to the Russians in 1792, 'but because the Great Emperor loves all humankind, he sympathises with your little people who are poor and miserable . . .'. In the eyes of the mandarins who governed China's foreign trade, Canton was far away, nefarious and difficult to monitor: if northern barbarians wanted to trade with the Middle Kingdom, let them come to Kiakhta.

And come the barbarians had. There were plenty of things worth buying from China, after all, including items as obscure as dried rhubarb root, from which popular medicinal infusions were made. Twenty-five tons of the stuff was being shifted through Kiakhta each year, destined to fetch a 1500 per cent profit in St Petersburg (and in London and Paris, more profit still). Other goods sought by Russian traders included fine Chinese cottons and silk. A million yards of cotton entered Russia through Kiakhta every year during the eighteenth century, destined for the courts and salons of Europe. But by far the greatest Russian need satisfied at Kiakhta was its thirst for tea. At the end of the eighteenth century, Russia's tea imports from China stood at two million roubles annually. The larger part of this was a loose-leaf, luxury product for the upper classes; a significant and growing proportion comprised rock-hard bricks of tea, to be consumed by the common man.

But if the Chinese could offer a variety of goods, the goods which Russians came to offer in Kiakhta must have seemed overwhelmingly monotonous: furs, furs and more furs. Supplying the world's need for fur was as much a tradition to Russia as the drinking of vodka. Sable furs had kept the Russian government in revenue from the twelfth century to the present day. By the seventeenth century, the governments at Novgorod, and later Moscow, were collecting an annual tribute in furs. It is not possible to overstate the importance of this 'soft gold' for Russia's economy: already by the end of the seventeenth century, the tsar's fur tribute had amounted to 100,000 pelts a year. Furs literally paid the expenses of the imperial court. They also paid for the costs of government, and were used as gifts for foreign sovereigns and ambassadors. It was fur that had helped make Russia the powerful country it had become.

In the old days, Russia's largest market for fur had been Europe. Now it was China. The mandarins all wanted it, for hats and for trim on their garments, to help them survive Peking's drab and bitter winters in style. By the beginning of the nineteenth century, Siberian furs would be a mandatory part of winter dress throughout northern China.

Traditionally, the furs traded had been those of forest-dwelling creatures, which could be tracked and trapped in the snow. The fur-bearing animals had included the Siberian squirrel, fox, muskrat, beaver, domestic cat, ferret, rabbit, ermine and sable. But now, since the discovery of the Great Land, a new fur had come onto the market. And this fur, that of the fabulous sea otter, once introduced, would become the most valuable of them all. The hunt for the sea otter, more than anything else, inspired the Russian invasion of Alaska. In 1790, a sea otter skin could fetch $100, that was to say, a year's income for a Pennsylvanian farmer. Among its qualities was its surprising size. The pelt of a fully-grown mother sea otter could measure five feet by two feet. The best furs were rich and thick and nearly black, interspersed with silver. 'Excepting a beautiful woman and a lovely infant', William Sturgis, the hardened Bostonian seafarer, declared, 'they are the most attractive objects produced in nature'. And the prices that the insatiable Chinese traders were willing to pay for furs exceeded by ten times the prices required by the trappers and hunters, back in the freezing wildernesses of Yakutsk, Okhotsk, Kamchatka and (eventually) northwest America. No other product the Russians could offer, came anywhere near it.

The city of Irkutsk—regional centre, and capital of eastern Siberia—had rapidly got rich on the Kiakhta trade. By the time Catherine came to the throne in 1762 it already had a stone cathedral, several wooden churches, half a dozen trading arcades, numerous taverns, a brewery and public baths, not to mention plenty of government buildings and a thousand privately owned dwellings and shops. Which is not to say that furs represented a free lunch. Sea otters had one drawback: although naturally numerous, they produced only one offspring per year, and would quickly succumb to extinction wherever they were hunted. It comes as no surprise to learn that rapid diminutions in populations of fur-bearing animals resulted wherever Russians decided to settle—to the despair of a few early conservationists. In 1792, Martin Sauer compared the dwindling sea otter population to that of the stellar sea cow, first described by Stellar in 1741, but now already extinct. 'There are no more [sea otters] on the coast of Kamchatka', wrote Sauer gloomily, 'they are very seldom seen on the Aleutian islands; of late they have forsaken the Shumagins; and I am inclined to think, from the value of their skin having caused such devastation among them . . . that fifteen years hence there will hardly exist any more of this species'. Only narrowly did he turn out to be wrong.

But as the supply of furs had dwindled, so had the costs of collecting them grown. In the old days, private fur trappers had simply set off, following sable tracks through the snow. Hunting had progressed since then. Now it was about launching fleets of ships onto the north Pacific, or even importing shipments of Canadian pelts when Siberian supplies ran short: the exclusive domain, in short, of big business.

All the big fur-trading enterprises, naturally enough, had their headquarters in Irkutsk, including Shelikhov-Golikov, as well as its rivals Mylnikov and Lebedev-Lastochkin. Two major fairs were held annually in the city, already worth two million roubles by the beginning of the 1780s, even before Shelikhov began filling up the arcades with his latest Alaskan imports. Soon the trade would grow to seven million roubles. By the beginning of the nineteenth century the population of Irkutsk would reach 15,000 or 20,000, and enjoyed such facilities as a forty-piece orchestra, a seminary, a library containing a 'collection of curiosities', a centre for smallpox vaccination and a theatre, where, according to Martin Sauer, 'pieces were got up . . . with astonishing propriety' (the less ebullient Langsdorff, twenty years later, merely commented that he saw some Russian pieces there, 'not ill-played'.)

Of all Siberian towns, this was Martin Sauer's favourite. 'The society established, and the liberal hospitality of the first order of inhabitants, is superior to that in any part of Russia', he wrote, with apparent amazement, before describing it as a place of humanity and good spirit, in thanks, not least, to the local tutors 'who generally consist of Poles, Swedes, French, and some of the Jesuitic order . . . who are under the need of travelling'. John D'Wolf, the amiable Bostonian seafarer, would also describe it as a 'handsome' town, by the banks of the 'beautiful' Angara River; a place which had become 'the great commercial emporium of the eastern part of the empire'. Even Langsdorff, at first glance, commented that 'the number of stone churches in the town, with their glittering cupolas and towers, communicated a pleasing impression from the idea they gave of wealth and prosperity'. Despite subsequent reservations, he was also impressed to note that 'even the best foreign wines were . . . to be obtained at a very reasonable price'—something which is surprisingly true of Irkutsk to this day. Above all Irkutsk had a spirit. All who possess merit here, declared Sauer, 'meet with liberal encouragement'. There were no inns or coffee-houses, 'but no stranger who behaves himself with common civility will ever be at a loss for a home . . .'.

In such a classless milieu, several clever men had done exceedingly well. But one above all had come to stand out. He was no nobleman, but he was a tireless opportunist. He was also a self-publicist and a traveller. And in the massively profitable fur trade, he was undisputed king. This, of course, was Shelikhov himself. Born in the provincial town of Rylsk, in landlocked southwestern Russia, young Shelikhov had not seemed destined for a life on the high seas. But from the day in 1775 that he had married a rich merchant's daughter named Natalia Alekseevna, he had shown his talent for sniffing out money. And eastern Siberia, where the couple would spend most of their married life, must have seemed the ideal place to put that money to good use.

A man like Shelikhov could not, of course, confine himself to the comforts of Irkutsk. His great desire from the outset was to reach Okhotsk on the Pacific coast; a place of which the mere mention, for most sensible Russians, evoked disgust and despairing thoughts of the edge of the world. But Shelikhov, staring east beyond the floating ice and the monotonous grey swell off Okhotsk, seems to have been drawn by thoughts of what might lie beyond that edge. Soon he would be sending ships in the direction of America, in search of sea otters.

One can easily imagine what might have prompted the anxious restlessness of a man such as Shelikhov. Back in St Petersburg, Siberian fur traders (even the rich ones) would have no social status at all. They were regarded as wild people, *nouveaux riches* at best, who dwelt lawlessly beyond the fringes of civilisation. Rumours now trickling back to the court of the Empress Catherine, furthermore, told of their abominable behaviour towards the natives—people who were now subjects of the Russian Crown and entitled to imperial protection. The hardest challenge for Shelikhov was always to win social acceptance from an aristocratic, disdainful St Petersburg.

And back in 1783, when he had embarked upon the radical plan of his life—to ship an entire colony of settlers across the cold ocean and build a town on the unknown and rain-swept shores of northwest America—people must have shaken their heads in disbelief. As a private, speculative venture, the investment looked so colossal and the return so unsure. Until then, Russia had had no overseas colonies. Supplying Siberian ports like Okhotsk with food and commodities was difficult enough. How much more difficult would it then be to supply America? To pass from St Petersburg to the projected new colony on Kodiak Island would require travelling more than half way round the globe. Even from Irkutsk (as Shelikhov's own journeys would prove) the travel time to Alaska might be as long as a year.

But Shelikhov was not a man to set himself modest goals. As already mentioned, he was later to publish an entertainingly self-important account of his exploits in establishing the colony of Three Saints Bay, on Kodiak Island, Alaska. The Empress Catherine may once have described fur traders as 'irresponsible and malignant people'—which most of them probably were—but Shelikhov refused to be thought of as a mere trader, or hunter of sea otters. He had far greater ambitions than that.

Merely to make money was plebeian; to be a *discoverer* was something noble. Such were the aspirations of Shelikhov. His fervent desire was to be seen as a man of honour, class, religion and good morals, spreading Russian goodness around the world. A statue he commissioned, of himself, showed him posing in the outfit of an English gentleman seafarer, decorated with a sword and ribbon, in a frogged coat, wearing a powdered wig complete with curls and a plait. The man it resembled most of all was the greatest explorer of his time, Captain James Cook of Great Britain. This reverence for Cook was fundamental to Shelikhov. In the preface to his book, he describes its contents as including 'a circumstantial account of the discovery . . . of two new islands, Kuktak [Kodiak] and Aphagnak, to which even the famous English navigator Captain Cook did not come'. This was the honest truth insofar as Cook had not visited these islands— a dishonest lie insofar as Shelikhov had not discovered them either. But being the man who built the first Russian town in America, Shelikhov felt entitled to the historical credit anyway. Not as some savage conquistador, but as an eighteenth-century gentleman, to be remembered for bringing civilisation and a love of God and the Russian tsar, to the natives of America. Never mind that some of these natives were proving recalcitrant. Fifty years into the future—with a little help from Baranov—Russian churches and colleges and palaces and granaries and forts and docks might fill up his new land.

It is hard to say that his hopes were groundless. In the 1780s, others willing to accept Shelikhov's extravagant perspective on his American colonies could already be found. An ode composed by the celebrated Russian poet Gavrila Romanovich Derzhavin (known for writing syco-phantic poems to the Empress, as well as a famous 'Ode to God') would lionise him as a 'Russian Columbus'. Perhaps a more suitable name, given his role in establishing the first Russian colony in America, might have been 'Russia's Pilgrim Father'. Shelikhov would have seen himself in no lesser a light. By his own admission, after he had finished subjugating the 'savages' on his very own Alaskan island, he enjoyed almost priestly rela-tions with them. 'I tried to bring them gradually into an awareness of their heathen condition', he later recalled, without irony, '. . . as a result, they at last began to call me their father'. Native bafflement in the face of such technological 'sorcery' as lamps, mirrors or written notes, would be equally charming to him. So Shelikhov had begun bestowing upon them the advantages of Russian homes, Russian clothing and Russian agricul-ture. 'Not knowing how to please me, they brought me a great many of their children as hostages . . . in order not to disappoint them, I accepted many of them, and sent the others back, after giving them appropriate trinkets . . .'.

Baranov was not the only person on whom Shelikhov's gigantic egotistical energy would leave a considerable impact. Native Americans, fur-hunters, sailors and classical poets: none were left unscathed. And despite inflicting a life of unimaginable hardship on his wife Natalia, Shelikhov seems to have retained her loyalty as well ('she always went everywhere with me', he once boasted, 'and was never daunted by any hardships'). Some saw his eccentric insistence on dragging a wife around, as a public relations stunt, aimed at hoodwinking the Russian authorities, and potential investors, into believing that Alaska was not an inhuman place. Either way, Grigori and Natalia would spend many a winter of unstinting bitter cold and darkness 'on business' together, dashing across Siberia on dog-sleighs, followed by brief summers on storm-tossed ships, with Natalia often the only woman aboard.

As for his grand project—the first colonial settlement on the north-west coast of America—he had successfully established it on the jagged shore of Kodiak Island in the year of 1784. In its first years, the European population of Three Saints Bay would comfortably outnumber that of its nearest neighbour, a tiny Spanish *presidio* and mission, newly established by a fine natural harbour in the region known as California, some two thousand miles to the south. The future destinies of these two rival settlements would be very different. But with Baranov now heading for Kodiak, under instruction to expand the colony, Shelikhov would have seen little reason to be intimidated by the neighbours down at San Francisco Bay. The truth was that he faced far more immediate problems than that. One was a question he had been asking for years: why, after all his petitions, and all his good work, was the Russian government still so reluctant to commit itself to supporting him?

St Petersburg, it seemed, had not kept up with the times. The imperial court was still too conservative and unwieldy a body to comprehend the future value of western America. Shelikhov may have been conquering America, but even now Catherine and her ministers were not able to make out what this unusually ambitious fur trader was up to. Was he acting to promote the glory of Russia and the empress? Was a Pacific empire worth investing in and fighting for? Or was Shelikhov, despite all his protestations, just another fur trader trying to gain an advantage over his commercial rivals?

It was three years since Grigori and Natalia Shelikhov had hobbled into Irkutsk, boasting of their death-defying return journey from Kodiak, and ready to tell the world that they had begun the Russian invasion of America. These years had been tantalising ones for Shelikhov. His hopes to win government backing had been on a knife-edge. We can assume that he concealed the details of such matters from Baranov: he would not have wanted to suggest to his underlings that he was desperately short of cash. But when it came to submitting petitions to the empress, begging for support with his great colonising project, he had been far from reticent.

His own actions, he had argued—with much sycophancy and embellishment—spoke for themselves. At his private expense, he had extended Russia's empire into a whole fresh continent. He had overcome the opposition of 'thousands' of 'ferocious savages' to teach them 'about Her Majesty, her mercy, authority and power, and how fortunate those persons are who come under Her authority and find themselves under Her laws, and conversely how miserable those are who desert Her or act contrary to Her instructions'. So he, Shelikhov, 'the lowest subject of my empress', had begun steering new races of men from darkness into light. The Russian Orthodox faith too had been given a foothold in America. Even now, a worthy new manager was being sent to the colony, to continue the work of expanding Russia's possessions southwards. The glory of Russia was at stake.

And there was that other awkward matter. Yes, Shelikhov wanted honour for the empress. But right now, as it happened, his company needed cash. Future profits were inevitable, once the investments in Alaska finally began to yield their anticipated harvest of sea otters (in 1789, indeed, the first shipment had arrived at Okhotsk); but in the meantime, the fur market had gone dead. For reasons unclear, Peking had closed its border to Russian trade at Kiakhta. At this rate, Shelikhov would soon be heading for insolvency.

The closure of Kiakhta had been potentially disastrous for all Irkutsk fur traders; indeed, for the whole city of Irkutsk. Between 1785 and 1792 traders would have nothing to do here except count their existing stock. In all these years, not a single pelt would be sold to China through Siberia. Given that Russian traders were also barred from operating at Chinese ports such as Canton, this only left the somewhat speculative option—for those in any position to try it—of shipping cargoes to Macao, and haggling with middlemen or smugglers. But that was an air-project, a mere possibility. For now, Shelikhov, who had a colony to run and salaries to pay, would have no income.

One problem for him was that, by tradition, the Russian government had kept scarcely any presence in those remote eastern dominions. The 'conquest' of the Pacific, as of the whole of Siberia, had not been achieved by Russian armies or fleets, but by *promyshlenniki*: fur hunters. These comprised private citizens, traders, adventurers, thieves and exiles, largely drawn from the ranks of those fiercely independent frontiersmen known as Cossacks. Tiny groups of ruthless people had thus subdued vast swathes of Siberia. The Russian state had then scurried along behind, imposing order and collecting taxes. Such had always been the pattern of Russian expansion in the east.

Another problem was that Catherine the Great herself had, for ideological reasons, been cool to the idea of intervening in the free market on behalf of merchants. 'It is for traders to traffic where they please', she was on record as saying. As for the colonisation of America, she would furnish 'not men, ships, nor money'. Later she was even supposed to have observed that the English experience with ungrateful American colonies stood as a warning to other nations. This is not to say that she had taken no personal interest in her remotest possessions. In a memo written to the governor of Eastern Siberia in Irkutsk, Denis Ivanovich Chicherin, dated as early as 2 March 1766, she had described her delight at hearing of the 'six hitherto unknown Aleutian islands, which have been brought under my sceptre'. She had added excited comments on the native handicrafts that had been sent over for her inspection, which included bags woven of grass, thread made from twisted fish gut and bone hooks.

But for all her personal interest—and despite the fact that Russia had its private back door onto Alaska—America had never shown itself in a promising light to Catherine. Expeditions that she had commissioned to the area never seemed to yield anything of value. The first, under Ivan Sindt, a Baltic German, had been bad enough, producing nothing other than a bizarre map showing numerous non-existent islands. The second, a grandly ambitious affair under the command of Captain-lieutenant Petr Kumich Krenitsyn and his assistant Lieutenant Mikhail Dmitrievich Levashev, dispatched in 1764, had turned out almost comically disastrous from the start, suffering from shipwreck, disease and attacks by natives. It was, in part, these negative experiences—proof of America's inaccessibility and indefensibility—that had turned Catherine into such an adamant free trader when it came to that continent.

Shelikhov did, however, have one more argument to unleash: the suggestion of foreign threats. Now it was not only Russians in the race to capture the American trade. A few months before dispatching Baranov to Kodiak, in February 1790, Shelikhov, had submitted a report to the new governor-general of eastern Siberia, IA Pil, referring to the growing menace. 'In the past two summers', he explained, 'thirty foreign vessels have been sighted from our factories'.

Shelikhov was probably right to suspect that Catherine's interventionist instincts might resurface in response to a foreign threat in the north Pacific. They had done so before. Dark rumours, it turned out, had long been circulating of foreign intrusions in the north Pacific, a region nominally claimed by Russians as theirs by right of first discovery. And Catherine had not liked these rumours one bit.

The trouble, in her eyes, had started with the publication in Paris, as long ago as 1771, of a sensational book, *Memoirs and Travels*, by a Polish adventurer by the name of Benyowski. The book had told the extraordinary tale of Benyowski's escape from imprisonment in Russian Kamchatka of all places, and of his subsequent journey on a stolen ship to Europe. Through the early 1770s his daring exploits (greatly embellished in the telling) had been the talk of the salons of Paris. To the fury and embarrassment of the ever-paranoid Russian authorities, not only had

Europe learned how tenuous Russian rule really was in the East, but rumour had even come back to Russian ears that the French planned to present this Polish scoundrel with a frigate, in which to return and seize Kamchatka for the King of France.

Nothing had eventually come of that (Benyowski had gone to Madagascar instead), but the threat of foreign intrusion had not gone away. The next shock had been Captain Cook's visit to Alaska and Siberian Kamchatka in 1778, followed by British claims that Cook had 'discovered' much of northwest America himself. This had been a serious insult to Russia. As had been explained to Catherine, Cook had not only had the temerity to cruise coasts claimed by Russia, but he had even published maps—far superior to any pre-existing Russian map—with new British names on them (and Cook's names, it was known, tended to stick). Shortly after Cook's death in Hawaii in 1779, the *Resolution* and *Discovery*, now commanded by Clerke and Gore, had then dared to return to Kamchatka to obtain water and provisions. The final affront had been their presentation to the local Russian governor, Magnus von Behm, of a packet of reports—asking if he would be so kind as to send it overland to London for them. Von Behm had obliged, in a most cordial manner.

Back in St Petersburg the reaction to this news had been anything but cordial. This double visit of the British was regarded as highly suspicious. Even as more guns were being rushed overland to Kamchatka, the Empress was resorting to fluttering her eyelashes at Sir James Harris, the British ambassador to Russia, and asking him to provide her with copies of Cook's maps. An amused Harris had subsequently written a long and ironic dispatch to the First Lord of the Admiralty, the Earl of Sandwich, dated 7 January 1780, remarking how keenly the Empress had felt 'the great utility' of Cook's voyage and how anxious she had been 'to promote its success', such was her enthusiasm to acquire British maps of *her own* empire.

But the single worst result of Cook's visit to the north Pacific, from Catherine's point of view, was that it had inadvertently revealed more of Russia's precious trade secrets to the world. Without intending to make money, Cook's men had casually collected a few otter skins during their trips along the American coast. Only on their subsequent arrival in Canton, did it become apparent to anyone how much money these skins could fetch. An astounded Lieutenant James Trevenan was said to have got $300 for furs that he had acquired in exchange for a single broken shoe-buckle. And unlike the unfortunate Russian merchants, whose

Chinese trade was confined (by treaty) to remote Kiakhta on the edge of the Gobi Desert, the British had their own helpful compatriots already stationed in Canton. A fortune, then, was waiting to be made by those who could get there first. At least two of Cook's crew with dollar signs in their eyes had gone so far as to jump ship on the spot, in the hope of being fastest to enter the Alaska-to-Canton fur trade.

Meanwhile, the British had not been the only ones daring to affront the dignity of Her Imperial Majesty by sailing illegally in her waters. The Spanish, too, had still not abandoned their lofty claims to possession of the whole littoral of western America: and Juan Francisco de la Bodega y Quadra had made a surprising appearance off the coast of Alaska in his ship *Favorita* as recently as 1779. Worse still was the news from France. In the summer of 1785, the Comte de La Pérouse had been detected preparing a naked bid for America's northwest coast. This seems to have been the last straw for Catherine. Just nine days after La Pérouse's departure from Brest with his two ships *La Boussole* and *L'Astrolabe*, she had announced the departure of a brand new state-sponsored expedition to America, namely, the 'Northeastern Secret Geographical and Astronomical Expedition' under the surprising leadership of an Englishman, one Joseph Billings, recently in service with Captain Cook. But this had hardly helped. Billings and co were to spend years idling around in Siberia before they even got to America. Meanwhile, in the spring of 1786, La Pérouse had already arrived off the coast of Alaska, where, entering Lituya Bay (in the vicinity of today's Yakutat), he had promptly claimed it for France, deeming it a suitable post in which to base a fur-trading company.

Then had come tidings of a veritable flood of British merchant ships, all seeking to muscle in on the fur trade that should have been Russian by right. Captain James Hanna, in 1785, in a daring trip to the northwest coast, had managed to persuade the local Indians to sell him 560 furs in exchange for trinkets and trifles. He had then sold these in Macao for a staggering $60 each, realising over $20,000. Catherine did not yet have up-to-date figures. But no fewer than seven foreign merchant ships had come to the northwest coast in 1786. The governor-general of eastern Siberia, IA Pil, had spent much of his time now ranting about the 'greediness for trade' of the foreign merchants, and their 'audacity . . . in the pilfering of Russia's treasure'. Shelikhov—still in Alaska—had known nothing of this commotion. But to judge by what happened next, his hopes of state intervention had, for a few short months, looked like coming true.

First, an oleaginous memo had been sent to the empress from Count Alexander Vorontsov, head of the Russian ministry of commerce, and Count Alexander Bezborodko, Catherine's own secretary, presenting to her their own 'humbly formulated' ideas on the need to declare Russian rights in North America. Given that such a declaration 'might in some ways even undermine the dignity of the court' if not backed up by force, so they 'humbly' submitted to her Imperial Majesty their view that the navy should be sent. What they meant was that the perfidious British merchants of the East India Company understood no argument better than the roar of cannon.

Catherine's answer had been obliging. Her order had gone at once to the Ministry of Foreign Affairs, complaining of 'unauthorised penetration by English merchantmen . . .' and demanding that an armed naval squadron be sent to the north Pacific 'to preserve our right to the lands discovered by Russian seafarers'. She had sent Joseph Billings on his way to America just the year before: now she would send a different kind of expedition. On 22 December 1786 Catherine made the decision, as definitive as any yet, to assert Russia's claim to the western part of America.

The new Pacific squadron was to have been quite unlike anything that had gone before. It was to comprise four brand-new three-masted ships, all fully armed. A crew of 600, skilled in trades such as carpentry, joinery, boiler making and foundry work, would man the ships, along with the best officers of the day. The naval squadron was to sail under the command of one Grigori Ivanovich Mulovskii. Mulovskii's route, as outlined by Catherine and the Admiralty, would also have been a significant choice in Shelikhov's eyes. First he was to take the ships from St Petersburg, round the Cape of Good Hope to New Holland (today's Indonesia). From there he was to set out across the Pacific to Hawaii. Anyone interested in mastering the west coast of America would have wanted a close look at these islands, discovered just eight years earlier, by Captain Cook. Equidistant between Alaska and California, they offered a station to revictual for ships crossing this ocean in any direction. Visionary men could already suspect their value. So it was that Mulovskii had been asked to reconnoitre them, while taking water and provisions on board. Something of their strange internal politics might have been investigated; leaders like the war-chief Kamehameha, encountered by Cook and his men in 1778, might have been courted. Sailing on from Hawaii, one pair of Mulovskii's ships was then to have consolidated the Russian presence in the Kurile Islands and Sakhalin north of Japan, as a prelude to opening trade with that closed country. The other would proceed straight to America's northwest coast.

The objective in America had been unprecedentedly assertive. Mulovskii's first task would have been to head for Nootka Harbour, located in the southern part of today's British Columbia, on Vancouver Island. From Nootka they were to sail north 'to take that coast from the harbour of Nootka to the point where Chirikov's discovery begins, as possession of the Russian state, if no other state is occupying it'. As a matter of fact this coast did indeed remain unoccupied by any European power.

The second task had been to reassert for once and for all Russia's sovereignty over Alaska itself, that is to say, all the Aleutian islands, and the 'whole littoral' north of 55°, using force if necessary. This required making sure that Chugach Sound (which Cook had now named 'Prince William Sound') and Kenai Inlet (which Cook had had the effrontery to rename after *himself*) were not frequented by foreign vessels or outposts. If any such foreigners were found, they were to be 'evicted' and their markers of sovereignty 'levelled'.

Siberian fur-traders must have been overjoyed at the thought of frigates being sent to increase their profits. And if the foregoing had not already been enough to demonstrate the fierceness of her commitment to a Russian America, Catherine, in early 1787, had even gone so far as to approve a third expedition, to run concurrently with the other two. This was to have been led by yet another Englishman from Cook's last expedition, namely, the British naval lieutenant, James Trevenen (he of the $300 shoe-buckle). In the words of his brother-in-law and biographer, VC Penrose, Trevenen had 'contracted a violent antipathy towards the gentlemen [in charge of the British Admiralty] . . . and was not very moderate in his anger, at their not employing him in the way he wished'. Thus it had come about that 'his ardent mind embraced the world as his country . . .' and he had decided to apply for a job in the Russian navy. The 'North Pacific Project' that he had then presented to the Russian ambassador in London, was to send three vessels from St Petersburg to 'deal with' British fur-poachers. Catherine, all then knew, was in an aggressive mood. Who better, it was agreed, to deal with British poachers, than yet another ex-servant of the British Admiralty?

Nobody could have been better pleased at this moment than Grigori Shelikhov, on his arrival in Irkutsk, from Alaska, in the spring of 1787. Talk of fleets and assertive action had been precisely what he wanted. The time (it must have seemed) was coming when he, and the Russian state, would merge their affairs. With ships of the Russian navy cruising the Pacific, he would no longer fear foreign poachers stealing his profit; a glorious spotlight would fall on his efforts to colonise the American coast; and the way for a rapid expansion to the south would be clear. So where, he would still be asking in 1790, was the acclaim (and the money)?

In fact, it had turned out that Shelikhov's arrival back in Siberia had coincided with a disastrous turn of events over in Europe. Catherine's interest in America had been about to evaporate once more. A nasty war with Sweden had flared up. Suddenly the defence of the Baltic was at stake. Mulovskii's frigates had to be requisitioned for the new war, and Trevenen, in his haste to reach Russia, had broken his leg: America was about to be relegated to the sidelines yet again.

Shelikhov's disappointment, as this news had filtered through to Irkutsk, must have been intense. He might have guessed that it would foreshadow the rejection of his petitions for help: all he would have to show for his efforts, three whole years later, would be a 'citation' from the governing senate, and an honorary presentation of swords and medals. Now, in 1790, with his new manager on the way to America, Shelikhov still had no spare cash for his colony, either to plan expansion or to stop foreign ships from poaching in his waters. And, worst of all, the chance remained open for rival powers to encroach on the unclaimed parts of the coast.

At the very moment that Catherine was cancelling her plans to send the navy to the Pacific, another ominous development had been about to occur. For in that same summer of 1787, on the other side of the world, private merchants of a new power had been outfitting their first expedition to the northwest coast of America. The substantial sum of $50,000 had been pooled and invested. Two ships were involved, both hoping to cash in on the supposed profits of taking furs from the northwest coast to China: one was named the *Columbia*, under a Captain John Kendrick, and the other was the *Lady Washington*, under Robert Gray. The two men were both veterans of the American War of Independence: both were as hard as nails. Their ships, as they sailed out of the port of Boston, Massachusetts, were stuffed full of goods for trading with the Indians: hoes, axes, hammers, knives, combs, mirrors and glass beads. They were flying the flag of the United States of America.

The projected journey of these Bostonians (as the Russians soon began calling all their compatriots) had been an awesome one. To reach the west coast of America from New England required sailing all the way to the bottom of South America and up again. For more than a year the ships would be at sea. Not until September 1788 had they sailed safely into Nootka Sound, Vancouver Island.

Nootka, in these years, was fast becoming the marine headquarters of the Pacific northwest. Nobody had yet established a settlement here, but English, Spanish and Portuguese ships, anchored side-by-side, could be found wintering in its waters (Britain and Spain, in fact, were soon to come to blows over the question of whose claim to Nootka was pre-eminent). During the summer of 1788, the British sea captain John Meares had managed to build a small ship here, the *Northwest America*—the first to be constructed anywhere on this coast. And now the two Bostonian ships had quietly added yet another flag to the multinational scene.

Both Kendrick and Gray had stayed for the winter, before exchanging ships for the 1789 season. Kendrick, it seems, had wanted the smaller ship, for creeping close along the shore of this unknown coast. Perhaps he hoped to stumble across the mouth of the fabled 'Great River of the West', assumed to flow from the western Rockies to the Pacific somewhere along this coast. Otherwise his mission, over the coming months, had been to make deals with natives of the Vancouver area; in 1789, as a matter of fact, he had even 'bought' several tracts of land from them, drawing up legal documents to be 'signed' by the natives in the process—the legality, or otherwise, of these deeds, would still be under discussion two centuries later.

The two ships, travelling separately, then headed across the Pacific, both making stopovers in Hawaii. Kendrick, once there, would become the first foreign seafarer to take on a cargo of sandalwood (which would soon excite the Chinese market as much as sea otters had). But his fellow-adventurer Robert Gray, meanwhile, now in the *Columbia*, was already delivering in Canton the thousand or so furs that he had collected on the northwest coast. With the profits, he would literally fill his ship with expensive Chinese teas.

So it was, in August 1790—exactly at the moment when Baranov was about to commence his own journey to America—that Robert Gray finally sailed back into Boston harbour with his precious cargo, to a hero's acclaim. His achievement had been immense: in circumnavigating the globe, he had covered no fewer than 48,889 miles, according to his own log. He had become the first American to land at Hawaii (and was bringing back a real Hawaiian, by the name of Attoo, who paraded the streets of Boston in a red and yellow feather cloak to prove it). As it turned out, half of the Chinese tea in Gray's hold had been contaminated by seawater. But this was almost beside the point. Once news had spread of the possible profits to be made on the northwest coast, a flood of Bostonians would soon be on its way, led by Gray himself, returning with the *Columbia* to accomplish yet more historic feats.

Baranov's job, though he did not yet know it, had just become very much harder. But the journey that he now faced was a trivial one compared with what the *Columbia* had just achieved. At around 1800 nautical miles, the gap between Okhotsk and Kodiak could, in a good ship, have been traversed in a month or two. The trouble lay in the old and unsound vessels usually used by the Russians. We do not know whether Shelikhov had described to Baranov the details of his own journeys to and from America. He would have been unwise to do so, if he had not wanted to frighten his new recruit. Nevertheless, the difficulties that Shelikhov later described in his book, surrounding his prior journeys between Okhotsk and Kodiak, give us some idea of what Baranov had in store.

Shelikhov's outward journey to America had taken place seven years earlier, in 1783. He and his wife had left Okhotsk at exactly the same time of year and in exactly the same ship as Baranov was now sailing on; with the advantage that the Shelikhovs had travelled with two sister ships in company. Nevertheless, within a few days of their departure, Shelikhov later recalled, 'we ran into a storm that lasted two days . . . the storm was so bad that we almost despaired of our lives . . .'.

In consequence of delays and damage occasioned by this storm—nothing unusual in the north Pacific—Shelikhov and his men had subsequently anchored at Bering Island for the 'winter', that is to say, until 16 June of the following year. On the island there was no hunting to speak of except for a few foxes. For food they had caught fish, sea lions and fur seals. But, as Shelikhov recounted, 'blizzards were almost daily occurrences' and scurvy, in the absence of fresh greens, could not be prevented. Not until the late summer of 1784 would they eventually reach Kodiak (and even this was not bad going: one of the three ships in their party had not arrived until 1786, three whole years after setting out).

But Shelikhov being Shelikhov, we cannot be certain that he would have wanted things any other way. His return journey from Kodiak, three years later, had been just as spectacularly horrific. On this occasion, the troubles had begun after he and his wife had put ashore at Kamchatka, 'to buy fresh fish'. No sooner had they disembarked than their ship broke anchor, and disappeared in an easterly wind. Thus stranded, the couple had been obliged to make their way to Irkutsk overland from Kamchatka, although it was, by now, mid-winter.

This journey had proved to be the usual mix of farce and horror. In his autobiography, Shelikhov regaled his readers with stories of 'unreliable' tribes and 'terribly fierce' north winds. On being stranded in desolate places, he wrote, they 'would hitch the sleds together with leather thongs and on such occasions only saved our lives by lying in the snow for two, three or even five days, without leaving, without water, without cooking food. Since it was impossible to build a fire, we ate snow to quench our thirst. In place of any other food, we ate dry biscuits or iukola [dried salmon], which we chewed while lying in the snow. The last part of the journey from the Aldan to Irkutsk was so difficult the dogs and reindeer were exhausted. The horses too were exhausted by the snowdrifts, often to the point of collapse. In order to make the journey more quickly, I went on foot . . .'.

Shelikhov, however, wanted us to know that he had more stamina than either dogs or horses. But Baranov was a different kind of man. Anxious and alert to every threat, he must have known that his 100-foot-long ship the *Tri Sviatitelia*, on which he was now sailing to America, was the self-same vessel that Shelikhov had sailed in. It was now seven years old and no doubt in a fairly dilapidated condition. Filled to the gunwales with supplies for the colony, it would certainly not have been safe by any modern standards. In addition to Baranov, 52 men were aboard. Also in the ship would have been live cows and sheep, hogsheads of sugar, salt, rye meal, tea bricks, bales of tobacco and Chinese cloth. On deck, there are known to have been a few old pieces of artillery.

The most disconcerting news for Baranov, though, may have been the identity of the vessel's captain, Dmitrii Ivanovich Bocharov. The man was an old-timer but a well-known drunk. He 'has been drinking ever since the day he arrived', Shelikhov himself had recently complained about him, in a letter to a previous manager, 'and I do not hope for anything better for the future . . . I cannot sober him up'. But this had not stopped him from putting this dangerous liability in charge of the vessel, now due to convey the new manager to the colonies. A difficult crossing seemed almost inevitable, and there was nothing Baranov could do to prevent it.

Not that the trip started badly. Initially, winds were very much in their favour. The Okhotsk Sea was crossed and the southern tip of Kamchatka rounded without mishap. Then began the long sweep through the eastern Aleutians. Only one thing was against them: a shortage of fresh water, probably owing to defective casks. This was the problem, it seems, that forced the captain to drop anchor at Koshigin Harbour on the island of Unalaska some time around the end of September.

To make an unscheduled stop in the Aleutians at this time of year was unfortunate to say the least. They were more than four-fifths of the way to Kodiak, but winter storms would soon be howling through these islands, making any further progress extremely hazardous. And as skies darkened over Unalaska, Baranov must have felt his fury rise at his drunken captain. Why had proper water-casks not been carried? He was still unaware of the extreme economies to which employees of Shelikhov were obliged to resort. Two days later the inevitable happened. A huge storm hit the island. No shelter would have been adequate to protect an old, flimsy ship in conditions like these: after breaking anchor, the whole vessel came crashing and splintering onto the beach in the night.

By the standards of the day, it was not a tragedy. Nobody drowned. Some of the provisions were saved. The natives of Unalaska were by now thoroughly familiar with Russian visitors, and did not attempt to attack them. Nevertheless, for Baranov, it was a predictably grim start to his spell in charge of the American colonies. He was now stranded with more than fifty men, without a ship, on a wild and treeless island in the middle of the north Pacific, with winter coming on. It was certain that nobody would rescue them before the following summer, if at all. Apart from a few quarts of cranberries preserved in candlefish oil, presented by the locals, they were now obliged to live off what foxes or sea lions they could catch, plus the surviving stores intended for the Kodiak Island colonists—and these stores, according to Shelikhov's strict rules, were being charged to all of their accounts.

It was to be the first of many ghastly Alaskan winters for Baranov, cooped up in makeshift, dripping shelters of sod and wood, amid the stench of fish and rotting whale blubber, watching storms roll in from the sea, worrying about money and sources of food. 'Sometimes two months passed' he later grumbled, 'without a possibility of going any distance'. He became accustomed 'to think no more about flour or bread'. Not until the following May, nine months later, were he and his men in any position to risk an escape from the island, using three native style boats of seal skins stretched over wooden frames, built from the wreckage of the *Tri Sviatitelia*.

While a handful of men stayed behind to guard the remaining stores, the three improvised craft set out on the risky journey to Kodiak, staying as close to the shores as they dared. Two of the three boats took a more northerly route via Bristol Bay, while Baranov and sixteen men stayed south of the mainland, aiming straight for Kodiak. They carried no provisions, but would rely on whatever seal, birds, salmon or clams they could catch en route.

From an account left by Martin Sauer, who had come with the Billings Expedition on this same route just a year before, we have a sense of how things looked to contemporary travellers. First Baranov would have seen Unimak Island bobbing above the swell, with its three mountains, including one 'rent and broken' and the other 'a perfect cone, towering to an immense height, and discharging a considerable amount of smoke from its summit'. Approaching the mainland, they would then have run into the 'innumerable' islands of the Shumagin group, with their rugged cliffs, sharp capes and bluff heads. Only once these hazards had successfully been negotiated, would it have been time to stand in for land. By now, native hunters would have been spotted paddling past in their baidars. And two days later, through the heavy clouds and drizzle, Baranov would have glimpsed 'the lofty mountains on the island of Kodiak'. From this point, natives would have escorted his boat through the harbour entrance of Three Saints Bay.

But one wonders how much of the scenery Baranov would have appreciated, as he finally set foot on Kodiak Island, Alaska, on 8 July 1791. He was a middle-aged melancholic, unfamiliar with the sea. Along the way, he had fallen ill with pneumonia, presumably as a result of constant soakings. His prospects here for any kind of prosperity seemed distant. 'My first steps into these regions were attended by misfortune', he later wrote, with uncharacteristic optimism, 'but perhaps I shall be permitted to conquer in the end . . .'.

CHAPTER THREE

KODIAK ISLAND, ALASKA

Last time, Baranov had been asked to build a ship
without resources; this time he was asked to build an
entire city on the northwest coast.

Permanently wet and cold, living off dried fish, without light for reading or paper for writing: Baranov's grim winter on the island of Unalaska had hardly made him feel as though he was conquering America.

Even now that he had arrived at Three Saints Bay, his pneumonia would keep him low for weeks, long enough to miss the current hunting season. The darkness of yet another winter when little effective work would be possible was looming. Only in the following spring, once he had fully recovered, would Baranov start taking over the duties of the outgoing manager, the man referred to by Shelikhov as 'the Greek', Evstratii Ivanovich Delarov. In the meantime, he doubtless spent that first autumn and winter trying to familiarise himself with his new headquarters in Russian America.

As later events would show, Baranov was a depressive but he was no defeatist. On rare sunny days, there may have been moments when he could feel that Shelikhov's enthusiastic portrait of Kodiak had not been overblown. The island was after all, and still is, one of Alaska's most verdant places. It was no Elysium, and it rained most of the time, but compared with the treeless, semi-frozen tundra of Okhotsk, it was not unpromising. On the low lands round the coast, Baranov would have seen elder, low willows, some brushwood, ginseng, wild onions and plenty of berries, including currants and abundant raspberries. The fog-shrouded hills and mountains of the interior were thick with pine.

Being an island, Kodiak also had the advantage that it was easy to defend. And yet at the same time the mainland was conveniently accessible on baidarkas (one or two-man native boats), through relatively sheltered waters. North from here, furthermore, the coast of the mainland was fissured with two great natural inlets, both allegedly teeming with sea otter—Kenai Bay and Chugach Bay, today known as Cook Inlet and Prince William Sound, respectively.

As for Shelikhov's Three Saints Bay settlement, it did not yet bear the marks of a great Russian city of the future. But considering that there had been nothing at all here seven years earlier, it could have been worse. Martin Sauer who, along with the whole Billings expedition, had passed through in the year prior to Baranov's arrival, has left us drawings and some detailed descriptions of the Three Saints Bay area. His drawings show perhaps twenty structures strung along the beach of a small curving spit; this included the 'travelling church' and 'astronomical tent' of the Billings expedition, and a mixture of wooden and sod-and-grass built structures. Tied up in the harbour were a couple of narrow galiots. The colony, as Sauer described it, had five houses 'in the Russian fashion', barracks 'somewhat like the boxes of a coffeehouse', a rather splendid-looking courthouse, the commissaries' department, a counting house, the manager's house, another building for 'the hostages', storehouses, warehouses, a smithy and a carpenter's shop. And unlike in Okhotsk, where everything was falling to pieces, the houses here were at least relatively new.

To Sauer, furthermore, Kodiak had seemed to be full of people, in comparison to the Aleutian Islands that he had already visited. Sauer noted that the population of Kodiak, 'according to Shelikoff's [sic] register', comprised 1300 adult males and 1200 young males, with an equal number of females. The vast majority of these were Native Americans, referred to indiscriminately by the Russians as 'Aleuts', regardless of whether they were originally from Kodiak itself, or from the Aleutian Islands to the West (in fact these were two unrelated peoples).

At the time of Baranov's arrival—this being summertime—the adult male Aleuts would have been largely absent, hunting for furs in the service of the Russians. So when he first saw it, the settlement must have contained nothing but women: Sauer, the year before, had observed them curing and drying fish, digging, washing and drying edible roots, collecting useful plants and berries, and making clothes, laying in a winter supply for the whole population.

These Kodiak natives had not excited Sauer in the way that the people of Unalaska had done, but he found them curious enough. He liked, for example, the fact that their houses had small apartments attached, 'which serve for a vapour bath'—that is to say saunas, into which guests were conducted, and given bowls of melted seal or bear fat to drink. He also noted the women's extreme fondness for their offspring. Such was their dread of the effects of war, he wrote, that some mothers resorted to bringing up their males in a 'very effeminate manner', and were even happy 'to see them taken by chiefs, to gratify their unnatural desires'. Other aspects of tribal life that intrigued him included their festivities: from February to October, he reported, they were kept busy hunting and fishing, before partying all November long, 'visiting each other, feasting . . . and dancing with masks and painted faces'.

Few Russian descriptions of the Kodiak natives would ever be as sympathetic. Much merriment in particular would be focused on their eating habits. 'There is almost nothing that the islanders do not eat', mocked the Russian naval officer GI Davydov, a few years later. 'When an American is fishing and he feels hungry, then he catches a cod or plaice, and eats the head or tail while the fish is alive. Rotting, or as the expression goes, "bitter" fish, is more popular than fresh; the Kenais [ie natives] deliberately let it lie in a heap for several days until it begins to rot and smell nice to them . . . this food creates such disgusting flatulence that it is impossible to stay under the same roof as a man who has eaten his fill of this splendid repast'.

Davydov could talk for hours on this subject. He chuckled elsewhere over their 'rotted or fermented caviar', a great delicacy among the Americans, which 'gives off a revolting and unbearable smell'. The islanders, he alleged, had 'even been seen in the summer time to collect bears' droppings and cook them with berries'. This was not to mention the ubiquitous whale blubber, which 'smells so revolting' that 'you will never get used to it'. He described the system of preparing the blubber, which required 'a gathering of old men, old women, and children . . . they cut the blubber into strips, chew it and spit it into some kind of receptacle. Then they cook it with berries and add several ground roots . . .'.

By comparison to these eccentric Aleuts, those of Russian origin on Kodiak were extraordinarily few. In the estimation of Sauer, the whole community round Three Saints Bay was 'ruled' by about fifty of them (in fact the total number of Russians in Shelikhov's America at the time of Baranov's arrival was about three times this number: some were out hunting, while others occupied small outposts of the main colony on the mainland). From this tiny population of Russians, Sauer had been interested to note that one of them had married a native, who kept an 'extremely clean' house, and very healthy children; who seemed, in fact, a 'perfect mistress of Russian economy . . . Several of the Russians have their wives with them', he added, 'and keep gardens of cabbages and potatoes'. He had also spotted at least four cows and twelve goats. Delarov had told him that corn would later be grown here too.

Viewing all this in the autumnal days of 1791, the anxious Baranov might have had some grounds for guarded optimism. The weather of Alaska was vastly milder than that of Siberia and most of the men would be away on hunt until October—which meant there would still have been fresh food around.

And as it turned out, once this winter was through, one of the first tasks he would face in the coming spring would indeed be the relatively pleasant one of dispatching 300,000 roubles-worth of furs to Shelikhov in

Okhotsk. Admittedly these pelts, the fruit of two years' hunting, had been collected, not by himself but by his predecessor Delarov (who would himself also be departing in the same ship). Nevertheless, insofar as they meant large revenues for the Company, the dispatch of the *Sviatitelia Mikhail* represented good news for Baranov. Hunting sea otters and shipping them back to Siberia was, after all, the main job for which he had been recruited. On the success of this grubby but lucrative business would Russia's American Empire rise or fall.

Delarov no doubt spent that first winter explaining to Baranov the whole hunting system, as he had explained it to Martin Sauer the year before. During the summer months, it was possible to keep a veritable armada of 600 double baidarkas on the go, with the co-operation of native chiefs. It had been Delarov's habit to divide this mass of people into six parties, each of about 200 natives and each to be supervised by a single Russian. The separate fleets had then set out from Kodiak, across open sea, aiming for their own inlets and quiet bays and beaches on the mainland, where marine animals lurked. The top prize of all hunting expeditions, as ever, was sea otter. But different varieties of seal were also hunted for their furs; and for food, giant halibut was taken.

In fact it was hazardous work. At open sea, beside a rugged and mountainous coast, populated by suspicious natives, mishaps could and did happen. Later, as Baranov was obliged to send his teams greater and greater distances in search of bays still frequented by sea otters, these mishaps would become ever more likely. He would soon have seen how dependent he was on the native Aleuts. Without them these hunts could never have started. Russians were in no position to catch marine animals by themselves: not only did they lack the manpower, but they lacked the skills.

The unique expertise possessed by the islanders was that of boating on rough seas, and harpooning sea animals—from sea otters to whales—with poison-tipped darts as they went. Adam Bril, erstwhile governor of Irkutsk, had long ago seen the remarkable agility of the Aleutians at sea: 'One man sits in the baidarka', he had noted, 'and fastens to it an inflated bladder from a whale or another sea creature; then he puts his wife in the bladder. They can then move about the sea boldly and freely . . .'.

To Martin Sauer, who had passed right through the Aleutian chain, stopping in various points, the Aleuts were more like amphibious animals than human beings, 'going among the breakers, and under water, without concern'. Even when sunk, he had noted, no water could get into their baidarkas, given that the men sat so snugly inside the openings. And although they might be 18 feet long, on land they could be carried in one hand with ease. It was the baidarkas of the main Aleutian Island of Unalaska, above all, that had impressed him. They were, he wrote, transparent as oiled paper. 'If perfect symmetry, smoothness and proportion constitute beauty', he enthused, 'they are beautiful; to me they appeared so, beyond anything I beheld'. Considering the natives' light waterproof dress, their painted and plumed bonnets, and their perfect ease at sea, 'their first appearance struck me with amazement beyond expression'.

Maintaining good relations between the Russians and these fabulously useful natives was to be one of Baranov's main responsibilities. Not so many years before, as was well known, the Aleuts had been virtually enslaved for their skills. The early Russian *promyshlenniki*, based in Okhotsk, coming out to raid the sea otters of the Aleutians, had simply ordered them to work or to be shot. The Aleuts, many of whom had had no martial traditions themselves, were unable to defend themselves. Only lately, after an angry intervention from the empress herself on behalf of 'her subjects' the Aleuts, had matters quietened down somewhat in these seas. The Commandant of Okhotsk, as recently as June 1787, had been obliged to send an open letter of apology to the citizens of the Aleutian Islands, pleading the 'maternal benevolence' of Catherine, and referring to the petitions he had received from islanders, concerning maltreatment at the hands of Russian seafarers. 'With deep regret I noted the inhuman deeds of the hunters from these ships', he had written, 'deeds of which the government was until now unaware; otherwise their insolence and lawbreaking would have been stopped. . . . Meanwhile I ask you to be calm and not to despair of the high benevolence of the Great Empress of all the Russians, who, knowing that you are her true subjects, will protect you from all harm. . . . They must realise that you are just as much human beings as they are, and that you too are subjects of the same Empress'.

In theory then, islanders were no longer to be moved from one place to another against their will—and they were to be paid for what work they did. One of the secret purposes of the Billings expedition, in visiting this part of America the year before, had been to investigate allegations and rumours of abuses carried out by Shelikhov and his employees. Baranov would not have been aware of this. But he could see that hunting needed to be a co-operative affair, in the mutual interest of both natives and Russians.

Not that 'mutual interest' should be taken in any modern sense. This was the eighteenth century, after all. To judge by Martin Sauer's report from the year before, the system still relied on intimidation of the weak by the strong. Back on the island of Unalaska, he had noted, the Russians 'lord it over the inhabitants with more despotism than generally falls to the lot of princes; keeping the islanders in a state of abject slavery'. Subsequently, sailing in the direction of Kodiak, his ship had run into a crowd of Aleuts in baidarkas, under the supervision of a Russian. This must have been one of Delarov's hunting parties. Sauer recalled that the natives had boarded his ship and 'complained bitterly' of the treatment they had had from the Russians.

On Kodiak itself, Sauer had been less censorious, and more inclined to credit the good work of the Company. The main problem here, in fact, to Sauer, had been the Billings expedition's own 'illiterate and more savage priest', brought with them from Siberia. Sauer had referred to his 'zealotry' in burning the locals' masks and forcing them to be christened. He had also recalled a time in Siberia when this same priest had beaten two Tartar guides on the misplaced suspicion of theft. One had died. Sauer's own words convey his astonishment: 'The priest said, *there was no harm done; they were not Christians*'. Besides the arrogance of the Orthodox Church, the regime on Kodiak may have looked relatively benign at the time of Baranov's arrival. It was certainly not open warfare as in years gone past; the natives had indeed been 'pacified'.

But worrying features still remained. One was the Russian custom of taking native 'hostages' as security on the promise of good behaviour. Sauer had remarked on this. Right here in Three Saints Bay, for example, there were no fewer than 300 native girls being held hostage, the daughters of native hunters currently out working with the Russians. After their capture and confinement—wrote Sauer—native opposition to Russian rule on this island had ceased: as far as he could learn, the hostages too were 'satisfied with the treatment they meet with' and now seemed 'reconciled to the rules introduced by the present chief of the company, Delareff [*sic*], who governs with the strictest justice'. On such a wobbly mix of co-operation and threats then did Russian rule depend. These were important lessons for Baranov. At Kodiak the system seemed to work; on the mainland—as he soon saw—it would run into trouble.

Of the other difficulties to test Baranov's fragile patience, two would have been apparent almost from the moment of his arrival at Three Saints Bay. The first was the declining sea otter catch. Kenai Bay, the 250-mile long inlet (today known as Cook Inlet, leading up to the modern city of Anchorage) had for a short while promised an easy prosperity for the

Three Saints Bay settlement. Now those hopes were already fading. In the late 1780s Delarov had been able to catch 3000 otters here in a single season; by the time of Baranov's arrival this figure was down to 800. 'The hunting in Kenai Bay', Baranov would be reporting gloomily within a year of his arrival, 'already does not amount to much . . .'. New, accessible hunting grounds needed to be found fast.

The other anxiety came from hints concerning the personality of Shelikhov himself, and by implication, the whole enterprise of a Russian America. Baranov would see it soon enough, in the grim demeanour of his Russian employees, as they returned from their hunts. Martin Sauer had noted it too. In Irkutsk, Yakutsk and Okhotsk, he had written, it had always been a 'matter of amazement' to hear of the high wages that Shelikhov paid to his common sailors and workers—that is to say, between 600 and 1000 roubles yearly. Through such inducements had men been tempted to apply to him for work, without ever paying attention to the fine print on his contracts. Only when they were already at sea (as Sauer had seen) did such men realise that from these salaries, would their own provisions have to be paid—at prices set by the Company. With brandy at a rouble a glass and tobacco at 50 roubles a pound, the men's expenses were rapidly outstripping their incomes. In time, such details would serve to confirm Baranov's growing suspicion: that he would soon come to hate the man who had employed him.

In the best of circumstances, 1792, Baranov's first full year in America, was likely to prove a difficult one. But even as he prepared to organise his first hunting season in the spring, more black clouds were beginning to gather from faraway lands.

One threat had emerged a year earlier while Baranov had still been encamped in the rain on Unalaska. On 1 April 1791 a grand imperial expedition, to follow in the wake of Cook's voyages, had departed from Falmouth, England on the other side of the world. In charge of the two ships, *Chatham* and *Discovery*, was a former lieutenant of Cook, George Vancouver. His mission was to survey the Pacific Coast of North America, with a view to claiming parts, or all, of it for the Kingdom of Great Britain.

The Pacific expeditions of Great Britain's Royal Navy might have been designed to make men like Baranov look on his own leaky vessels, drunken captains and inaccurate maps with shame and despair. For equipment and expertise, the British had no rivals in the world. Thus it was that Vancouver's stately journey over the past year had taken him from the

Atlantic to the Pacific via southern Africa and Australia, and then on to Tahiti and the Hawaiian Islands, without mishap. And when finally, on 17 April 1792, his men had sighted the misty, west coast of North America, bearings showed that they were at 39° north, in other words, that they had hit land one hundred miles north of San Francisco. The expedition was on time and on target.

As a leader of men, Vancouver was no James Cook. By personality he was insecure to the point of ridicule. But the meticulousness with which he would insist on examining this coast was quite unprecedented in the history of seafaring. As he moved steadily north over this spring and summer, he would take soundings and readings in every tiny intricate inlet and channel of Vancouver Island, naming (among hundreds of other features), Puget Sound and the Gulf of Georgia. By August he would be at Nootka Sound, negotiating the final surrender, by the Spanish, of their tenuous claims to this whole coast.

Grigori Shelikhov would have been livid to hear of Vancouver's activities. Five years earlier the Empress Catherine had planned to send her man Mulovskii to these waters to claim Nootka for Russia. Now George Vancouver was claiming it instead.

And even as the British were bidding to grab the lion's share of this coast, another equally momentous and (for the Russians) threatening voyage was underway. Also in the same spring of 1792, was the Bostonian trader and navigator Robert Gray, for a second time, reaching the Northwest coast in his ship *Columbia*. On this occasion the trip from Boston to Nootka had taken him a mere eight months rather than the previous twelve. With a long summer still ahead of him, he found time to cruise the coast of what is now Oregon; it was while turning north for Nootka that he first noticed what seemed to be the out-flowing current of a great river from between two capes. Might this have been evidence of the fabled 'Great River of the West', so long postulated by European cartographers but never yet seen by a white man? Gray was sure of it. Some days later, indeed, encountering George Vancouver's expedition near the Strait of Juan de Fuca (by today's Vancouver Island) he went so far as to tell the British explorer what he had noticed. Vancouver, who had just come up from the same coast, must have been disconcerted to hear it. How could he, the world's most careful surveyor, not have noticed such a feature? He informed Gray that he himself had seen a solid line of surf between the same capes. If any river had existed there, he would not have missed it.

So while Vancouver then departed to circle the island that now bears his name, Robert Gray returned south. If this was indeed the Great River, it would be a tremendous discovery: for almost two centuries, after all, Europeans had been looking for a highway into the interior of northwestern America. And explorers of the calibre of Cook, and now Vancouver, had denied its very existence.

On 7 May he entered a large harbour on the coast of what we now call Washington State, naming it Gray's Harbour. Natives came out to greet them. 'They appeared to be a savage sett and was well armed', crewman John Boit wrote in his journal, 'every man having his quiver and bow slung over his shoulder—without doubt we are the first civilised people that ever visited this port, and these poor fellows view'd us and the ship with the greatest astonishment-their language was different from any we have yet heard . . . they are stout made and very ugly'. That this was a populous, well-watered, well-fed region was fast becoming obvious to the crew of the *Columbia*. On 8 May Boit noted: 'Vast many canoes alongside, full of Indians. . . . I've no doubt we was at the entrance of some great river, as the water was brackish and the tide set out half the time'. But this was also a nervous time. During the night, they fired upon and killed a crowd of natives in a canoe, for getting too near ('I am very sorry we was obliged to kill the poor devils', wrote Boit). Gray, anxious to move on, raised anchor and continued along the coast, in search of the source of the increasingly fresh and reddish-coloured water in which they found themselves. Finally, on 12 May 1792, in calm waters, he succeeded in slipping over the breakers between the two capes.

As events would show, this had been no easy matter. The Columbia River, for its last thirty miles to the sea, is an estuary, varying in width from three to seven miles. The area was exceedingly dangerous to ships, because of its unpredictable shoals, winds and currents. Nevertheless, once safely over the sand bar, wrote Boit, soundings revealed ten fathoms of 'quite fresh' water. The crew of the *Columbia* found themselves staring up the length of a river, which 'extended to the NE as far as the eye could reach'. There was no doubt that this was indeed the Great River of the West. In fact it was the largest river flowing into the Pacific from any part of North America. Its mouth was the first deep-water harbour north of San Francisco. Here in the estuary, in its spring flood, it was nearly four miles wide. Entire trees could be seen floating towards the sea. Its banks, furthermore, were thickly populated. The inevitable crowd of Natives in canoes soon appeared by the ship offering furs and salmon for trading; at a village on the north side of the estuary, Gray's men were able to purchase four otter skins for a single sheet of copper. Later they sailed a few miles upriver, where Gray and Boit went ashore, 'to view the country', as Boit wrote; later interpolating, in different ink, the crucial words, '*and take possession*'. Spanish explorers had probably sighted it in 1775, and numerous Native American peoples had inhabited its basin for thousands of years. But Gray it was who now won the right to name this river after his own ship: the Columbia River.

The magnitude of what had been discovered by these Bostonian merchants was obvious. 'Found much clear ground, fit for cultivation, and the woods mostly clear from underbrush', enthused Boit in his journal, as if already thinking ahead. 'The river abounds in excellent salmon and most other river fish, and the woods with plenty of moose and deer . . . and the banks produces a ground nut which is an excellent substitute for bread or potatoes. We found plenty of oak, ash and walnut trees and clear ground in plenty, which with little labour might be made fit to raise such seeds as is necessary for the sustenance of inhabitants, and in short a factory [ie a fur-trading post] set up here and another at Hancock's River in the Queen Charlotte Isles would engross the whole trade of the NW coast . . .'. Even the local Natives, it seem, were amenable types. 'The Indians are very numerous, and appear'd very civill (not even offering to steal)', mused Boit, before adding, later, that 'the men at Columbia's river are strait limbed, fine looking fellows and the women are very pretty'. In all, Gray and his crew spent eight days in the river, trading for 150 otter and several hundred other furs. That same summer he returned to Nootka, generously handing out charts of his discovery as he went: he was a merchant, not an imperialist.

With George Vancouver, it was the other way round. And given his obsessive preoccupation with detail, he must have been furious at Gray's charts, when one reached him some months later. How could he have missed the honour of discovering and naming one of North America's greatest rivers? This did not stop him from sending Lieutenant William Broughton in the *Chatham* back to chart its course, and to claim it for Britain.

All of which would have been reason for Grigori Shelikhov, back in Irkutsk, to begin petitioning the government all over again. If only Catherine had sent the navy as planned in 1787! For seafarers in 1792, this river represented a whole new highway into—or out of—the interior of the continent. From the moment of Gray's discovery, the Lewis and Clark expedition, twelve years hence, opening up a trans-continental route from the United States to the Pacific, had become inevitable. The mouth of this river would not only give its owner a fine port for his ships, it would also allow him to control the traffic from the other side of the continent. And once again, it seemed, the Russians had missed an easy chance of staking a claim.

Back on Kodiak Island, of course, the unfortunate Baranov as yet knew nothing of these great events taking place further down his coast. 'Expansion' or 'discovery' were concepts that were hardly relevant to him in his current situation: and all the less so, after what was about to happen to Kodiak Island. This was to be a misfortune that no Russian, not even Shelikhov, could have anticipated. But Kodiak, as a place to erect the headquarters of a great new empire, was about to reveal its most serious drawback. And unknown to Baranov, strange forces, even now, were trembling beneath his feet.

We know from more recent history how strong these forces can be. Twice in the last hundred years, Kodiak has suffered sudden devastation. On 6 June 1912, after five days of violent earthquakes on the Alaska Peninsula, one of the most gigantic volcanic eruptions in recorded history blasted more than seven cubic miles of volcanic material into the atmosphere, right next door to Kodiak. After the fall-out, the entire island had been buried under a foot of ash and cinders. And in more recent memory, the Kodiak earthquake of 1964, again exceptionally violent, lowered the topography of the entire island by five to six feet, resulting in colossally destructive tidal waves.

It can be assumed that when the earthquake of 1792 hit, Baranov was in the act of organising his first hunting season. Large numbers of Aleuts from Kodiak and the neighbouring coasts and islands would have been assembling with their baidarkas. Baranov's delicate task would have been to impress his authority upon the local toions, or chiefs, as they arrived, one by one. He would have had to persuade them that it was in their interests to let their men work for him. And then this. It is impossible to believe that large numbers of people were not drowned when the catastrophe struck. Many of the baidarkas would have been washed away. The natives would have been devastated. It could not have come at a less auspicious moment for Baranov. Worse still were the aftereffects. As would happen again in the 1964 quake, the lie of the land on Kodiak was radically altered: 'Our old harbour has become hopeless as a place for men to live in', Baranov was groaning, a year later, in his report to Shelikhov. 'After the earthquakes, the ground settled and became so low that there are regular straits between the buildings, and during extremely high tides there is very little dry ground left . . .'.

It was maddening but true: the brand new town of Three Saints Bay, so lovingly planted and nurtured over the preceding decade, would have to be abandoned. Some time in May 1792, paddling round the island himself on a baidarka, Baranov found and selected a new location for the company headquarters. The name he gave to the future settlement was Pavlovski Gavan, 'Paul's Harbour', in honour of Catherine's son, and the heir to the throne. Whether he drew any pleasure from the notion that the founding of the capital of Russian America could now be credited not to Grigori Shelikhov but to Alexander Baranov, we cannot know. All we know is that the building of new houses and facilities, at the new harbour, would be a massive drain on flimsy Company resources.

As Baranov prepared then, for a second time, to organise the hunting teams for the season, more alarming news of a different kind began coming in from the various ships he had out on service. This concerned the activities of a rival Russian fur company that had recently been installed in Alaska by a man called Lebedev, and was now threatening Shelikhov's monopoly. Lebedev, in fact, was another Irkutsk fur-trader in the mould of Shelikhov. The two had sometimes worked together in the past: and it was not Lebedev's intention now to let Shelikhov garner the whole American market. To stymie his old colleague and rival, Lebedev's men had recently managed to establish a couple of trading posts of their own, in Kenai Bay, on the mainland north of Kodiak. The first of these, St George, had appeared in 1787, and the second, St Nicholas (near present-day Anchorage), in 1791.

By all accounts, these forts were a good deal nastier even than the Kodiak settlements. Thanks to the subsequent arrival of George Vancouver we have a description of St Nicholas. It comprised a few miserable wooden huts within a stockade, and a front gate decorated by a carving of the imperial arms. Vancouver described how, on their arrival, after a cannon salute, they were met by 'two Russians who came to welcome us and conduct us to their dwelling by a very indifferent path, which was rendered more disagreeable by a most intolerable stench, the worst, excepting that of the skunk, I have ever had the inconvenience of experiencing . . . we were however constrained to pass some time in this establishment . . .'. For food they were obliged to eat cold boiled halibut and raw dried salmon: the cooking of the Royal Navy was not its strength, but it was better than what the Russian settlers of Alaska had to eat.

And unlike on Kodiak Island, where—so far—dissent had been managed and Russian relations with the Natives had been prevented from boiling over, the fort of St Nicholas had recently exploded right out of control. In August 1791, Lebedev's latest ship had arrived here, carrying Grigorii Konovalov, a shareholder in the company. After his disembarkation, he had proceeded to seize power from the existing manager. All hell had then broken loose.

The character of Konovalov is hard to discern precisely through the passage of time. By most accounts he seems to have been psychotic. Conflict followed wherever he went. He was a *promyshlennik* of the unreconstructed school, following the old dictum, 'God is high and the Tsar is far away'. Where Shelikhov's aim had been to 'pacify' or 'subdue' the natives, Konovalov's had been to terrorise and brutalise them. Furthermore, he regarded commercial rivals such as Baranov as his blood-enemies. This chaos had not lasted a year, when Konovalov's own men had managed to arrest him and have him shipped back to Okhotsk. But the damage had been done. Kenai Bay was now a place of midnight raids, piracy, ambuscades and gang-warfare. Men lived in constant fear of one another, behind wooden fortifications. The aggravation unleashed by Konovalov had already left these permanent scars and Baranov was still complaining of them years later. Now the Lebedev men would be determined to oppose the Shelikhov men, by force, at every opportunity.

Far from expanding, Baranov's domain seemed to be rapidly shrinking under this pressure. Years later, Baranov told the historian VN Berkh that 'if only he had had two hundred of such brave and energetic men as were in Lebedev's Company, he could have conquered all the American tribes as far down as California'. In fact, Lebedev's men were soon acting as if the whole of Kenai Bay belonged to them, and the following year they would move to dominate the second of the two great inlets, Chugach Bay, as well. 'They have already begun hostilities', lamented Baranov in 1793, 'beating men of two of our hunting parties . . . they took from the natives their baidarkas, hunting darts and seal skins, and beat them up and crippled some of them'. Thus something approaching a reign of terror had begun in Chugach Bay, with entire village-loads of natives being kidnapped and enslaved.

Open warfare with other Russians was not something for which Baranov was prepared. How, he must have asked himself, could hunting possibly take place in such a poisoned atmosphere? Which is not to say that he would get no hunting done this summer. In the event, Baranov, in person, decided to lead a party of up to a thousand men; and the hunt was to take place in Chugach Bay, that great bite-sized hole in Alaska's coast, dotted with islands.

Thanks to Lebedev, the atmosphere would indeed be tense out there. All the natives of Chugach Bay were now suspicious of the white man. But entering the bay, like so many tourists after him, Baranov cannot fail to have been struck by the scenery. The jagged mountains, the cataracts, the precipices and the crunching glaciers of Prince William Sound are still the highlight, for many, of a visit to Alaska. For Baranov, in his tiny native boat, the effect would have been awesome. And here it was, on the small island of Nuchek that he now stopped and waited for his hunters to assemble.

Nuchek is in the eastern part of the sound. For some days, it seems, Baranov would have held court here with leading toions of the area, all in their wooden hats and visors, and long waterproof outer-coats of stitched seal-gut; we have to imagine them in discussion, surrounded by noisy geese and spring-grouse, crowding both the land and the water. But in the midst of all this, an unexpected development occurred. A large ship with a broken main mast was suddenly detected creeping into the bay. It was the first foreign ship that Baranov had ever seen.

The Russian chief and a fleet of natives in baidarkas immediately paddled out to greet these strange visitors. The vessel turned out to be a ship of the East India Company, from Calcutta, called *Phoenix*: from the perspective of its crew, the oncoming bustle of boats, paddled by men in paper-thin parkas of seal-gut and visors ornamented with walrus-bristle, could only have contained potentially hostile Natives: we have to imagine the astonishment of the two Irishmen, Captain Hugh Moore and First Mate Joseph O'Cain, when Baranov finally stepped on board and shook back his hood to reveal the dishevelled face of a white man. This meeting proved highly memorable for Baranov. Joseph O'Cain in particular was to become a familiar face for him over the coming years. Although Baranov spoke no English, and the visitors no Russian, they eventually found they could get by with German. Hospitable and convivial, as he always would be with foreign visitors, Baranov later wrote of spending 'five days on board' with Moore, and having all his meals with him, while he helped the men from the East Indian Company to fix their damaged masts. 'Although it was difficult because we did not know each others' language', wrote Baranov, later, 'we eventually talked about many things'. We can imagine what these things were. Moore had sailed from Calcutta, to Canton and then across the Pacific to Nootka Sound, where he had 'accumulated a big quantity of furs'. To hear firsthand accounts of these places must have captivated Baranov. Few if any Russians had ever seen them. Above all he would have wanted to hear about the land down the coast of America to Nootka Sound. Had the British occupied any of this area? Or was it still up for grabs?

Moore had no grounds to hide things from Baranov. He would have told him about the abundance of sea otter along this coast right the way down to California. He knew nothing as yet of the discovery of the Columbia River, but he could have explained what he knew: that there were still no permanent settlements on this coast, between Kodiak and San Francisco—perhaps pausing to point out the feat of the Englishman Meares, who had stayed at Nootka long enough in 1788 to build a forty-ton ship, in which he had then sailed across the Pacific.

At some point conversation must then have turned to the islands of Hawaii. Baranov may have been a jaded old fur-trader, but having spent twenty years living in Siberia and Alaska, it is inconceivable that he would not have enjoyed tales from lands of such fabulous abundance, where colourful flowers grew all year round, where the surf was a luminous blue, where food could be plucked from trees, where the local women swam naked and happy to the ships of visiting seafarers. If anything could awaken his enthusiasm for the concept of a Russian America, it might have been this.

In the end, a regretful Baranov wrote, 'we parted good friends, and he gave me a salute from his cannons'. Moore also left, as a 'gift', his Bengalese cabin boy, Richard, to be an English interpreter and servant. For Baranov, it had been an extraordinary few days of respite from the unpleasantness of everyday life.

And now it was time to get down to some hunting. But what a short season this would turn out to be. For just a month, it seems, Baranov worked with the Natives to supervise the collection and temporary storage of pelts. One night he was camping by the shores of Chugach Bay, when, he later recalled, 'during the darkest hours of the night, before daybreak, we were surrounded by a great number of armed men . . .'.

His first assumption may well have been that these were local natives seeking vengeance for the abuses of the Lebedev men. They had come up so stealthily that the sentries hadn't seen them. But now 'they began to stab and cut down the natives who were with me . . .'. Self-defence, in these terrifying moments, seemed hopeless. 'They were about ten paces from us, but we shot at them without any result', Baranov later wrote, 'because they had on thick armor made of three and four layers of hardwood and sinews, and on top of that had heavy mantles made of moose hides'. Their appearance, in the half-light of an Alaskan summer night, was awful to behold. 'On their heads they had thick helmets with the figures of monsters on them, and neither our buckshot nor our bullets could pierce their armor. In the dark they seemed to us worse than devils'.

It was a nightmare. They were thus besieged for two hours, with arrows and spears ricocheting off the trees and the rocks. Men were falling all around as Baranov, in his nightclothes, rushed around directing the men to point the cannon in what seemed the likeliest directions. 'God shielded me', he wrote, 'for although a spear ripped my shirt and arrows fell around me, I was unhurt'. But once the carnage was over, nine of their own natives and two Russians were dead. Around and about lay twelve dead and dying Native Americans. One of these, whom they found still breathing, had some advice for Baranov. Kenai Bay, he gasped, would also soon be attacked. From the dying testimony of this man, it appeared that their attackers had been Native Tlingit, who had travelled from Yakutat Bay to carry out a revenge attack on the local natives, but 'finding out we were Russians, attacked us hoping for a rich booty'. Baranov had the presence of mind to collect a couple of suits of the Indian armour, for the possible interest of future ethnographers; otherwise this incident seems to have shaken him to the core. He returned to Kodiak in haste and fear. 'Finally, on July 17, 1792, I reached Paul's Harbour', he later wrote, in an apparent fury, to Shelikhov, 'experiencing during this trip many other inconveniences and dangers besides those I have described. But here they are very common'.

When he arrived at Paul's Harbour, he might have been gratified to find that work was progressing on a blacksmith shop, a warehouse, a store with living quarters, and a place to store the rigging during winter. Even better than that would have been the sight of a ship in dock, bearing much needed supplies from Siberia. It was the *Orel* ('Eagle'), under the command of Shelikhov's latest recruit: an Englishman, one James Shields. But what might have been a moment for celebration soon turned black. Enclosed in the cargo were Shelikhov's latest letters and instructions. Baranov's bitterness at what he had experienced during the year since his arrival in America seems to have overflowed. The most astounding of Shelikhov's new demands was that Baranov, out here in the wilds, should build an entirely new ship from scratch, starting this very winter, using the shipbuilding skills of James Shields. 'I was astonished', he burst out, in his written reply to Shelikhov, 'by your instructions . . .'.

The fact was that there were no larch trees either on Kodiak or indeed in the Kenai area, of the variety suitable for shipbuilding. As Baranov later wrote, in fury, 'the local fir has too many knots and is too brittle for shipbuilding. . . . We have half a flask of pitch, not a pound of caulking, not a single nail, and not enough iron . . .'. Building materials were short. Goods to pay the natives for hunting were short. Food was short. Men were short. The list of complaints went on and on.

Shelikhov would have had little time for his manager's bellyaching. Back in Siberia, things for him were looking up. In 1792 the Chinese authorities, for their own reasons, had decided to reopen the trade at Kiakhta. Shelikhov, with his massive stockpile, including an entire shipload of priceless sea otters despatched by Baranov that same spring, was in a perfect position to take advantage of the change in policy. His furs began pouring through the arcades of Kiakhta by the thousand, leaving all competitors standing. Just as important as this were the dividends now beginning to be paid by Shelikhov's tireless networking. He had recently found an invaluable accomplice to help him in St Petersburg. This was a man who was not only enthusiastic regarding the colonisation of America, but possessed a very important attribute lacked by Shelikhov himself: class.

Nikolai Petrovich Rezanov was destined to play a vital role in this story of Russian America. Far from wintering in smelly wooden cottages in Alaska, by the wild, freezing waters of the north Pacific, this young man was more used to living in a marble-lined palace, travelling in a carriage, wearing a full-dress uniform aglitter with orders and gold lace, and being universally feted. Drawings of him show an aesthetic, even fastidious face, with a long Russian nose and blonde hair. Twenty years younger than either Shelikhov or Baranov, he was to bring not only patronage and royal influence to the project, but also imagination, youthful zest and an unlikely touch of romance. Compared with the coarse merchants of the Company, he had enjoyed a privileged upbringing surrounded by the 'elegant fashions, gorgeous dresses, sumptuous repasts, splendid fêtes and theatres' of St Petersburg, in the time of Catherine the Great. At the age of fourteen he had been enrolled in the prestigious Izmailovskii guard regiment in St Petersburg. There, in the heart of the capital, he would have paraded in elaborate uniforms, training to become part of Russia's elite. It may well have been his alienation from the military—he dropped out of the regiment after only two years—that contributed to his subsequent love for adventure in far-flung locations. Fortunately for Rezanov, his dislike of parading did not ruin his subsequent career. His family was not of titled aristocracy, but it certainly qualified as lesser nobility, and had well-placed friends. One of these family-friends, the famous poet and courtier GR Derzhavin, asked him to be the chief clerk of his office in 1791.

Thus did young Rezanov acquire a toehold in the intimate, feverish world of the imperial court. Once there, an ambitious young man's opportunities for cultivating contacts were boundless. Unlike some of the more indolent members of the nobility, Rezanov seems to have been a creature of high energy and inquisitive mind. Before long, we know that he was serving on the staff of the Prince Platon Zubov, the latest lover of the Empress Catherine. He was also being employed by the empress herself to carry out specific assignments relating to tax and company law. He began to accumulate honours and wealth.

At what point, and where, Rezanov's path crossed that of Shelikhov is not entirely clear. We know that Rezanov's connection to Siberia ran deep: his father worked in Irkutsk as a judge for many years, and it is likely that Rezanov had spent his childhood years there. Through his father he would have learned about Shelikhov. The two men had probably come into contact in 1788, during Shelikhov's petitioning visit to St Petersburg. Knowing Shelikhov's eye for a business opportunity, we can well imagine his enthusiasm for nurturing relations with the high-placed young nobleman. What better means existed for pursuing the right to run his company in America as a monopoly? Through Rezanov, doors were soon being opened to Prince Zubov himself. Such was Shelikhov's enthusiasm to flatter Zubov that he even went so far as to organise for a new group of islands to be named the 'Zubovs' (they are now known, after their discoverer, as the Pribilofs).

By the early 1790s, it seems that Shelikhov's sycophancy was beginning to pay off. Privileges for his company had begun to be granted. And in 1793 a particularly significant letter reached him from St Petersburg. It had been decided, by the approval of Her Imperial Majesty, to send a mission of distinguished churchmen to his Russian American settlements. We know that this news was intensely gratifying for Shelikhov. It meant the beginning of the russification of America; with hindsight, we can say that it was the climax of his career. He had long been seeking to curry favour with the authorities by impressing upon the empress his zeal for spreading the Orthodox faith, and for annexing territories and peoples to the Empire of Russia. And here at last was the official recognition of his struggles.

One has to give Shelikhov credit for taking the long view. He was not, in fact, a man noted for Christian piety. But his expedient involvement with the church seems to have dated back to his visit to St Petersburg in 1788, when he paid a pious visit to the monastery of Valaam, to talk to the fathers there about possible missionary work for the benefit of 'his' Natives in America. Now, he had gone so far as to apply to the Metropolitan of St Petersburg for a priest and a church, by which to convert the American natives of his colonies. And here was the fruit of his efforts. 'Thanks to the Lord', he later wrote, slavishly, to the head of the mission, 'it is, by His will, your lot to propagate the Christian faith in America, a land as yet untouched by Christianity . . .'. Those on their way to Kodiak Island would include the Archimandrite Ioasaf, two hieromonks, two hierodeacons, two monks and two servitors. Alongside these, furthermore, a labour force of exiles and serfs with their families was being granted, for service as agricultural colonists. That Baranov was having a hard time feeding the people he already had, does not seem to have concerned Shelikhov. The opinion of a manager was unimportant where these mighty affairs of church and state were concerned. Anyway, turning down the gracious offer of the mission and the settlers would have been unthinkable. All in all, 150 new people would be heading for Kodiak.

Thus it was in the year 1794 that the mission, bound for America, set out on its laborious journey from St Petersburg, bearing the archimandrite's mitre and cross as well as icons and holy books. On their arrival in Irkutsk, a great service would have been held in the cathedral, under the auspices of the bishop, praying for the success of the first Russian mission overseas. Praises of Shelikhov's work would have been sung, platitudes about replacing darkness with light would have been uttered. Subsequently the entire unwieldy party—missionaries, settlers and Shelikhov himself, along with one hundred packhorses—would have continued on their sanctimonious way down the River Lena to Yakutsk and then Okhotsk. A serene Shelikhov handed the archimandrite a letter as a send-off. 'Without flattery, we rely upon you when we think of the future of this remote country', he had written; '. . . the position that you will occupy there will curb turbulence of all kinds . . .'.

Whether it was during this bizarre pilgrimage to Okhotsk that the family alliance between the Shelikhovs and the Rezanovs was finally sealed, we cannot be certain. But it seems likely. We know that Rezanov came to Irkutsk in 1794, possibly in some official capacity as overseer of the men now being despatched to America. Marriage may not have been on his mind, especially not to the 15-year-old daughter of Shelikhov, who had not a drop of noble blood in her. But the girl was certainly wealthy, and her father no doubt did everything humanly possible to encourage the alliance. So it was, some time during the course of that summer, that Nikolai Petrovich Rezanov and Anna Grigorevna Shelikhova were married in Irkutsk. As a relationship between a man and a woman, it was to be sadly short-lived. As an advancement in the fortunes of Russian America, it was to have untold significance.

But while Shelikhov had now risen into the clouds, Baranov was still deep down in the mud. For him, these years were a time of mounting resentment. Cut off without news, without support, surrounded by bumpkins and foreigners, he seems to have teetered on the verge of insanity. He was a man with a fearful sense of duty, who now found that his duties had become quite unmanageable.

From the parts of his correspondence with Shelikhov that have survived, it is possible to piece together a picture of his deteriorating state of mind during this period. The frustratingly slow speed of these communications was a story in itself: a two-year time lag between sending a letter and receiving the reply was nothing out of the ordinary. To miss the post by five minutes was to condemn oneself to another year of waiting. In such circumstances the cheerful request for a ship to be built in Alaska seems to have been what tipped Baranov over into his long rage with Shelikhov. To add insult to injury, Shelikhov had requested that the shipbuilder Shields merely prepare the work and then leave, taking his own ship with furs directly to Canton. Baranov was not having this. 'Such an important affair as building a ship cannot be left to careless hunters without the supervision of an experienced man', he wrote, scornfully. 'Not a few of the men are sick, unfit to work, or old'. Shields, the young Russian-speaking Englishman, was staying to see the project through, whether he liked it or not. Baranov hated being unable to carry out his tasks correctly and on time. He was a conscientious manager. He would certainly have understood what was at stake: news that Russians had been building ships in America would cause jaws to drop right round the world. And as events would show, the more difficult a task, the more grimly determined Baranov was to demonstrate that he could do it. This did not mean he would get any joy in the process. The letters he wrote to Shelikhov in these years give us the impression of a man almost deranged with anxiety.

He had already decided, with extreme reluctance, not to start work on the ship in the autumn of 1792 as requested, but to delay it until the summer of 1793. But his bitterness at having been asked to do something impossible almost scorches the paper. Chief among his grievances were materials: the complete lack of them. Iron for example, indispensable for nails, hinges, rings, windlasses, chains and anchors, was simply unavailable in Alaska. They only had one blacksmith, who happened to be in very poor health. 'And the iron that we have', Baranov added bitterly, 'must be used for axes and a great many other things'.

The situation with the sails was no better. Baranov simply had no canvas. He had already used up his supply of canvas to make tents and sails for baidaras. 'The old ones', he almost spat, 'became so worn-out that it was difficult to make out of them ten pairs of pants for the native workers, and even these pants fell to pieces after they had been used for two days'. And then there was cordage. 'You sent very little twine', Baranov could not help pointing out, icily, 'so we are short again'. But even this was to overlook the most basic constituent of all: wood. The shortage of suitable trees on Kodiak meant that any shipbuilding would have to take place in Chugach Bay, two hundred miles away. A whole new settlement, effectively, would have to be built for the purpose, running the gauntlet of both the local Natives and the rebellious Lebedev men. And how was Baranov to supervise both Chugach and Kodiak at once?

Not that the ship was the only problem in his life. As he also went on to point out—most irritably—he was also badly short of goods to pay the natives for the produce of their hunting, now that good clothes, rather than mere beads, were demanded. There was also the small matter of the earthquake, not to mention the ongoing quarrel with the Lebedev men.

If Baranov could have identified one general problem in his situation, it might have been his lack of resourceful, healthy Russians workers: of the 162 Russians that had been left to him, ten so far had died—two killed by Tlingit Native Americans, and eight drowned in a storm. Of the 152 remaining, wrote Baranov, fifteen were 'sick and old' including, perhaps, himself (but he later described the men that Shelikhov subsequently sent him as 'parasites, sent to make up the numbers'). In response to Shelikhov's accusation that he had been sending back insufficient shipments of furs, meanwhile, his (exaggerated) retort was that the vessel *Simeon* was now so old for use that his experienced Captain Izmailov refused to sail it. As for the *Orel*, Baranov conceded that it might eventually be dispatched. 'I will try to send off according to circumstances', he wrote, sulkily. He himself had received no shipments in months.

As a matter of fact the poor fur harvests were a genuine worry to him, though he was keen to dispel any suspicion that these might be his fault. He referred constantly to the fact that Kenai Bay was now almost hunted out. 'With many partners in the company, this should be considered unsatisfactory', he wrote of the total number of furs obtained the previous summer. As to foxes, otters, and 'all other trifles' gathered during the latest winter, he was unable to give the exact number caught, because 'I have no books here and am writing from Chugach where I am supervising the construction'.

Just to ensure that Shelikhov could not possibly underestimate his misery, under a leaky roof, in half-light, with scarcely a scrap of dry paper to write on, he now proceeded to explain in detail why he was not sending these letters in duplicate or triplicate, as was customary. 'You can make the copies yourself', he wrote, rudely, before pointing out that his assistant Ivan Kuskov was the only literate man at Chugach and anyway, that they lacked paper. 'We've used it all up on accounts and notebooks in the harbour and in the crews . . . and above all for correspondence, as well as on the formal office books'. 'Rainy weather is frequent here, and lasts a long time', he added, as if Shelikhov might have forgotten the incessant rains of coastal Alaska. And anyway, he wanted to know: where were the ten stacks or more of new paper that he had been expecting? 'Even now . . . receipts and bills would be made out correctly everywhere, if things were sent from Kodiak and if I was not in such a hurry, burdened with so much work and papers . . .'. He finally signed off his letter, dispatched on the *Simeon* in the summer of 1793, with a morbid flourish. 'My respects to all my friends . . .' he wrote. 'Tell them that I am still alive'. Which then seems to have prompted the afterthought: 'Please ship all the chain mail or armour you can. Guns and bayonets are very useful in time of danger, also we need more grenades for the cannons; and more cannons'.

As things turned out, any kind of shipment at all would have been better than none. And yet for the whole summer of 1793, the Russians in Alaska waited for supplies. Surely Shelikhov would not be so callous as to let an entire season pass by without sending a single ship? Hurrying back to Kodiak in the late autumn, risking high seas and autumnal storms in the process, Baranov had been convinced that he would find the long-awaited shipment. But it was not to be. No new ship had arrived. 'We reached Kodiak on November 7', he later wrote, 'and my desperation on not finding a transport from Okhotsk was extreme . . .'. For another long winter there would be nothing to pay the natives, no materials for the ship and no treats at home.

In the end, it was to be the same story throughout the following spring and summer as well. The colony was ticking over on starvation rations when a ship finally did sail into view in September 1794. But when it came, its principal cargo—a group of severe-faced, long-bearded men in black robes and tall conical hats—was not one that Baranov had been hoping for. If anything, the arrival of these clerics, followed by a second ship of convict-settlers a few weeks later, seems to have plunged Baranov into an even worse mood than before. Shelikhov's first letter in two years, brought off the ship by the Archimandrite Ioasaf, was highly critical of Baranov, belittling his anxieties, accusing him of being afraid of 'mice', telling him not to complain and not to be wasteful. The issue with the Lebedev men, Shelikhov had declared, was a trifling matter, to be dealt with by 'tact' and 'diplomacy'. Fraternising with the Englishman Captain Moore, on the other hand, had been wrong-headed and irresponsible. Then there were the shipments: 'In the future', wrote Shelikhov haughtily, 'send ships earlier and do not think that sending a ship here is just as easy as sending one across a river. The very best and most trustworthy men should be assigned, not drunkards'. Baranov's bile must have risen to boiling point as he read this (in his reply, he would explain that he had read Shelikhov's letter 'with extreme politeness, in spite of the fact that you consider me not as a friend but as a lowly slave'). But yet to come were Shelikhov's latest instructions. 'It remains now', ran the letter, 'after finding a good location on the mainland, to build a well-planned settlement . . .'.

Last time, Baranov had been asked to build a ship without resources; this time, he was being asked to build an entire city on the northwest coast. Which meant that, in effect, he was being asked to do what Peter the Great had done ninety years before: found a new city, on the edge of a wilderness, in impossible circumstances. Yes, there was the small matter of Baranov not being Peter the Great, and not being able to mobilise the resources and labour of the entire Russian Empire. But if St Petersburg on the untamed Gulf of Finland had grown into the grandest city in Europe in less than a hundred years, why could the same thing not happen in Alaska? Foreigners, Shelikhov wrote, must not be permitted to think that Russians live in America 'in the same abominable way as at Okhotsk'.

Shelikhov's tone as he addressed Baranov was sometimes malicious with sarcasm, but he was also deadly serious about his idea. 'Please dear friend, for your own pleasure and satisfaction', his letter went on, 'plan it to be beautiful and pleasant to live in. Have public squares for meetings and gatherings. The streets must not be very long, but wide, and must radiate from the squares . . . leave the trees in the streets in front of the houses. The houses should be well separated to make the town look bigger. The vegetable gardens must be separated from the street by good fences. For God's sake don't do things in the small village style. . . . The public buildings such as the church, monastery, office of clerical affairs, guardhouse, warehouses, store etc, must be planned and constructed, and their sites chosen, in the style of big cities . . .'.

We have to remember that Shelikhov, writing these words, had not only just acquired a new nobleman for a son-in-law, but he had recently won himself the backing of the Russian Church for the russification of America. He had always been an optimist; now there was something messianic in his tone. Regarding his great new city of the future, he began pondering the details. '. . . [T]o impress foreigners and the natives', he mused, 'it wouldn't be bad to dress the hunters in some coats of military pattern and give them, when needed, some weapons to carry, such as, for instance, bayonets to be worn on the side'.

Was this a description of a future Russian city on the American mainland? A Russian rival for Boston, perhaps? 'You can have these coats made out of the woollens sent to you this time, choosing the best . . . have the boys trained to play musical instruments, to beat the drums at daybreak and at sunset . . . good habits once established, stay forever. In time, this small settlement will become a big city'. Even that was not the end of it. Shelikhov went on to speak of copper bells to ring the hours, solemn courthouses, redoubts for the artillery, turnpikes, high palisades, big strong gates with names like *Glory of Russia* or *Glory of America*. 'Everything must be impressive', he concluded, 'and look important, especially when a foreign ship arrives'. Once reports of this new settlement began to get out (he reminded Baranov cheerfully), Russians would want to flock there, and 'your achievements will become known, and will create a sensation at court'.

If only Baranov had been able to explain the torture he had been suffering, merely in trying to get his ship built, not to speak of an entire new city! The previous summer he had in fact established a shipbuilding location in Chugach Bay, and set men to work there. In theory, the men were to labour for the duration of the winter, while he, Baranov, returned to Kodiak to look after affairs at Paul's Harbour. But the whole experience had been traumatic. In his letter of 1794, we see him complain bitterly of the difficulties he had faced in building a ship, as requested, more than 200 miles from Kodiak, despite being short of steel, iron, hemp, caulking material and pitch. He wrote of worrying about the ship 'all winter long'. 'I flattered myself', he added, cynically, 'that you would help me out as you promised . . . but the month of July arrived and nothing happened'.

More than half of his Russians had had to spend the winter in Chugach, preparing the lumber and constructing the ship. In the sub-zero temperatures of the Alaskan mainland, on very limited food supplies, without adequate shelter, these men had had to cut trees and plane wood, using defective tools, for months on end. As Baranov saw, they had almost started a mutiny rather than do this, giving as reasons an 'insufficient number of men, danger in the places not yet subjugated, and obstacles put up by Lebedev's men'. Baranov seems to have sympathised, but been unable to help. Food supplies were a major problem. Instead of nasty iukola, it seems, the men began to request flour everyday. Subsequently, during Baranov's wintertime absence on Kodiak, '. . . they made a lot of trouble and divided into factions . . . the situation became dangerous'. The men, it seems, held secret meetings, wrote resolutions and even decided to quit the work. 'Some rascals' he said elsewhere, '. . . insisted on having . . . cakes from white flour when there is not enough of it to be used every-day for everybody'. On Baranov's return the following spring, he wrote, 'the scoundrels made an attempt on my life'.

It is hard to guess from the furious and bitter way in which Baranov spoke of this building project, that a brand new ship was in fact now ready to sail: it had finally been launched, a miracle of improvisation, as the *Phoenix*, in September 1794. Many of the problems had been overcome by Baranov's own resourcefulness, including that of how to coat the wood. After experiments, he had found that 'from the pitch of fir trees, with the addition of ochre or iron ore, I made a good coating with which we painted the whole ship'. Not that this had been a small labour—to make it, nearly 500 men had had to busy themselves gathering resin at Kenai. Meanwhile, he had procured steel from what iron they had, despite the fact that the blacksmith Tsypanov was 'very often ill' and that Baranov had had to treat him himself. The successful completion of this first ship had been an almost unbelievable triumph, and was, in fact, celebrated by a party at which Baranov's sole surviving ram was eaten, washed down by copious draughts of liquor. A year later, two more new ships would be launched here.

But all Baranov could talk of in his letters to Shelikhov were his grievances. 'My white vodka is gone', suddenly begins one sentence. He was referring to the recent shipments, and to the fact that his 'personal things'—vodka from his brother—had been left behind in Kamchatka. As he saw it, the vodka had been 'stolen by the hunters in loading and unloading'. Later he came back to it: 'I did not get a drop of vodka either on the *Orel* or with the recent transport'. Even three superior bottles from the Commandant Koch, sent as gifts, were reported to him to have 'leaked away' during transit. For a third time in the same letter, he returned to the subject: 'As for the vodka shipped to me . . . Pribylov while on the high seas swallowed a whole flask without leaving a drop'.

Melancholy, self-pity and premonitions of old age and death were beginning to dominate his thoughts. Now approaching his fiftieth birthday, he clearly felt that his Alaska sojourn was something more than his mortal frame could bear. 'The time has come when I am getting old', he told Shelikhov, almost in passing. 'The senses become gradually dulled. I have to use a magnifying glass when I read and write at night time. My energy begins to dwindle and I do not feel myself strong enough to fulfill all the new instructions nor do I feel that I have the ability . . .'. We get the impression of a man retreating into his own mind, to escape the stresses of his daily life. 'I hope that you will release me of all my duties with arrival of the next transport', he sighed, elsewhere, 'and then I will present you with a full accounting, provided I am still alive then . . .'.

It was unfortunate for him, in this state, that far from being allowed to retire, he instead had urgent new problems to face. One of these, as already mentioned, was the question of the new settlement. Where and how was he going to establish it? The other problem was the newcomers, and in particular the clerics. If life prior to their arrival had not already been hard enough, Baranov now had the tall, critical figure of the Archimandrite looming over his shoulder all the time in Christian judgment.

A censorious letter from the Archimandrite to Shelikhov, written in 1795, provides a fascinating record of this. The letter does not beat about the bush. Among the Russians in America, thundered the Archimandrite, almost from the first sentence, a 'French licentiousness' prevailed. Far from encouraging the Americans to be baptised, the Russians were in fact actively discouraging them, by flaunting their 'depraved life' beside the 'good behaviour' of the Americans. Of the Aleuts, 'only five children attend the school. Most of the older pupils stay at home without supervision, and have turned again to their savage way of living'. And turning again to the Russians:

'everyone', wrote the Archimandrite in horror, 'openly keeps one girl or several'. 'Not only are the barracks full of prostitutes, but they have gatherings and parties and dancing on holidays and sometimes during the week too'. There was no doubt as to the chief culprit for all this unchristian debauchery: Baranov himself. 'He told me once, *we had a dance so the rain would stop*. His only pleasures are girls and dancing. That's the kind of Christian he is'.

He and his dubious foreign friend, Shields, it seemed, were personally 'licentious', and had 'spread French free-thinking among the others'. As the Archimandrite saw it, Baranov had instructed men to 'keep mistresses openly' and 'the members of his staff, following his example, are not afraid to scoff publicly at the church regulations'.

Blissfully unaware of Shelikhov's own failures to send adequate supplies, the Archimandrite speculated in vain to uncover the reason for Baranov's bitterness. 'To this day', he began, 'I do not know if it was my arrival, or your biting remonstrance [by letter] that so enraged Baranov. He incites all the hunters against you, writes calumnies, and persuades everyone to sign them'. As far as the Archimandrite could see, Baranov was furious with everyone: the 'good-for-nothing' hunters, the new farmer-settlers, and above all the company directors back in Siberia (including Shelikhov himself), who had been 'growing rich' at the expense of the company. 'I see nothing good in his business management', summed up the unbending cleric. 'There was starvation from the time of our arrival here, and throughout the winter'. The cooks were 'half-naked, bare-footed and dirty'. Hardly any collective fishing was done, and in response to requests for food, Baranov reportedly went around saying that he was 'not a servant to provide food for the settlers'. The nets were left lying on the ground near the beach all winter; the cowhides were being allowed to rot; dogs had been allowed to get the calves and goats. 'I have never seen him go out to see how things are, the way a boss should', added the Archimandrite. 'He sits, day and night writing all kinds of chicanery . . .'.

Through the passage of time, it is hard to take these charges completely seriously. Clearly there was a feud between the two men. Towards the end of the same letter, the Archimandrite goes so far as to accuse Baranov of murder. Not only does he 'deal cruelly' with all the Aleut hunters, in the view of the Archimandrite, but, 'he has already sent many people to the world beyond, so he would not be scrupulous about killing me'.

Was Baranov such a monster? Conditions under his stewardship were certainly grim, insofar as the Kodiak colony failed to live up to Shelikhov's glowing portrayals. But much of the Archimandrite's disgust may have stemmed from the sudden shock of having to fend for himself in such harsh circumstances. The clerics had to make their own clothes and do their own laundry. 'We too pack wood on our shoulders, bringing it from the forest for our needs', he grumbled, elsewhere in the letter. 'It is funny that during the entire year, not a single block of firewood is laid by . . . when he [Baranov] asks for tea, his servants will run out and chop a corner off a house, or take a pole out of the warehouse roof'. It was the same with food, of which there was always a shortage. 'From daybreak we have to think about food. We have to walk about five versts to find clams and mussels . . .'. In contrast to this, according to the Archimandrite, 'Mr Baranov and his favourites do not go hungry. They shoot birds, sea lions and seals for him'.

To his credit, in fact, Baranov would strongly rebuff these allegations. He did not, after all, see himself as a Russian ambassador to the world, but as a much-abused employee. In a letter dispatched to Shelikhov simultaneously with the Archimandrite's criticisms, he fiercely rejected the notion that he had favourites, that he was idle or that he embezzled money. As regards his supposedly debauched life-style, he preferred to describe it as 'good clean fun on some of the holidays'. Baranov would never allow anyone to deprive him of his small pleasures; diversions from the rigours of life on a savage coast. On the subject of these, he could not help elaborating: 'For example, we have music in the evening and dancing with the Americans, six or eight couples dancing the kazach'ka, the contredanse and others. The islanders watch these dancers with interest. Some of them are learning different steps, and astonishing others. The musicians have lots of practice, and do not forget how to play. The girls learn how to be sociable, and besides pleasure, we have exercise, so needed in wintertime as a preventative against scurvy'.

This then led him back to a subject even closer to his heart, namely, alcoholic beverages. 'It is not true that we drink vodka all the time', he suddenly burst out. 'Nobody with the exception of myself and Izmailov makes it . . . but I make it only once or twice a year'. It was typical of Baranov that, having raised the subject of vodka, he then somewhat undermined his own protestations by dwelling on it in such loving detail. 'On my birthday', he conceded, 'I make a bucket, and treat everyone to it. Sometimes on Christmas and Easter I make half a bucket out of snakewood roots, and this is all'. But this was not to mention wine of course. 'Berries, certain roots and bracken are very suitable for making wine', he added, wistfully; '. . . and now that I remember it, when we were laying out and launching the ship in Chugach, I twice made a bucket of vodka out of berries and roots. The second time, I added six *puds** of the company's flour in your honour, and we all had drinks and I was drunk . . . if you can call it vice, it was vice'.

With that off his chest, he came right out and admitted his other vice: 'I have for a long time now been keeping a girl', he wrote, shortly. 'I have taught her to sew and be a good housekeeper'. Yes, it was an unchristian liaison, insofar as Baranov had a wife still living back in Russia. But in truth it was far from the rampant promiscuity described by the Archimandrite. Later, when news came through of his first wife's death, Baranov would eventually marry this same girl, the daughter of a Kenai toion (sometimes romanticised as a 'Kenai Princess'). He would also ensure her welfare for the rest of his life.

And in spite of the shortages and the humiliations, Baranov never quite forgot what he was supposed to be doing here: spreading the glory of Russia into America a little further each year.

Not that he could quite believe in Shelikhov's vision of great new Russian cities, springing up along the coast towards California. 'Your plans for the construction of settlements seem to surpass human strength', was Baranov's rather understated response to Shelikhov's latest demand for a new settlement on the mainland. Unlike Peter the Great, who had recruited thousands to build St Petersburg, Baranov had only eight carpenters. And despite agreeing to discuss its location with Ivan Grigorevich Polomoshnoi, the man sent out by Shelikhov to manage the new city, Baranov made little attempt to conceal his contempt for the newly arrived settlers. Writing to Shelikhov, he referred with evident *schadenfreude* to their 'sedition and revolt', 'shouting' at 'your' Polomoshnoi and threatening to loot his stores.

One can only feel pity for the wretched human beings whom Shelikhov had dredged up to be his settlers: none were equipped for the ghastly hardships involved in providing for themselves in the unfamiliar climate and environment of Alaska. Years later, the naval officer Vasilli Mikhailovich Golovnin, a stern critic of the Russian-American Company, pointed out that of the thirty-five families of 'mechanics' (as he called the settlers), only three men and one woman remained alive in 1818. Shelikhov, in his view, 'had used the name of Christ and this sacred faith

---

* *Pud*: Russian measure of weight, approximately 16.3 kgs.

to deceive the government and entice thirty-five unfortunate families to the savage shores of America where they fell victims to his avarice and that of his successors'.

But in 1795, Baranov was more worried about their use than their welfare. 'From among those sent recently', he wrote, 'very few are capable of glorious deeds. They owe so many sea otters that they are in bondage, and have no clothes or footwear. We will perish if we have to depend on such men'. This was not to say that he spared them no sympathy at all. He also expressed the view that they had been cheated into believing that they would be receiving proper rations, whereas the sad truth was that 'they do not get them at all, or very little, and that they cannot get used to the local food'.

Anyway, there was no doubt that Baranov would be relieved to pack off such riffraff, along with the clerics, to remote and insecure outposts on the mainland while he remained behind at Kodiak. 'We decided . . . that two families should be settled at Kenai Bay on the Cape to make experiments with agriculture', he told Shelikhov. 'One or two of the rascals will also be left there and a third in Chugach or near Cape Elias . . .'.

The Archimandrite Ioasaph was very much afraid of precisely this. What might he expect to find at the new settlement, he protested, in his own letter? Baranov, he claimed, had told him that he planned to go down the coast, dropping off settlers and clerics here and there; some at Kenai, some at Chugach, some at Yakutat. The Archimandrite would be among them. And 'though he will not instruct the natives to kill us . . .', the cleric wrote, fearfully, 'the natives will kill us of their own accord'.

As events would show, the welfare of the settlers was indeed at risk and Baranov was indeed looking for ways of getting certain people out of his hair. But this was not to say that his only interest was in leading a quiet life. Far from it: he cared about expanding the colonies. His love of Russia, it seems, still outweighed his hatred of Shelikhov.

In only his second summer, 1793, after all, he had sent out one hunting party of four Russians and natives in 170 baidarkas, under a man called Purtov, as far as Yakutat Bay. Yakutat was the next major bay along the coast from Chugach. The Russians knew they were getting close to it when they saw the snow-capped bulk of Mount St Elias looming up in its hinterland. It was the only way they knew to go: further along the coast, in search of glory, and new otter-hunting waters.

Yes, the distances to be covered were huge. From Kodiak to Yakutat, travelling the coastal route was at least four hundred miles, virtually due east. In the two-man kayaks used by the otter-hunters, it was a back-breaking trip to say the least. Nevertheless, according to Baranov's brief report, his 1793 hunting party was successful. Tlingit natives gave them a fright on several occasions, and 'they lost much time in looking for shelter from stormy weather' owing to their unfamiliarity with this part of the coast. But, in the words of Baranov, 'thanks to Purtov, we made this experiment in hunting beyond Cape Elias to the glory of the empire'.

Later that same summer, returning from Yakutat Bay, Purtov had reported to Baranov his encounter with a three-masted English vessel in Chugach Bay. The Captain of the ship, James Baker from Bristol, had given Purtov a cordial reception and questioned him as to how far the establishments of the Company extended. Purtov had replied that they stretched from Kodiak all the way to Lituya Bay (about a hundred miles further on from Yakutat). He hoped to imply that the whole coast teemed with Russians. Baranov was delighted to hear of it. Such exaggerations were a standard method of intimidating foreign rivals. In his report, the chief manager later wrote with satisfaction of how 'the Englishmen were surprised at seeing such a big fleet of native baidarkas with Purtov'.

Following the tentative success of this first hunting trip to Yakutat, moreover, Baranov once again dispatched Purtov in the following summer, of 1794, with no fewer than 500 baidarkas, carrying two or three men each, for the same bay. About ten Russians in total were in charge of this huge party, carrying plenty of guns and ammunition. On the way across, somewhere in the Chugach area, they had a dispute with some people of the Lebedev Company who told them to get off their territory. They passed anyway. But what happened as they approached Yakutat was more exciting. Purtov himself later told the story of how they came face-to-face with the tribe who had attacked Baranov and his men in Chugach Bay with such ferocity two years earlier.

By all accounts it was a remarkable encounter. The two groups sat down and 'talked over' their differences. The Russians heard the explanations offered by the natives of what had happened. Somehow, a kind of friendship was sealed. Later, reported Purtov, 'we left in the village a proclamation stating that from then on they would be subjects of Russia'. The next stop was the main village of Yakutat itself. To ensure a felicitous arrival, presents were sent forward to the chief toion. And the gesture was reciprocated: 'as a sign of friendship, they sent us also three staffs decorated with eagle feathers, and sea otter skins'. The exchange of hostages for security, as was customary, accompanied all these proceedings.

It was here, on 13 June that Purtov and his men spotted an English naval ship. This turned to be none other than the *Chatham*, under the command of George Vancouver. Once again, conviviality and friendship prevailed all round. At least, it did in all accounts, bar one. The Archimandrite Ioasaph, who was not there, begged to differ. According to him, the English gave Purtov presents and were kind to him, 'but he behaved like a churl and was so impertinent that when he arrived on board the frigate, he shouted: "Hey, quickly, tell the Captain that I want coffee!"' Purtov's own view seems closer to the mark: 'we brought them about thirty halibuts, and they gave us a fine reception, with whisky'.

Anyway, alongside all this bonhomie, it seems that territorial matters were also discussed. The British apparently asked Purtov how long the Russians had owned this territory. Purtov told them that the whole region had belonged to Russia since the first sighting of this coast by Aleksei Chirikov, back in 1741. Vancouver's men did not accept this at face value. They instead put forward a polite assertion of their own rights, based on the discoveries of Captain Cook. And there in the rain, they made a proposal. To discuss these matters further, and perhaps to settle a definitive border between the Russian and British areas, should not a meeting be arranged between Vancouver and Baranov?

Baranov, back in Kodiak, would do anything to avoid this meeting. Three times an appointment was made, and three times it was broken. 'They were very eager to get information from our people and wanted to see me', he later recalled, with pride, 'but I was detained at Kodiak on business and could not see them'. Baranov, it seems, saw no advantage for the Russians in settling the border, when further unlimited expansion to the south was still so eminently possible.

Meanwhile, the presence of the massive armed ships of the British Royal Navy seemed to give added confidence to Purtov and his men. At the village of Yakutat, over the coming days, numerous tribes greeted them with ceremonial dances. 'Then', recalled Purtov, 'the toion invited us to his yurt and offered us a meal, which consisted of halibut and berries with fat, served on fir bark'. Presents were exchanged and a reciprocal invitation extended. Finally, when their chief had been persuaded to visit the Russian camp, 'with fifteen of his best men', a conference was held, at which the attack of 1792 was raised once again.

'They admitted their guilt', reported Purtov '. . . we made them understand that we wanted their friendship, and to prove his feelings, their chief presented us with Yakutat Sound and the small islands that are in it'.

Thus, in the time it takes to spear a fish, were four hundred new miles of American coastline added to the Russian Empire. And the question of where on the mainland to build Shelikhov's projected great new city seemed to have been solved: Yakutat Bay was the answer.

Subsequent to these agreements, natives came from all over the bay, and the Russians presented them with 'various articles of copper, kettles, big and small rings and plates of copper to be worn on the chest'. Purtov's only worry concerned the fact that the natives had 'lots of guns, lead and powder in their possession'. How had they acquired these? They told the Russians that they had bought them from foreign trading vessels 'that used to come every year'. To the astonishment and anxiety of the Russians, it seemed that the Bostonians had been selling arms to the natives. Baranov would have much reason to complain of this new practice in years to come.

Later, the natives were asked if they knew of any other peoples further down the coast 'who were subject to, or had given hostages to, other companies, from Europe or from Russia'. The natives replied that as far as they knew, there were no other establishments further down the coast. So in spite of everything, it seemed, Baranov's grim hopes of conquering the American northwest were still alive. A year later, in the summer of 1796, two years before the first convict settlement was planted in Australia, he personally oversaw the founding of the new town by Yakutat. Thirty or so settlers and their families began building homes and planting fields under the rule of Polomoshnoi. The town was called Slavorossiya. Whether this fragile enterprise would ever become the great city of Shelikhov's dreams, remained to be seen.

CHAPTER FOUR

THE RUSSIAN-AMERICAN COMPANY

Baranov's name is heard all along the west coast as far as California. The Bostonians respect and honour him, and the Natives fear him and offer him their friendship.

Until now Baranov had not been able to run his empire as he saw fit. The war of complaint and counter-complaint that he had waged on Kodiak with the Archimandrite Ioasaph in the summer of 1795 was intended for the attention of Grigori Shelikhov, the mighty pioneer whose decisions still governed the destiny of Russian America. And Shelikhov, the lucky man, lived thousands of miles away in Siberia.

But change was coming. The pioneering colossus would turn out to be mortal after all: Shelikhov was not destined to see Baranov build great Russian cities for him along his coast down to California, or build an empire to dominate western America in perpetuity. Only the years could tell this, and for him at least the years had run out. By the time Baranov's latest missives from Kodiak had arrived in harbour at Okhotsk and then been hauled over 2000 miles of mule-track to Irkutsk, Shelikhov had expired—apparently of an intestinal complaint. He was forty-seven years of age.

It is hard to imagine that Baranov, in the rainy wilds of Kodiak, surrounded by rotting whale-blubber and savages, would have been sorry. Had he heard it, one suspects that he might have brewed up a celebratory bucket of raspberry vodka. But as yet he knew nothing. The next mail from Siberia, informing him of the news, was still two years away. So he remained encamped in his ignorance, continuing to curse his old boss for the rain and the shortages and the vile food.

Little did he suspect the dramatic developments that had now been placed in motion back in Russia. Within months, Shelikhov's newly bereaved wife Natalia was writing a pleading letter to Count Platon Zubov, the lover of the Empress Catherine. 'To whom could I turn', she lamented, 'a widow with small children, if not to your highness?' In theory, ownership of Shelikhov's company had fallen into her sole hands. But a single woman in Russia (then as now) was unlikely to prosper for long. Natalia needed a supportive man behind the scenes. This was where her blonde, upright, aristocratic son-in-law began to show his worthy hand.

It is improbable that Natalia's plea from Siberia would have been heard without the help of Nicolai Petrovich Rezanov. St Petersburg, with its bridges and spires, its noblemen on horseback, its elegant sail ships filling the Neva skyline, its gilded carriages and sledges, and its beautiful women in silk stockings, was still a world where nasty Siberia (let alone brutish America) was extremely easy to forget and ignore. In such a milieu, Rezanov was still unusual. He was a nobleman and an aesthete, but he genuinely believed in the benefits of international commerce. He

PLATES

PLATE ONE

Alexander Baranov

PLATE TWO
Grigori Ivanovich Shelikhov

— PLATE THREE —
Nicolai Petrovich Rezanov

PLATE FOUR
Kamehameha, King of Hawaii

PLATE FIVE

Early settlement buildings at New Archangel

PLATE SIX

Baranov's castle (a replacement for the original building)

PLATE SEVEN

Kodiak, the first colonial capital of Russian America

seems to have been in love with the mercantile idea that ships criss-crossing the oceans could generate massive profits (which partly explained why he had married the daughter of a wealthy Siberian merchant). The business of killing marine animals to collect their furs may have had a squalid edge to it, but Rezanov's own aims retained an aristocratic grandeur: he foresaw a role for the company analogous to that of Great Britain's successful overseas enterprises, simultaneously safeguarding the imperial dignity of the monarch and expanding the territories of the empire, at the same time as earning the shareholders an income.

The British East India Company was a startling example of such an enterprise. But the Canadian fur companies offered models that would have excited Rezanov still more. As was well known, King Charles II had chartered the famous Hudson Bay Company, operating in eastern Canada, as long ago as 1670. But in recent years the Canadian fur trade had undergone a huge expansion. After the expulsion of the French from Canada by Great Britain in 1762, new fur trading opportunities had opened up right across the top of North America. On the scent of easy money, bands of freelance traders had promptly headed off into the wilds, spreading drunkenness and 'sordid and ruinous contentions' wherever they went, much in the style of Russia's Cossack *promyshlenniki*, in their own rampage across Siberia and the Aleutian Islands.

But such anarchic conditions were entirely at odds with the imperial goal of bringing civilisation to new lands and new peoples. Free trade was all very well, but only insofar as it did not jeopardise imperial dignity. And Rezanov would have heard how the British had successfully squashed the anarchy in western Canada just a few years earlier, by chartering a new monopoly—to be known as the Northwest Company. The principal British fur traders of Montreal had finally joined forces in 1787, to exert, in the words of Washington Irving, 'a lordly sway over the wintry lakes and boundless forests of the Canadas'.

This Northwest Company consisted of 23 shareholders, and had 2000 employees, including clerks, guides, interpreters and 'voyageurs' or boatmen, whose job was to take goods by internal rivers from Montreal all over Canada. The main partners of the Company, no matter how wintry and inhospitable the environment, lived in a style with which Rezanov would have been delighted (though of which Baranov could as yet barely conceive). Washington Irving depicts them as 'a kind of commercial aristocracy, living in lordly and hospitable style'. Elsewhere, he calls them 'hyperborean nabobs' or 'chieftains of Highland clans', taking their cooks and bakers and wine tasters into the wilds to cook up banquets of venison, buffalo tongues and beavers' tails.

Could Russia emulate the British in constructing such a company in northwestern America? A company that would combine the commercial aims of investors, with the imperial aims of the tsar of Russia? Such was Rezanov's hope in these years following Shelikhov's death. If one man in the parochial Russian establishment could dream of such a venture, it was he.

He began to act. His first move, at the end of 1795, was to forward Natalia's requests for support to the Empress's favourite. One of these letters to Count Zubov survives, in which we find Natalia writing with desperate enthusiasm, of the settlers and clerics even now braving the rains of Kodiak, waiting to spread out and settle the mainland of America. 'Remembering your benevolent protection of the American Company', she had obediently gushed, in a manner of which her late husband would have been proud, 'I have the temerity to beg your highness to help me get trained seafaring men . . . we have great need for trained seamen for further exploration, discoveries, surveying and transportation'. Finally she had dared to ask Zubov if he might bring the company's needs to the attention of the Empress: the need, for example, 'to ship for the settlers and clergy a great quantity of merchandise, seed grain, cattle and other necessities . . .'.

While waiting for the reply to her requests, she got on with constructing a worthy memorial for her husband in Irkutsk, a fine tomb topped with a seafarer's globe. But when news finally came back from St Petersburg, it did not pertain to the American colonies. Instead it was the grim news that most Russians had been dreading for years: that the long and glorious reign of the Empress Catherine had finally come to an end. And the newly anointed tsar was her emotionally damaged and snub-nosed son Paul, whose favourite activity was playing with toy soldiers. This was a thought to make the whole of Russia tremble. But for the Shelikhov enterprises, it was potentially catastrophic. It now looked as though Rezanov's contacts at court might turn out entirely counter-productive. The well-known reason for this was that Paul had always detested his mother. Now, on acceding to the throne, his chief ambition would be to reverse every policy she had ever had. All her old favourites were banished from court, while her old enemies were invited back in.

Given this, Rezanov's friendly relations with Catherine's last lover Zubov suddenly looked to be of very dubious merit. And when rival fur merchants in Irkutsk now began queuing up to wrest Natalia's business out of her hands, the new tsar seemed minded to help them. It had already been suggested that Shelikhov's company should be punished, for the abuses its founder had allegedly perpetrated on native Aleuts during his lifetime; for such reasons, snub-nosed Paul was soon expressing an interest in breaking up the company and cancelling its existing privileges.

Rezanov had to act fast to stop this. He was the chief protector of the company. We also know that he had considerable aristocratic charm: unlike most men of the age, he had so far managed to keep close relations with both the imperial mother and the imperial son. Far from being banished from court, within months of the new emperor's enthronement, he had in fact been assigned to the Senate as secretary. A month later, he was chief secretary. But would he find sufficient charm to persuade Paul of the merits of Natalia Shelikhov's requests for help? As it turned out, the smooth courtier had one easy card to play: he reminded the tsar of Catherine's famously implacable opposition to commercial monopolies. The ploy worked. The insecure tsar promptly declared himself to be resolutely in favour of commercial monopolies. The fact that the one Siberian fur company to benefit most from monopoly status would be the one Rezanov himself was most involved with does not seem to have troubled anyone at all.

In devising the new policy, the tsar was encouraged, in part, by a recent report from a government committee which had stressed the need for a single company (rather than many) to operate in the north Pacific, to combat 'disorders, outrages, and oppressions of the natives, caused in the colonies by parties of Russian hunters . . .'. In the view of this committee—based partly on the findings of the Joseph Billings expedition, but also lobbied by the energetic Rezanov—there was reason to hope that 'placing the business of that distant region in the hands of one strong company would serve, on the one hand, to perpetuate Russian supremacy there, and, on the other, would prevent many disorders and preserve the fur trade . . . affording protection to the natives against violence and abuse . . .'.

This was of course to overlook the trifling consideration that a principal agent of this 'violence and abuse' had been Shelikhov himself. But in July 1797, less than a year after Paul's accession, the process of uniting the old rival fur companies had already got underway. It worked out in exact parallel to the British formation of the Northwest Company in Canada ten years earlier. A preliminary agreement to merge the two biggest companies, those of Shelikhov and Mylnikov, was first reached; this was followed, on 3 August 1798, by an imperial *ukaz*, issued to confirm the merging of most of the fur companies under one umbrella. Among the stated purposes of the newly merged company was 'the search for new lands and islands in the North Pacific and the Southern Seas, and the attempt to convert newly discovered peoples to Orthodox Christianity and bring them under the suzerainty of His Imperial Majesty . . .'. Thus was the United American Company formed, under Imperial protection—with special privileges and a controlling interest for the Shelikhov Company of course.

Natalia's charming son-in-law had indeed been busy. A year later, on 11 August 1799, another Imperial *ukaz* took the process one step further, sanctioning the formation of the 'Russian-American Company' (RAC), endowed with a monopoly over all hunting and mining 'on the coast of America from . . . latitude 55° to Bering Strait and beyond it, also on the Aleutian Islands, the Kuriles and other islands situated on the Northeastern Sea'. 'The company may undertake to make new discoveries', continued the decree, 'not only above 55° northern latitude, but to the south as well; they may occupy lands they discover and claim them as Russian possessions . . .'.

Even this was not the end of Rezanov's good work. As it turned out, the establishment of the Russian-American Company heralded the beginning of a boom in investment. In 1800, Rezanov would manage to persuade the tsar to permit him to switch its headquarters from Irkutsk to St Petersburg, where he could run it with more convenience to himself and his family. Before long, company officials found themselves lodged in smart, centrally located premises on the bank of the Fontanka, overlooking the fortress-cum-palace being built by the tsar himself.

Not even the assassination in 1801 of the unfortunate Paul (in his night-clothes, in his newly-completed fortress-palace) was to derail this smooth progress. Once again Rezanov would handle the transition with aplomb. Within a year he would be talking the latest tsar, Alexander I, along with many of his family and staff, into buying shares in the Company. Instantaneously, the number of shareholders would rocket from less than 20, to 400 or more. Baranov would have found this laughable: the company he managed was becoming fashionable in high society. The Russian-American Company would no longer be a mere commercial enterprise. In the six years following Shelikhov's death, it would be transformed into a branch of the government of Imperial Russia.

The first Baranov knew of any of these momentous developments, in fact, was when he received a gratifyingly large shipment of supplies from

Okhotsk on the *Phoenix* in the summer of 1797, along with four trained navy officers, presenting themselves at his service. For Baranov, the common trader from Kargopol, to be served by naval men trained in St Petersburg was already extraordinary enough. But now that Shelikhov's belligerent, critical letters had ceased, he suddenly began receiving brief and sensitive missives signed by Natalia and other company partners instead. A letter dated 19 July 1797 supplied the pleasant tidings that the United Company had been formed, with 800,000 roubles of capital. It then went on to state, that, 'we are very glad to have you for a manager in the northeast. We beg you to stay and let us see our plans executed . . .'. After years of feeling like a forgotten outcast in Alaska, at the mercy of vindictive clerics and a charlatan employer, Baranov's status was showing remarkable signs of revival. He would no longer be a 'lowly slave'. The company for which he worked was soon to be a monopoly by imperial decree. By 1799 he would not just be a manager, but a governor.

Commensurate with these changes of status, daily life inside his Alaskan colonies had in fact started to improve by 1797. One improvement had been occasioned by the news that the Archimandrite was being summoned back to Irkutsk, to be ordained as the first Bishop of Kodiak. Another sign of progress had been the removal of the threat of war with the Lebedev men. Chugach and Kenai had once again become Baranov's exclusive preserve, thanks, it seems, to help from the local natives who 'rose up because of their [Lebedev] cruelties and wiped out two of their artels [working groups] . . . killing twenty-one Russians'. Baranov approved this, insofar as it relieved him of a five-year headache. After the slaughter he wrote to Polomoshnoi at Yakutat in April 1798: 'thanks to the Almighty, everything is now quiet as far as we are concerned'.

But the best news was that foreign encroachments on his coast now seemed to be diminishing. This was largely thanks to Napoleon Bonaparte, and the ever-increasing chaos on the European continent. Already back in 1795 Baranov had got wind of revolutionary events from Paris (in the last letter before his death, Shelikhov had complained that the French were 'forcing the whole world to fight them'). Since then, it seemed, war involving the main European powers had become almost endemic. Britain and France had become locked into a bitter stalemate. Spain was France's vassal. Russia too was involved. But unlike his rivals, Baranov was not handicapped by the need to travel across thousands of miles of ocean simply to get here. He lived here. And he was now the acknowledged ruler of a thousand miles of coastline, stretching all the way from the Aleutian Islands down beyond Mount Elias.

None of this is to say that Baranov was about to mutate into a cheerful human being. To some extent his persistent gloom reflected a reality: that life in Alaska was hard at the best of times. The Slavorossiya settlement at Yakutat, for example, had hardly got off to a flying start. During its very first winter, no fewer than twenty of the settlers, 'not counting the women and children', had died of scurvy.

Another factor, perhaps, was that Baranov was a typical Russian. Melancholia seems to have been in the blood. In March 1798, writing to an old friend Emelian Grigorevich Larionov, now installed as company manager on Unalaska Island, we find him less interested in explaining the burgeoning prospects of his empire than in describing an injury he has suffered to his leg. 'I suffered terribly for three months'. he complained, 'and could not go out of the house . . .'. Then, in January, as the leg was beginning to improve, a servant girl dropped the samovar on it, scalding it severely. 'Again,' he declared, mournfully, 'I had to stay indoors and doctor myself'.

It was a familiar pattern. Once stimulated by maudlin thoughts, Baranov found himself unable to stop. In the same letter to Larionov, he complained of being cheated out of money by 'our highly honourable Okhotsk office'. Then there were his various business interests in Siberia, all of which were going terribly badly. 'Besides these interests', he moaned, 'I have to pay on my debt, make payments to my wife, and satisfy the demands of unscrupulous men . . . so you will see why I want to get out of here'. Which brought him to the main point: his profound longing to get out of America for once and for all. Shelikhov's death had not changed this. The directors of the Company, he grumbled, had sent no one to replace him and were 'asking me to stay till they find a reliable man, and that will never happen. I cannot quit because the company's business is connected with the interests of the state . . . in the meantime, I have become old and am becoming older. My health and senses become weaker . . . it would be wise to retire now so as not to end my life in turmoil and sin'.

This was classic Baranov, forecasting his own imminent death, speaking of wanting to quit and abandon the project. But at the same time—just in case—he was also planning his next advance along the coast: he knew better than anyone that half of America was still up for grabs. He also knew that rival powers, especially the English and the Bostonians, would move in as soon as they could. 'Only the revolution in France, and wars, are keeping them from doing so', he wrote, bleakly, in 1798, 'but as soon as they have peace, we will find ourselves in danger of losing this territory which was explored by our seafarers a long time ago'.

To pre-empt this possibility, his latest project was to found a new city of his own a couple of hundred miles further down the coast from Slavorossiya. He needed it. This area now yielded the best hunting, and yet it was too far from Kodiak for his hunters to get there and back in a season. Moreover, this part of the coast was at present highly dangerous for itinerant hunters. The local natives were hostile, and possessed large quantities of firearms. According to Khlebnikov, Baranov knew that they were formidable enemies. 'He foresaw that it would not be easy to occupy their territories and it would need a great effort to subdue them. But the more obstacles and difficulties there arose, the stronger burned his desire to overcome them and to achieve the proposed goal'. A fortified city was required.

Baranov, characteristically, emphasised its defensive purpose, to protect his hunters from these natives who 'have guns, cannons and ammunition in abundance, from the English and from the American republicans in Boston, who aim not only at trading but at occupation of this territory as well'. But it is easy to imagine that he also remembered some of Shelikhov's ambitious talk of great new cities, of leafy streets radiating out from grand squares full of imposing buildings. He already wanted the new settlement to be his capital. He would later call it Novo'Arkhangelsk: New Archangel. If any town in Baranov's Alaska had the potential to grow into a world city, this might have been it.

Deciding on the general location was not a big problem. As usual, Baranov simply chose the next otter-rich bay down the coastline. He found it on the west-facing shore of one of the many islands that crowded the shattered shores of the coast below the 58th parallel. The name of the bay was Sitka.

A promising place to live? Everything was relative of course. When the naval officer Iurii Fedorovich Lisiansky glimpsed the country round Sitka from his ship just three years later, he wrote, that 'nothing presented itself to our view but impenetrable woods, reaching from the waterside to the very tops of the mountains. I never saw a country so wild and gloomy; it appeared more adapted for the residence of wild beasts than of men'. Rezanov on the other hand would see Sitka in a more positive light: 'Innumerable wooded islands in the bay provide good shelter for ships and a fine view', he wrote of his first view, when he arrived several years later. 'There is a lighthouse on one of the islands. A magnificent mountain, Edgecombe, is in plain view, ten miles distant . . .'.

But whichever way you saw it, the Native Americans of Sitka did not seem any less hostile than Baranov had feared. A Bostonian merchant, Captain Cleveland, on the *Caroline*, had visited Sitka just weeks before Baranov turned up to build his city. 'A more hideous set of human beings in the form of men and women, I had never before seen', was how he described the natives in his journal. Some of them had looked 'really as if they had escaped from the dominions of Satan himself', thanks to the terrifying paintwork on their faces which, in Cleveland's words, must 'daily require more time than the toilet of a Parisian belle'.

But it was in the home of such people, in the summer of 1799, that Baranov set off to found his city. Nothing would be easy. Before leaving with his own fleet of Aleuts, he had sent one of his naval officers, Gavriil Terentevich Talin, ahead, to get food ready, and to survey the important coast south of Sitka down to the Charlotte Islands. 'But what do you think was the result of my diligence in performance of my duties for the interests of my company?' he asked Larionov. 'Talin got angry at me . . . because I, a plain citizen without any titles, was requesting a navy officer to obey my instructions'. Having endured for years the malice of the clerics, the newest challenge facing the fractious and over-sensitive Baranov, it seemed, was the snobbery of the very navy men who had been sent to serve him.

Meanwhile, paddling for Sitka, he and his fleet of canoes made a stopover at Slavorossiya. 'I found everything here in bad shape', he wrote, with a heavy heart. Barely able to feed themselves, the men at the new settlement had taken to feuding with one another. In Baranov's impatient view, 'all of it was hearsay and women's gossip'. At best, it was an example of what was not wanted at New Archangel.

Nevertheless, he pressed on south to Sitka, finally arriving on 8 July. The disdainful Talin was waiting, but—as Baranov perceived the situation—'he avoided seeing me and threatened to tie me to the mast and torture me if I came on board'. It was not that such threats would deter him. Instead he began the job of selecting an exact site for his fort. 'I gave presents to the toions', he wrote; 'and saw many good harbours'. He wanted a piece of level ground, with facilities such as fresh water, timber for shipbuilding, and hunting grounds nearby. It did not take long. 'After making our plans, we started to fell trees and begin construction'. The mountains behind were soon echoing to the sound of axes.

Baranov, on this occasion as on others, made no attempt to romanticise what he was doing. Had he been Shelikhov, he might have talked of laying the first stones of a new St Petersburg. Instead he declared that he 'lived in the bath-house all winter suffering from the effects of smoke and a leaky roof'. Nor did he shirk from pointing out the frequent setbacks. 'On the day after they left Sitka', he reported, of the hunting party that had accompanied him here, '. . . they ate some small black mussels. Two minutes later, half of the hunting party had a feeling of nausea and dryness in the throat, and in two hours' time about one hundred good hunters were dead'.

What was more he could now see, more clearly than ever, the effects that foreign ships were wreaking on this Russian coast of his. Two European ships, he noted, had already visited the Sitka area earlier in the same summer; one more appeared just days after his own arrival; and three more would arrive the following spring. 'At Sitka alone, before our very eyes they bartered about two thousand sea otters'. Baranov was outraged at the audacious behaviour of these men. Baranov was also alarmed to note the high prices Bostonians were willing to pay. 'They will give a gun with ten cartridges, powder and lead for one sea otter'. The English, he saw, were already being driven out from this business, on the grounds that they could not compete commercially. 'From the time the Bostonians started to visit these coasts, their [the English] trading has been ruined'. For how much longer would he be able to keep acquiring furs from this coast before his trading was ruined?

To Baranov's credit, he spent much time trying to understand how the Bostonians made their money. When they sailed out of the port of Boston, they would be carrying in their holds blankets, coarse cloths, great coats, firearms and ammunition, rice, molasses and biscuit, cottons, cutlery, hardware and literally thousands of gallons of rum. The trick, it seemed, was to add value to this cargo twice per voyage: once, on the northwest coast, when they exchanged the goods for otter skins; and then again, in China, when they exchanged the otters for tea, silks and cloth, goods which were 'badly in demand in the American Republic'. Most of a ship's eventual profit, he reckoned, would come from the Chinese products subsequently sold in Boston for cash.

Baranov was not one normally to get carried away with big ideas. But sometimes, even he could be inspired to take the long view. With most of the world at war with Napoleon, he had to admit that he was in the driving seat on this coast. 'Seeing our strong buildings and establishments', he told Larionov in 1800, 'they [the Bostonians] expressed the opinion that in two years time it would be impossible for them to do anything more here'. He seems to have felt a modest touch of pride about this. 'They were surprised at our fortitude and endurance', he confessed, 'and above all at our ability to exist on local food and to drink only water . . .'.

He spent the whole of that first winter at Sitka, helping prepare the lumber and erect the basic structures. By May of the following spring, Baranov was already able to report that the rudiments of his city were in place. 'It was not without trouble, but we pacified and subjugated the people there, founded a settlement and built a fort', he was writing. 'Some of the buildings are already completed, such as the manager's living residence, two stories high . . .'. There were also barracks, a bathhouse, a smithy, a kitchen and a cattle-shed. Scurvy had made an appearance during the winter but 'only two died'. Except during November and December, 'we had an abundance of halibut and meat . . . we were catching so many [herring] that we and the natives could not eat all we caught'. There were also plenty of seals and sealions, as well as sea otters. 'It seems to me that a strong foundation is laid there, not only for occupation by us, but by our descendents, which will be in the interests of the state also'.

The apparent success of this winter had been feeding his newfound confidence. No sooner had the first buildings been erected at New Archangel, than he was speculating on the next move, down to what is now the Vancouver area of British Columbia. 'Just now Nootka is deserted', he explained to Larionov, 'and there are no English or Spaniards there'.

The mere thought of moving down to occupy Nootka on behalf of the Tsar of Russia, while Britain was at war with France, was enough to boggle anyone's mind. This would have extended the borders of Russia to the edge of what is now continental USA. Even Baranov was excited. 'We could earn big profits there, and our country would gain millions', he wrote. How many millions? Using what he described as 'very conservative' estimates, he reckoned that the British and American ships were, between them, making off with 10,000 otter skins per year, 'which in ten years time will make 100,000'. At 45 roubles per pelt at Canton, that would amount to 4,500,000 roubles. Take out expenses, he mused, and one would still be left with '3,000,000 clear profit in ten years' time'. This was the money that he could make available for the Russian-American Company, should he succeed in annexing the next few hundred miles of this coast down as far as Nootka Sound.

By 1801, the move seems to have been imminent. According to a report from the RAC to Tsar Alexander I, Baranov was eagerly eyeing his next jump south. Having 'brought under the sceptre of your Imperial Majesty the island of Sitka', the manager of the colonies was now considering a plan 'to annex to the Russian Empire the Queen Charlotte Islands and the Sound [Nootka] which the English have already abandoned'.

Some months later, writing to Baranov himself, the directors of the Company were still urging him 'to extend our claims also into Nootka'—and to avoid, at all costs, limiting the extent of his expansion south by settling a border with anyone. With the British, Spanish and French currently incapacitated by war, the only serious cloud on Baranov's horizon at this time continued to be the free-ranging, gun-selling Bostonians.

In the calm language of the head office of the Company, 'Citizens of the United States of North America trade to the local inhabitants all sorts of firearms and cold weapons, gunpowder and lead, showing them also how to use the latter, to harm our trappers . . .'. In the angry language of Alexander Baranov this sale of weaponry to the natives was 'shameless'. 'I have told [the Americans] many times that they should not sell firearms and powder to the barbarians, who not only are engaged in continuous bloodshed among one another, but are dangerous even to themselves . . .'.

The citizens of no country trading on the northwest coast, least of all Russia, were innocent of crimes against the Native Americans. But by 1800, Bostonians were showing themselves to be as bad as anyone in this regard. Cycles of attack and revenge-attack between themselves and the natives dated back to the very first Bostonian to cruise the northwest coast, John Kendrick, who in a savage dispute with the Haida back in 1791, had massacred at least sixty natives.

One such cycle of killing was unfolding in the year 1801, just down the coast from Sitka, on the Queen Charlotte Islands. The trouble had started after the local tribes had been provoked into attacking the Boston ship *Belle Savage* under Captain Ockington. This had promptly been avenged by Captain Ingersoll of the *Charlotte*, who had, however, inadvertently killed several members of a quite different tribe in the process. In October 1801, the fellow tribesmen of these unfortunates had in turn attacked an unrelated ship, the *Globe*, killing its Captain Magee and others. Survivors of the *Globe* were at this very moment planning the next revenge, probably on the wrong people.

When Baranov pointed out that the Tlingit sometimes turned their guns on the very Bostonians from whom they had purchased them, he was not exaggerating. In 1803 there was just such an incident in the Bay of Nootka, when Native Americans attacked and killed the crew of the ship *Boston* with guns, plundered its goods and burned the ship. One Bostonian would later admit to Rezanov that, since the onset of their trade on the northwest coast, they had lost six vessels to such violence (despite which, noted Rezanov, they continued to be 'driven by the love of profit every year'). But when Baranov tried explaining this to the men from the land of the free, they just laughed, and 'paid no attention to my arguments', saying only that they were traders and that they had come thousands of miles in search of profit, and that 'no one has told us that such trading is prohibited'.

It was hard to say that the reckless distribution of weaponry was directed specifically against the Russians. Nevertheless, it was exasperating for them. And, as Baranov already feared, it was a practice that was going to lead to trouble. Even while arms were proliferating by Sitka Bay, new moves were already afoot back in St Petersburg, to offer government assistance to Russia's new American colonies.

The first years of the century were a time when it was just beginning to be possible for titled Russian officers to take an interest in liberal, 'bourgeois' ideas of international trade and overseas colonies. Notions and understandings that had been commonplace for years with Siberian traders like Shelikhov and Baranov had finally begun to penetrate to the ministries of Commerce and of the Admiralty in the Russian capital. Rezanov had helped to pioneer this. But a new breed of worldly officers with international experience was following fast on his heels. Among these, were two young men who were to play an important part in the destiny of Russian America.

One was Ivan Fedorovich Kruzenshtern, the other Iurii Fedorovich Lisianskii. In 1800, both were around 30 years old. Both had spent years serving in a foreign fleet, namely the British; both had seen the British planters in action in the Caribbean; both caught a whiff of the fabled riches of places like Malacca and the East Indies. 'Never', wrote Lisianskii from Antigua in 1795, 'would I have credited that Englishmen could be so cruel to their fellow men'. But he could not deny that they lived better than most Russians could even dream of.

Of the two, the senior, by three years, was Kruzenshtern. History would eventually record him as one of Russia's greatest navigators; a statue of him still adorns the banks of the Neva in St Petersburg. By birth he was a Baltic German, who had fought with the British fleet during the war with France for much of the 1790s. In 1798, still in British service, he had been sent east, where, in Canton, he had witnessed an event that would leave a lasting impression on him. It was as he later recalled, 'a small craft of about 100 tons, commanded by an Englishman . . . from the Northwest Coast of North America. She had been fitted out in Macao, the venture had not taken more than five months, and the cargo, which consisted entirely of furs, was sold for 60,000 piastres'.

The thought of such easy money had eventually led Kruzenshtern to understand what the late Grigori Shelikhov had always been complaining about: namely, the massive disadvantages under which Russia continued to labour, in respect of its Pacific trade. The obligation to take American peltry by sea to Okhotsk and then 2000 miles by land to Kiakhta—losing two years in the process—was manifestly absurd. How could the Russians hope to compete with the British and the Americans, who were shipping their furs directly to Canton and Macao? Equally serious was the matter of provisioning Russia's American colonies. The present reliance on carrying grain from Irkutsk by land to Okhotsk, and then across the stormy north Pacific in leaky, locally-built, ships, placed a severe constraint on future expansion.

A couple of years before, he had sent a memo to the Admiralty outlining his observations on how to increase Russia's share of the Pacific trade. In his view, an old plan of the Empress Catherine was the answer: to start regular round-the-world sailings, from St Petersburg via Russia's American colonies. All the while Paul had been tsar, this plan had lain dormant. But now that the relatively sane Tsar Alexander had been installed, liberals were again taking charge of the Admiralty, and Kruzenshtern's ideas were getting the airing that they deserved.

The major outstanding difficulty was simply that not a single Russian ship had ever done this long journey before. All shipping to Alaska was still being done via the phenomenally inconvenient Siberia port of Okhotsk. In seafaring terms—in spite of Peter the Great's heroic efforts a century before—Russia remained a pygmy beside Great Britain, whose merchants, in the wake of Cook and Vancouver, were already treating parts of the Pacific as their own back yard. And even from a young country like the US, with its relatively small population, merchants of Boston were now regularly sailing round the world, trading on both sides of the Pacific as they went. When would Russian merchants be able to boast such accomplishments?

Kruzenshtern's memo was the place to start. In July 1802 Rezanov and the directors of the Russian-American Company issued an appeal: the advantages of pioneering round-the-world voyages, they declared, were obvious. 'First, the provisioning of the American colonies for many years at once would decrease the volume of goods passing through Okhotsk port; and this would lower the very great cost of overland transport. . . . Second, our company may well succeed in establishing a lucrative trade in furs at Canton . . . gaining the upper hand over foreign nations. On the return voyage we might even attempt trade in the settlements of foreign East Indies companies, eg Calcutta, Bengal, Batavia . . . in due course bringing sugar, coffee, indigo and other goods straight to St Petersburg . . .'.

By insular Russian standards, these were radical ideas. And yet their time had clearly come. Compared with the British and the Americans, Russians may have been backward, but this was not to say they could not catch up. On 7 August 1802, Kruzenshtern was formally appointed to lead Russia's very first round-the-world expedition, to reach the north Pacific via Cape Horn and Hawaii. He was to be accountable, in equal measure, to the Tsar, and to the directors of the increasingly powerful Russian-American Company.

Preparations took the best part of a year. Lisianskii set off for London to buy two large ships, the *Leander* (a 431-ton sloop) and the *Thames* (370 tons), to be renamed *Nadezhda* and *Neva*, respectively. The amount paid for both ships, including the costs of necessary modifications, was the considerable sum of £17,000. Once the deal had been concluded, both vessels were sailed to St Petersburg. By this time, the process of choosing a crew was well underway. Kruzenshtern wanted literate, intelligent men, including plenty of obedient Germans in his own mould, who could gel into a happy and committed team. On his instructions, good clothes and mattresses were to be issued to all crew, right down to the lowest cabin boy. Brand new rigging was acquired from the Admiralty, scientific instruments and splendid maps came from the Academy of Science. Tsar Alexander himself came to view the work in progress, and then awarded Kruzenshtern's wife a guaranteed income of 1500 roubles for twelve years.

All of which seems slightly to have gone to Kruzenshtern's head, prompting him to go hazy on why he had proposed the voyage in the first place. He did not intend to act as the mere agent of a vulgar commercial enterprise—he was now the appointed commander of a grand imperial expedition, bent on the noble, naval enterprises of science and discovery. The example of Captain Cook, circling the globe to view Venus from Tahiti, would not have escaped him. So while the Russian-American Company began pressing for *prikazshchiki* (clerks) and accountants to be sent, to assess commercial conditions, Kruzenshtern's thoughts turned to astronomers, zoologists and botanists. To an extent he would get his way. When the expedition finally sailed, numerous highly qualified scientists would indeed be on board, including Wilhelm Gottfried Tilesius von Tilenau, the naturalist, Johann Caspar Horner, the Swiss astronomer and Karl Espenberg, the surgeon.

Not that the Russian-American Company took this lying down. They lobbied hard for their own representatives to be included. And two *prikazhchik* of the company were eventually appointed to join the expedition, namely Fedor Shemelin and Nicolai Korobitsyn. But these two were not the only men on board with a particular interest in promoting the interests of the Russian-American Company. In the summer of 1803 the identity of a VIP passenger was unveiled. As personal envoy of the tsar, ambassador to Japan and Plenipotentiary of the Russian colonies in the New World, it was Nicolai Petrovich Rezanov himself.

Rezanov's decision to travel to America in person was a fateful one, which would have multiple unforeseen consequences. In part his motivation for travelling was professional: as the tsar's representative to Japan, he intended to use his diplomatic skills to open up trade with that closed country, to the advantage of the Russian-American Company. And then there was his lifelong fascination for America. To see at last, with his own eyes, the work that had been done by his father-in-law, and to meet, face-to-face, the legendary manager of the colonies, Baranov, would be the climax of his career.

But there was more to it. Rezanov also had other reasons for wanting to get out of St Petersburg in 1803. Just six months earlier, his beloved 22-year-old wife, Anna Grigorevna, daughter of Grigori and Natalia Shelikhov, had been pregnant with the couple's second child, and on 6 October 1802, she had given birth to a healthy baby daughter, Olga. But no joy had resulted. Complications had set in—and twelve days later Anna had died. For Rezanov, right now, in the throes of grief, a voyage to an unknown world could provide him with urgent emotional therapy.

But could he cope with this kind of adventure? That was another question. Now thirty-nine years old, refined, cerebral, he had no experience of seafaring. He had no idea of sailors' etiquette; he knew nothing of on-board discipline or hierarchies. Nevertheless, he considered himself, by imperial appointment, to be the overall commander of the expedition—a claim that Kruzenshtern and his officers privately treated as no better than a joke.

In short, Rezanov was in a vulnerable situation. The quantity and nature of the luggage he insisted on carrying with him (which included a library and numerous paintings for Baranov, as well as mirrors and trunks full of presents for the Mikado) were unlikely to endear him to the crew as an incensed Kruzenshtern later recalled watching Rezanov's possessions mounting up on the quay, which he 'was not a little puzzled how to stow'. Why, the captain must have wondered, would a man like this even think of coming to sea? To the officers, Rezanov, with no navigational or nautical skills, looked like a parasite, and an arrogant one to boot.

Even after getting underway, there was to be one more delay in the Baltic, at Copenhagen, where they picked up another passenger, a scientist who was offering to accompany the expedition without pay. This turned out to be Dr Georg Heinrich Langsdorff, a young German from the small town of Wöllstein, with a thin, intelligent face and an upturned nose. He professed himself willing to do any job to get to America; hence his appointment as Rezanov's private secretary-physician. It was in fact a role for which the independently minded, ambitious Langsdorff was ill-suited in the extreme.

When Russia's very first round-the-world expedition finally weighed anchor in August 1803, bound for the north Pacific, the mood on the *Nadezhda* and *Neva* was taut. The men were in for a long voyage.

The Russian-American Company, thanks to the efforts of Rezanov, may now have been all the rage in fashionable St Petersburg, but on the ground—in Alaska—life was as wet and miserable as ever. As usual, Baranov had no supplies. The last shipment had arrived in the *Phoenix*, as long ago as 1797. And by the spring of 1802, his hopes of expanding south to Nootka were not yet ready to come to fruition.

Instead, stuck on Kodiak, between snobbish navy officers and carping clerics, the chief manager had been facing a serious threat of rebellion from his Aleut hunters. This dangerous situation had arisen as a result of petty squabbles between himself and his navy men, over the question of who was really in charge of the colony. The navy men had wanted to start up their own private fur trade with the natives, and Baranov had told them that this was against company regulations. But by now the natives too were expectant. In squashing the illegal trade, Baranov was disappointing virtually everyone in the colony. Suddenly a revolt among the hitherto compliant tribes of Kodiak looked imminent.

Baranov's hysterical response was to write to his friend Larionov, predicting that 'disastrous and bloody events were bound to happen; the

Russians would be exterminated, all our settlements destroyed, the company would cease to exist and with it all advantages to our country . . .'. These prognostications may have sounded dire, but Baranov was never short of grounds for feeling insecure. In fact, he had not yet recovered from a previous disaster: in the spring of 1800, natives from Cape Chiniak had reported to Baranov seeing an object 'much like a ship' far out to sea on the horizon. But in the following days, a gale had blown in from the west, and the ship had been seen no more. People thought little of it until, as Baranov wrote later, 'our bird hunters picked up a flagon of rum at Shuiakh'. The curious thing about this flagon was that it had the word 'rum' stamped on it, in Russian. For the natives who found it, this seemed to be a matter for rejoicing. 'They were drinking it all the way here', wrote Baranov, miserably, 'and there was still about three pints left when they brought it . . . they tore the wrappings off, they told me, because otherwise they could not get it in the baidarka'. Nevertheless, they had had the sense to bring with them some of these wrappings, which Baranov now studied for markings of identification.

He must already have had a strong suspicion as to what had happened. And sure enough, pieces of boat timber now began to be found where the flagon had been picked up. Not long after, a whole beam of Chugach wood, with bolts attached, was found at Ugachek. Then planks were brought in from Ugak. The conclusion was agonising but inevitable: '. . . our *Phoenix*, carrying the transport', wrote Baranov, to a colleague, 'was wrecked'. It was an incalculable loss to the colonies. The *Phoenix* was the ship that they had laboured so long to construct in Chugach Bay. And now it had been smashed to smithereens. Two years' worth of food provisions were lost. And that was not even to speak of the loss of life. Most notable among the presumed dead were the clever English shipwright James Shields (who had lately become Baranov's closest ally) and the Archimandrite Ioasaph, returning from his ordainment in Irkutsk, as the first Bishop of Alaska.

We can imagine the pain that Baranov must have suffered over this. 'How we are going to live now, having but a few men scattered over great distances, and without supplies, I do not know', he wrote, glumly, to Larionov. 'We have but one ship and I cannot send it to Okhotsk with reports'. Once more he was on the slippery slope into self-pity. 'I can tell you frankly that I am tired, and during ten years of labours here have become old. My last exploit, the occupation of Sitka, ought to be considered a service to the country and to the company . . .'. It was the cue to begin begging Larionov to come and relieve him. 'I ask you to accept my resignation and enable me to leave . . . you would oblige me if you yourself would come here to take over the management'. In fact there was another reason for this sudden plunge into despair. Baranov admitted it elsewhere: 'Neither I, nor anyone else, has any vodka left. Enough was shipped with the last transport, but owing to my weakness it was all used up. At Sitka I used up five bucketsful not leaving a drop, expecting that the new transport would have arrived already . . . the raspberries are just beginning to ripen. Sometimes we make wine out of them to drown our sorrows . . .'. As it turned out, a shortage of vodka would soon be the last thing on his mind.

In 1802, New Archangel was three years old. Baranov regarded the founding of this town as his greatest achievement, and, in terms of increasing the fur-yield it had indeed shown good results. 'Thanks to providence we got more sea otters than we expected', he was able to write in the spring of 1801, with uncharacteristic piety, 'and by the generosity of the most gracious and omnipotent Creator we have this year almost 4,000, counting males, females and young'. For the time being, things seemed peaceful and quiet on that coast. Sentries kept a watchful eye, when parties went out to fish or to cut timber. Chiefs professed friendship to the Russians. All this was about to change.

As to the details of the shocking events at New Archangel, from late June 1802, we are indebted to a couple of eyewitness accounts from those who were unlucky enough to be there. Abrossin Plotnikof, a hunter, was one of them. He had been looking after cattle at the time, when he returned unexpectedly to find a 'great multitude' of the Tlingit Natives (called by the Russians, Kolosh) surrounding the barracks and being vocally encouraged by their chief. Fleets of canoes, too, were paddling up to join in the fun. Soon afterwards, Plotnikof saw that 'not only the barracks, but the ship recently built, the warehouse and sheds, the cattle-sheds, bath-house and other small buildings had been set on fire'.

Inside the barracks, the scene was one of utter terror. As settler Ekaterina Pinnuin recalled, 'the Kolosh broke the shutters that protected our windows and began shooting continuously through the windows'. Later, one of the Russians cut a hole in the ceiling, in the desperate hope of retrieving further ammunition from an upstairs room. 'Great flames shot from there as soon as he cut a hole', reported Pinnuin. It was a nightmare. The men forced to jump from the flames were immediately cut to death by the Indians. But it was not mindless destruction: attackers were then seen removing the company property, including up to 4000 otter skins.

In all, 20 Russians and 120 native Aleut hunters were murdered. Over the coming years, the Russians would work up their deaths into something of an epic tragedy; they began to acquire the heroic ring of a fall of Khartoum, or a Charge of the Light Brigade. Khlebnikov's account was typically pungent. In his words, 'the number of assailants may be estimated, without exaggeration, at over a thousand, and the few brave defendants could not long hold out against them. They fell, struck with bullets, daggers and lances, amid the flames and in torture, but with honour . . . and as the flames, fanned by the wind, leaped upward amid the unearthly howls of the mad, hurrying savages, the spectacle became hideous and awe-inspiring . . .'.

Meanwhile, an element of conspiracy was about to be added to the flames of New Archangel. From down the coast, a British ship was approaching, under the captaincy of one Captain Barber. He later gave the date of his arrival at Sitka, as 28 June 1802. Suddenly a group of American seamen were glimpsed on the shore, waving, and wanting to be taken on board. They identified themselves as deserters from the Boston ship *Jenny*, and told Barber that they had recently been living with natives. Then they gave their news: the Russian town at Sitka had just been destroyed. And these Americans themselves had been 'forced' to join 'on the bloody occasion'.

Barber himself later claimed to doubt their story. To take them on board his ship, he wrote, 'vexed me a good deal, knowing nothing of the characters of the above men, and their having deserted from their ship and residing with the Indians had a very bad appearance'. But hideous things had been happening here. Barber next went to where the fort had stood, and 'found the place utterly destroyed by fire, and the mangled bodies of about twenty men lying scattered among the ruins, a prey to the ravens and wild beasts of the forests, a sight as horrid and shocking as a human being could witness'. He waited awhile, as a few traumatised survivors began creeping out of the woods to be rescued.

Before long, quite a gathering of ships had collected at the sorry site. On 9 July, a couple of Boston skippers turned up, William Cunningham on the *Globe* and John Ebbets on the *Alert*. The three captains, none of whom were noted for their compunction in fighting natives, discussed what to do. And it was decided, apparently in the interests of white man's solidarity, that they had an obligation to punish the natives, and to rescue any Russian hostages currently being held. This did not turn out especially difficult. They simply tricked some native chiefs into coming on board, and then seized them. After a few days of anxious comings and goings (and one hanging), the natives around Sitka released the eight men, seventeen women and three children being held hostage. All were Creoles or Aleuts. Captain Barber now 'generously' offered to return them to Kodiak.

End of story? Not quite. When Barber reached Kodiak, it seems that he was unwilling to hand over the hostages without receiving payment for them. In the words of Rezanov, writing three years later, Barber 'insolently' demanded 10,000 roubles for returning the Kodiak islanders, and Baranov, lacking the cash, was forced to pay him in skins.

So the smoke surrounding the ruins of Sitka remained thick with skullduggery. The role of those strange American 'deserters' would never thoroughly be explained, nor would Barber ever clarify how he came to be so conveniently on hand to 'rescue' the captured Russians. And who ended up in possession of the huge number of furs plundered from Sitka? The Native Americans themselves, or some devilish conspiracy of Britons and Bostonians? Baranov had his suspicions. In trying to consolidate and extend Russia's grip on this coast, it seemed, he faced multiple, unseen enemies.

The treacherous destruction of the city in which he had personally invested so much hope was a severe blow for Baranov. He was a man of fragile temperament, at best. What hope was there now for expanding the empire further into America? If so solid a fortress as that of New Archangel could be swept away in a day, no Russian would be safe anywhere on this continent.

We have an insight into Baranov's state of mind at this time, from the boyish young naval officer, Lieutenant GI Davydov, who sailed into Kodiak just months later, in November 1802. Granted, he was seeing Baranov at a slightly better moment. Davydov himself, after all, was a famously gregarious and convivial individual and his mere appearance had the power to enliven any coast or continent. He and his close companion, the boozy Lieutenant Nicolai Alexandrovich Khvostov, would end up performing a role in this story that resembled something of a comic double-act. And as it happened, right now, the two were bringing with them a decent shipload of supplies from Okhotsk, vodka included—the first received by Baranov in five years—on their ship the *Sv Elisaveta*.

He and Khvostov were also bringing welcome news. The Russian-American Company, they reported, had received a new charter and fresh privileges; and Baranov himself had now been appointed shareholder and (by permission of the tsar) could henceforth wear the gold medal of the Order of St Vladimir. Such signs of official recognition, so few in Baranov's life, were capable of bringing tears to the old man's eyes. 'The undeserved favours which our great monarch has thus showered upon me', he confessed later, 'almost overwhelmed me . . .'.

But the visiting officers saw that the honours and the new shipment of vodka could not alone have sustained Baranov in the aftermath of the Sitka disaster. There was no doubt that they had before them a significant personality. 'All this work, these obstacles, sorrows, deprivation and fail-ures', Davydov observed, 'had not blighted the spirit of this rare man, although it naturally . . . made him rather sombre in manner . . .'. On arrival, the visitors were invited into Baranov's home, where Davydov found everything 'simple and clean'. Thanks to the recent visit of a foreign trading ship, it seemed, Baranov had been able to buy for his home, 'many goods and household utensils, and consequently he gave us a very decent meal, at least considering local conditions'.

And as it turned out, Baranov—the man who had spoken so much of wanting to quit America and throw in the towel—was now in a grimly res-olute frame of mind. 'He had already been in America for 12 years', recalled Davydov later, 'in the company of wild and primitive people, sur-rounded by constant danger. He had been struggling with the deep-rooted depravity of the Russians living here, working constantly in need of many things, often hungry, and at the same time almost without anyone who could work with him with the same energy. . . . It seemed as though he had been left completely alone to find within himself the means to make his lot better, and to support the settlements in America . . .'.

Far from accepting defeat, it seemed, Baranov was now planning a revenge of his own. The dream of founding a great city on the American continent had not been given up. 'Sitka is lost, and I cannot endure it', Rezanov later reported him as saying. 'I will go there and either I will die, or it will become part of the possessions of my beloved benefactor [the Tsar]'. His push south, down the coast to California had been postponed, but not abandoned.

As to the question of how New Archangel had been attacked, Baranov reserved harsh opinions. 'The cause of the disaster and of assis-tance to it', he later asserted, 'were the skippers of the Boston boats, Crocker and Cunningham, with their crews, since they not only enticed the islanders to do this deed, but also traded them the gunpowder and weapons. Later, after the massacre of the Russians, they seized from the savages all the skins trapped by the Russians . . . worth more than 300,000 roubles'.

His own assistant and good friend, Ivan Kuskov, currently managing the Slavorossiya settlement by Yakutat Bay, believed something similar. On 1 July 1802, just days after the attack, he had written to Baranov, explaining how the toions of many native tribes up and down the coast had agreed among themselves to destroy the fort at Sitka, and also to destroy the main Russian hunting party. The overall leader of the natives, Kuskov asserted, 'received all the arms and ammunition from the English or the Republican Americans'. Their reason for wanting to destroy New Archangel had been that the Russians were garnering all the otters. Men from American ships found themselves unable to buy skins in sufficient quantities. 'So they told the natives straight out, that unless they destroyed our New Archangel fort and our hunting party, they themselves would be the losers'.

Involvement of US, and possibly British citizens, to a greater or lesser degree, in the destruction of New Archangel, seems certain. How would Baranov, in his determination to recapture Sitka, respond to such adversaries in future? The answer was not obvious, but perhaps it was a clever one. He would employ them. Even prior to the fall of Sitka there had been signs that Baranov was entertaining this possibility. In the spring of 1801, a ship from New York, the *Enterprise*, had sailed into the Russian harbour of St Paul on Kodiak Island. It was the first American ship ever to do so. Baranov was not, strictly speaking, supposed to do business with foreign ships, but given that he had received no shipments from Russia for several years, he felt entitled to buy some essential goods. It helped, perhaps, that the ship's mate was a familiar face, the Irishman Joseph O'Cain, whom he had first met in Chugach Bay eight years earlier. In exchange for furs, he had therefore purchased a quantity of goods from the *Enterprise* (including the 'household utensils' that Davydov noticed in Baranov's house, the following year).

But this had been just the beginning. After the fall of Sitka, Baranov's business dealings with sailors from the United States would take on a whole new dimension. In the autumn of 1803, Joseph O'Cain visited Kodiak yet again, this time as captain of his own ship from Boston—a ship that he had named, rather endearingly, the *O'Cain*.

This was to be a highly significant meeting. Baranov was pleased, once again, to purchase 10,000 roubles worth of goods from Joseph

O'Cain. Much more important, though, was the pioneering agreement the two men now struck. O'Cain was planning to head south down the American coast to California to collect skins. The normal procedure, among the Bostonians, would be to buy their skins from the Tlingit natives in exchange for goods brought from Boston. O'Cain and Baranov now saw how things could be done in a different way. Instead of buying all his skins, the Irishman would hunt them. How? The solution was simple. Baranov would 'lend' him some of his Aleuts for the season, on condition that they were cared for and paid in the usual way. And the profits from the hunting, when O'Cain returned six months later, would be divided between him and Baranov.

For Baranov, the advantages of such an agreement were obvious. First, given his weaknesses, it was better to have the Bostonians as his colleagues than his enemies; and secondly, Bostonian goods could alleviate the constant shortages from which he had been suffering. Yes he would have to share his profits to achieve this. But of the two parties, the Bostonians were merely traders. He, Baranov, was the imperialist. 'His name is heard all along the west coast as far as California', Rezanov noted of him, a couple of years later. 'The Bostonians respect and honour him, and the natives, even in the most distant places, fear him and offer him their friendship . . .'.

This is not to say that Baranov could yet dictate to the Bostonians; but it was certainly true that the Bostonians would do anything for Baranov if it involved making a profit. One of the part-owners of the *O'Cain*, Jonathan Winship, who was also aboard in 1803, was a good example of this single-minded approach to the making of money. He and his younger brother Nathan were to strike many profit-sharing deals in the coming years with Baranov. They were the archetypal Bostonian traders, youths barely into their twenties, who counted among the hardest, most successful men on the northwest coast. Unlike Baranov, they would one day retire as rich men. But although they were good American patriots, they had few thoughts of disputing Baranov's possession of this coast.

Right now, in the autumn of 1803, O'Cain and Winship took about forty skilled hunters south with them on the *O'Cain*, as well as a couple of Russians to supervise the hunt and monitor the agreement. Timofei Tarakanov, Baranov's representative in charge of the hunting party, would also become a familiar character along the Californian coast over the coming decade. On this occasion, the Russian hunting party was taken down as far as San Diego, enabling it to capture 100 otters, which were duly returned to Kodiak in June 1804. The operation had been a conspicuous success. But what Baranov particularly appreciated was that Russians had now experienced the warm, pine-scented airs of the south. For the first time, Russian hunting parties, albeit on Bostonian ships, had been cruising and surveying the coasts of California.

The long journey of the *Neva* and *Nadezhda* from St Petersburg, down the Atlantic and around the Horn into the Pacific was a torturous experience for Nicolai Rezanov. Bad enough was the fact that he was still in mourning for his lost wife. But from the beginning, his role as commander of this whole expedition had not merely been questioned, but mocked. As the tsar's special envoy, he might have expected to be treated with respect. Instead, having occupied the largest cabin in the Nadezhda, for himself and his suite, he found himself the object of a persecution campaign. The longer the voyage went on, the worse the harassment and bullying became, to the point that thuggish young noblemen such as the twenty-one year old Fedor Ivanovich Tolstoi (according to Rezanov himself) were even threatening him with death. 'After travels of two years' duration with immoral men', he later wrote, in bitterness, 'I have become used to abominations of all kinds . . .'.

As for the man who considered himself the rightful leader of the expedition, Captain Ivan Kruzenshtern, he was entirely disinclined to help. In fact very few men on the expedition had any sympathy for Rezanov, cowering in his cabin, in constant fear of being murdered or shipwrecked. One who did was Fedor Ivanovich Shemelin, the clerk of the Russian-American Company, who left a sympathetic account of the trials of the man whom he referred to emphatically as the 'leader of our expedition'.

The taunting from the young officers and the stand-up rows with Kruzenshtern were only a part of Rezanov's misery. Besides those, wrote Shemelin, 'the torrid clime, and the coarse food aboard had lowered his spirits. In consequence he was imagining only the horrors of death and the constant dangers that could lead to it . . . at the slightest sound, knocking on the quarterdeck . . . his expression would change. He trembled and shook. He could not bring himself to take up his pen and write something with his shaky hand . . . in consequence of spiritual agitation and unease of some other kind, his health was so weakened that we feared we should lose him forever'.

It does seem as though the Russian-American Company's greatest asset, Nicolai Rezanov, was on the verge of losing his mind as a result of what he suffered during this trip. During a stopover in Brazil he spent his time writing letters to the government, demanding assistance 'for the circumstances which are causing me anguish'. Later, on reaching land for the first time after months at sea, at the Marquesas Islands, one of the lieutenants on the *Nadezhda* noted that Rezanov's face showed no relief. Instead, he 'looked pale and full of alarm' at the sight of cliffs and rocks. Even in such a paradise, he 'put on his suffering face'. The tone was not sympathetic.

Was it all Rezanov's fault? Had he been too arrogant and overbearing in his handling of the crew? Perhaps. But the atmosphere on board both ships seems to have been generally turbulent. Good food was lacking; Russian sailors were not accustomed to such long journeys in the open sea after all. An onboard cleric, Archpriest Gedeon, was having an equally unpleasant time, trapped amid 'sneering remarks' and 'people with unruly natures'. 'I was unfortunate enough', he later recalled, 'to spend my time for almost a year . . . on the vessel *Neva*'. He described Captain Lisianskii as being of 'troublesome character' and giving him 'much offence, against which my only cure was magnanimous silence'. Rezanov was not the only man having a bad time.

But at least they were on course. And before them now, north of the equator, rising from the waves, loomed the vast mass of the Mauna Kea volcano. The sailors may have been hungry to the point of faint-heartedness, but here at last were the fabled islands of Hawaii. It was on 8 June 1804 that the first canoes of native Hawaiians came paddling out to greet them. The Russians, not yet planning to enter harbour, had weighed anchor a mile offshore. As Lisianskii later recalled, they were approached by six boats, each holding two or three men. 'These persons accosted us with much familiarity, as if we had been acquainted with them for years', he wrote, in apparent disdain. 'They shook hands with everyone they saw'.

Even Rezanov, it seems, came out of his cabin, promptly to soar off into an aesthetic, almost ecstatic, fantasy. 'The closer we drew to the island', he wrote, 'the more pleasant it seemed. Mountains whose summits were lost in clouds inclined insensibly towards the watery horizon, forming an amphitheatre beautified yet further by coconut palms and other trees whose variegated greens made a lovely spectacle . . .'.

No wonder he coveted the view. But these islands offered more than just scenery. As he must have known, they also offered abundant food, and a possible solution to the problem of provisioning Baranov's colonies. They occupied a vital role in the protection and control of the north

Pacific. One day in the future a great Pacific war would explode from here. If the Pacific coast of North America were truly to become Russian, Hawaii would have to be part of the grand plan now.

Rezanov was not the only man already thinking ahead. Georg von Langsdorff, for one, had his eye on the sugar cane. 'If this were cultivated', he recorded in his journal, 'and a large amount planted, in time Kamchatka and all of Siberia could be supplied with sugar from here . . .'.

And all the hungry sailors understood what fresh food meant. Shemelin, aboard the *Nadezhda* with Rezanov, describes what happened next. A pig was glimpsed in one of the approaching canoes, 'a pig that, at that moment, no one would have exchanged even for the most beautiful woman, let alone for a savage girl'. The men seem to have been almost hysterical. 'There it is, in that craft under the leaves!' cried Shemelin. 'What a sweet and plump little piggy!' Later on, with the ships still anchored offshore, there was another encounter, featuring not pigs but women. Shemelin described a girl, 'about 18, quite attractive to look at', who, with 'amazing agility' leapt onto the ship by way of the side-ropes, and stepped on deck exclaiming 'Good morning!' Looking at all with 'merry eyes full of animation', she held out her hand to everyone approaching her. Her 'vivacity was matchless'; she was wearing nothing but a small sash covering her privates.

If men like Rezanov and Kruzenshtern and Lisianskii had cast their minds back to the desolate experience of cadet training in the ice-bound streets of St Petersburg, what would they have made of this place? The temperature, as always in Hawaii, was quite perfect. Soothing breezes assuaged the effects of a strong sun. From the ship, they would have glimpsed the steep hills of the nearest island, a little arid, perhaps, but dotted with pockets of banana and sugarcane; they would have seen villages of steep-sided thatch huts, and large cultivated gardens. Crowds of semi-naked people would have been jumping in and out of the surf without concern. And after months of ship's biscuit and salted meat, an abundance of fresh food was suddenly available. Over on the *Neva*, Lisianskii reported that 'we had acquired several hogs, ten fowl, as well as a cask full of sweet potato and a good number of coconuts, taro roots and sugar canes'.

There was no end to the pleasures offered by this bounteous country. A few days later, Lisianskii, still offshore, was noting how 'about a hundred women' swam out to their ship at sunset. 'It was with a degree of regret', he later confessed, 'that I felt myself obliged to give a damp to their joy, but I was firm . . . not to permit licentious intercourse on board'. Thus 'this troop of nymphs was compelled to return, with an affront to their charms'.

In fact Kruzenshtern and Lisianskii would have a hard time dissuading their men from relations with the island-women. Sexual fun with 'the uncivilised brunette in a state of nature'—women unshackled by Christianity—was one of the main perks of sailing the Pacific. This had been well advertised ever since the very first Europeans had started to arrive on these islands twenty-six years earlier. David Samwell, Captain Cook's physician, had noted within days of landing in 1778 that, 'the young women, who were in general exceeding beautiful, used all their arts to entice our people into their houses', and if these beauties encountered any resistance, 'they endeavoured to force them and were so importunate that they absolutely would take no denial'. Remaining offshore offered no protection from naked girls: they simply swam or canoed out to any ships they could see. 'When any one of us sees a handsome girl in a canoe that he has a mind to', Samwell had explained, 'upon waving his hand to her, she immediately jumps overboard and swims to the ship where we receive her in our arms, like another Venus just rising from the waves'.

Strangely enough, Russian morality turned out barely able to cope with such encounters. The God-fearing Russians of the eighteenth and early nineteenth century felt far more anxiety about fornicating with heathens than the British did. The same David Samwell of Cook's last voyage had noticed this very thing: in a journal entry from October 1778 he had written, of Russian fur-hunters in the Aleutian islands, that they 'always expressed their disapprobation of our intercourse with the Indian women . . . and seemed to lament our depravity in having connection with those who they said were . . . not Christians' (he had then added, with a snigger that is still audible across the centuries, that 'it is probable that this circumstance may restrain these godly people from meddling with any other Furr in these regions than that of the sea beaver').

Anyway, Cook himself had famously abstained from relations with the native women. It would not do for captains of respectable government-sponsored expeditions—of any nationality—to encourage their men to show weakness in front of the savages, and for Kruzenshtern and Lisianskii, dalliances with the island girls were something publicly to disdain. Apart from taking on fresh provisions, they had only one important task in Hawaii, namely to investigate the possibility of establishing a permanent Russian presence here. Rezanov would have shared this objective.

Which was why the first Russians in Hawaii all now wished to meet the famous King Kamehameha. As events would show, King Kamehameha—later called 'the Great' by his own people—had a pivotal role yet to play in the story of Russian America. But by the time Kruzenshtern and Lisianskii arrived in his country in 1804, he was already a living legend across the Pacific. 'According to all the information that I could gather, Kamehameha is held to be a man of rare abilities and extremely brave', wrote Lisianskii in his journal; 'ships call at his islands not only without the least danger, but in the full expectation of being kindly received'. All South Sea Islanders moreover regarded his army as 'invincible', supplied as it was by merchants of the United States of America.

Even by the standards of the day, the biography of this island king is an astounding one. He had grown up in a world that had more in common with Homeric Greece than with eighteenth century Europe. As a young man he would have taken part in ritualised individual combat with his enemies, involving sacrifices, prayers and exhortations from spear-flourishing orators. In battle, chiefs in feather cloaks and helmets would have directed phalanxes of spear-carrying men, before joining in with javelins and sling-stones, daggers and bare-hands. It was a world in which Achilles or Odysseus might have felt quite at home. But in his twenties, Kamehameha, along with all Hawaiians, had experienced an inconceivable trauma: the appearance of the white man, bringing with them a material culture thousands of years more advanced than their own.

From the time of Magellan's first journey from Cape Horn to the Philippines, it had taken Europeans 250 years to stumble across these islands. Cook's sighting of Hawaii in 1778 would prove to be the last significant island discovery anywhere on earth. But for the indigenous Hawaiians (estimated to have numbered between 300,000 and a million) the shock of discovering that they were not alone in the universe had been potentially cataclysmic. 'Their eyes were continually flying from object to object', Cook had written on the day that the first Hawaiians boarded his ship, 18 January 1778. 'The wildness of their looks and their actions fully express'd their surprise and astonishment . . .'. So great had been this astonishment, that, in the words of Samwell, 'the ship was followed by a great number of canoes, and the whole island seemed to be in motion, a prodigious crowd of Indians assembling from all parts, and running along shore abreast of the ships'.

As well as the brute fact of European technological superiority, ships, iron, European clothes, mirrors, clocks, guns and a myriad products were about to be revealed to them all at once.

But of all the thousands of Hawaiians who came shouting and singing down to the shore that day, none seem to have come with greater excitement than Kamehameha himself. Within days of the arrival of the white man, this colossal and unforgettable individual had begun adapting to the new reality. David Samwell was among those who noticed him, speaking of this 'chief of great consequence . . . but of a clownish and blackguard appearance', who 'came on board of us in the afternoon, dressed in an elegant feathered cloak, which he brought to sell, but would part with for nothing but iron daggers'. Others from among Cook's crew had also remarked on his terrifying appearance. According to one of the lieutenants, he was 'one of the most savage looking men I've seen here'. Another lieutenant, James King, had noted the same thing, referring to a young man called 'Maiha-Maiha, whose hair was now paisted over with a brown dirty sort of paste or powder, and which added to as savage a looking face as I ever saw'. On reflection, King had then added that this apparent fierceness 'by no means seem'd an emblem of his disposition, which was good natured and humorous; although his manners shew'd somewhat of an overbearing spirit . . .'.

In fact the Hawaiians had shown much friendship and hospitality to the British, until the skirmish in which Captain Cook had been killed. And when, in the early 1780s, private traders began arriving in Hawaii, relations were again set fair. A British mariner John Nicol, on the *Queen Charlotte*, noted the native enthusiasm to embrace English customs. 'They are among the worst people to pronounce English of any I was ever among . . .'. he wrote; 'yet they would make the greatest efforts, and look so angry at themselves, and vexed at their vain efforts'. And years later, Nicol could look back with deep nostalgia on his stay in Hawaii. 'Even now I would prefer them to any country I was in. The people are so kind and obliging, the climate so fine and provisions so abundant, all render it a most endearing place'.

Alas that not all visitors to Hawaii had been so appreciative. From the mid-1780s, the ships of foreign traders had begun arriving every year, touting western goods for sale: the highest profits being made on guns and cannon. Over the coming years, relations between the islanders and crews of foreign ships had deteriorated fast. On every island, shore parties from merchant ships were getting into fights with the natives, sailors were being killed, and anchors or entire boats were being stolen. Local Hawaiian wars had traditionally been fought using bare hands and spears: now the roar of gunfire could be heard among the taro fields and the fish ponds.

Total chaos had threatened to break out in January 1790, when the American Simon Metcalfe sailed in on the *Eleanora*, and anchored off the village of Honuaula on the island of Maui, to barter for food. One night, natives had swum silently to the ship, killed the sailor on watch and stolen the small boat tied astern. In response, Metcalfe lost all control. First he bombarded the village with grapeshot, and burnt its huts; then he turned his cannon on the small canoes of the native traders, killing about a hundred of them. The Hawaiians would not forget this atrocity. A short while later, the *Eleanora*'s smaller sister ship, the schooner *Fair American* arrived in Hawaii. Its largely Bostonian crew had already been thrown overboard and were being beaten to death by paddles before they apprehended their involvement in a blood feud. There had been just one survivor from the massacre: the Englishman Isaac Davis, who for reasons unknown to him, was taken prisoner rather than killed. Shortly thereafter, he found himself joined in captivity by a compatriot, John Young, boatswain of the *Eleanora*.

The Hawaiian who had now taken possession of the armed schooner *Fair American*, as well as of the two skilled seamen, was Kamehameha himself. And with the help of his new British counsellors (who were quickly allotted large estates and beautiful wives), this master of adaptation now proceeded to seize power over most of the islands of Hawaii. Already by the early 1790s, he had become the most powerful chief in the country. He had crowds of feather workers, wood carvers, healers, masseurs, chanters, dancers, orators, diviners and genealogists to assist and advise him. George Vancouver referred to him as 'the most renowned of Hawaiian warriors'. That is not to say that he was without rivals. Kamehameha's home base was the island of Hawaii, known today as the 'Big Island', on the far eastern end of the chain. On the more centrally located islands of Maui and Oahu, resided another chief called Kahekili.

Unlike in the case of Kamehameha, few westerners seem to have warmed to Kahekili, who allegedly roasted his enemies and used their skulls for filth pots. But the destiny of his island Oahu to become Hawaii's most important had become apparent in late 1792 when the English merchant William Brown finally found here what foreign sailors had failed to discover in all Hawaii over the previous fifteen years: a natural harbour. Natives had never liked this low-lying southern shore of Oahu, with its heat and humidity and its unpleasant beaches of mud flats and raised coral reefs. But for international sailors, there was no denying it. This was a genuine harbour, offering a navigable channel through the reef, a protected anchorage and deep water with room for a hundred ships. It was called Honolulu. Having made his invaluable discovery, the opportunistic William Brown had conceived an idea. In 1793, he had persuaded Kahekili to 'cede' Oahu to him, in exchange for substantial help against Kamehameha: Brown's thirty-gun frigate *Butterworth* was, after all, the biggest ship in Hawaiian waters at the time.

But still it was only a merchant ship. And in February 1794, Kamehameha had calmly trumped him, by agreeing to 'cede' the Big Island, in turn, to none other than the official envoy of the King of Great Britain, George Vancouver, in his two magnificent Royal Navy ships the *Chatham* and the *Discovery*. In exchange (according to Kamehameha), Vancouver had agreed to supply him with stores and assistance to build him his own ship, and furthermore had promised, on his return to Britain, to dispatch an armed vessel as a gift from King George III.

And luck, generally, now seemed to be turning in Kamehameha's favour. Kahekili had suddenly died at Waikiki in the middle of 1794. A civil war had then broken out among his supporters, with Captain William Brown intervening on behalf of Kahekili's son, Kalanikupule. Thanks to Brown's cannons, young Kalanikupule defeated his enemies. But by now Oahu was descending into anarchy. After his victory, celebrating on his ships in Honolulu harbour, Brown accidentally shot to death the pioneer of the northwest coast, John Kendrick, on the nearby *Lady Washington*, while the latter was at dinner. A kind of Wild West chaos had descended. In January 1795, it had been the turn of Brown himself to be killed in a fight with natives. Kalanikupule was fast running out of help.

And finally the inevitable had happened: Kamehameha, with the help of his British friends, invaded the island of Oahu. Total victory came after he had chased his enemies over the island's central ridge, where they plunged down jagged, wet, black cliffs to their deaths. From that day forth, Kamehameha had been the undisputed king of all Hawaii, bar one last, maverick island: Kauai. With its lush green undergrowth and cliffs and seabirds, no one could yet predict that the affairs of this small island would eventually come to dominate the thoughts of Alexander Baranov, of the directors of the Russian-American Company and even, briefly, of the tsar himself. Right now, in 1804, Kauai was simply the home to a scared and lonely 26-year-old king, the last chief still daring to hold out against Kamehameha.

The renegade King Kaumualii of Kauai had none of the diplomatic or political talents of his great rival. George Vancouver, who had met him when still a teenager, had found him to be courteous and intelligent; but otherwise, his destiny seems to have been to linger fretfully in Kamehameha's shadow, feeling neglected by history. Sooner or later, he feared, he would surely be conquered and killed. And he was right to be afraid: ever since the conquest of Oahu, nearly nine years earlier, Kamehameha had indeed been planning exactly this.

The reason for the delay was that Kamehameha was being highly meticulous in his preparations. In 1796 he had returned to the Big Island, to gather around him not only foreign experts in ships and armaments, but also wives, warriors and canoe makers, for building a new fleet of traditional twin-hulled canoes, rigged with sails. Not until 1804 did he feel satisfied with the size of his invasion fleet. Now it was that he sailed with his canoes to Oahu, ready to launch the invasion of Kauai. Which explains why his distinguished Russian visitors, Kruzenshtern and Lisianskii, were destined not to find him during their visit to the Big Island. Only on arrival did they learn of Kamehameha's absence, before being informed by his favourite British adviser, John Young, that he had taken with him to Oahu 7,000 troops and fifty armed Europeans, not to mention seven four-pound cannon, five three-pounders, a six-pounder, forty falconets, six small mortars and as many as 600 hand guns. In addition to a giant fleet of warcanoes, noted an astonished Lisianskii, Kamehameha had also taken 'twenty-one schooners of ten to thirty tons', all commanded by Europeans and armed with swivel guns. The destruction of the sad renegade, King Kaumualii, on his green island, seemed certain indeed.

All this was discomforting news for Captain Kruzenshtern. Considering that he had to get his VIP passenger, Nicolai Rezanov, to Kamchatka and Japan before the onset of the northern winter he was in a hurry. He felt he had no time to go looking for the king. So he made a decision: the *Neva*, under Lisianskii, could afford a leisurely few days to reconnoitre Hawaii, before cruising to the northwest coast of America. But his own ship *Nadezhda* would sail directly on to Kamchatka, without landing here at all.

This was unfortunate for Rezanov, in his cabin below deck, insofar as he would not now get a chance to walk through the taro fields of Hawaii, or chat with Kamehameha, or plan the Russian occupation of these islands, as dusk fell over Honolulu. In the words of the disgruntled Shemelin, who also wanted a stopover, 'the restoration of his health alone, or even some alleviation of his suffering, would have merited and justified the sacrifice of a few days . . .'. Instead, for those onboard the *Nadezhda*, it was full-speed ahead, to the colder, darker waters of the north Pacific. No new provisions had been taken on board, to the anger and incomprehension of many of the crew. 'God grant us health', grumbled one; 'for our diet will consist of salted viands, pease porridge and zwiebacken . . .'.

Meanwhile, Lisianskii was pointing the *Neva* west, to renew his search for Kamehameha. But once again, his luck was out. As he approached the island of Oahu, natives in passing canoes informed him that Oahu was in the grip of contagion and not a safe place to land. So bad were the conditions, it seemed, that even Kamehameha's invasion plans had been put in doubt.

So it was, on 19 June 1804, that the crew of the *Neva* found themselves unexpectedly anchored off the last island of all: Kauai. Against the odds, the first Hawaiian chief to meet the Russians thus turned out to be Kaumualii—the renegade king. Lisianskii seems to have vaguely enjoyed their meeting. The king immediately presented himself on board ship, speaking good English. He was 'portlier' than his subjects, and an attendant carried for him a feather fan, a towel and a small wooden bowl, which was apparently lined by human teeth. 'I was told that the king spat into the bowl, and that the teeth were those of his former friends', noted Lisianskii, before adding with apparent distaste, that, 'the king was meanwhile spitting almost constantly on deck'.

During their conversation, Kaumualii's woeful, lonely sense of living in the shadow of Kamehameha soon began to emerge. 'He assured me', recalled Lisianskii later, 'that he had truly attempted to win the trust and affection of the Europeans, but that he had had no success: no one visited him'. What—the king wanted to know—was he doing wrong? Why did everybody flock to Kamehameha while ignoring him? If this were not sad enough, the king then proceeded to show Lisianskii what he supposed to be certificates of recommendation, from commanders of different vessels; 'but on inspecting these papers I found that some of them were by no means in his favour', Perhaps indelicately, Lisianskii then advised him 'to earn the Europeans' trust by good and honourable behaviour' in the manner of Kamehameha, on whom so many ships now called each year.

But Kaumualii did not want lectures. He was begging for military protection and support. He explained that he was resolved to defend himself to the last drop of blood against his enemy, despite his meagre armaments. And his apparently hopeless plight seems to have aroused the compassion of some of the crew of the *Neva*. The officer (and future historian) Vasilii Nikolaevich Berkh referred to this 'unhappy king, who tearfully gave us to understand that he expected an attack from hour to hour . . .'. And while, in Berkh's view, the king of Kauai was 'civil and pleasant, as well as very able', his rival Kamehameha appeared to be a man of a 'vicious temper' and 'insatiable greed', whose object was 'to conquer a fifth of the world for himself'.

Over grog in the company of sympathetic foreigners, Kaumualii's mood may have improved a little. And once he heard of the disease on Oahu, and the disruption to Kamehameha's martial preparations, it improved a lot. 'I saw plainly that my words occasioned great joy in him', recalled Lisianskii. Nevertheless, the departure of the Russians later that afternoon rekindled his anxieties. 'So tearfully did he repeat his request for a final time', wrote Berkh, 'that Arbuov and I gave him our swords. . . . We left, not a little troubled about his situation and prospects'. These slight gestures of moral support from the visiting Russians on a single day in the summer of 1804 seem to have had an effect on Kaumualii that he would never quite forget.

Meanwhile, back on Kodiak, Baranov had been planning to recapture Sitka Bay and rebuild the fort of New Archangel, a plan which sounded highly rash to most. His faithful assistant Ivan Kuskov, based at Yakutat, cautioned against it. But recent business events had put Baranov in a positive and determined mood. In the spring of 1803, his two visiting jokers, Davydov and Khvostov were ready to return to Okhotsk, despite the fact that the latter had done 'nothing but drink and rampage' since his arrival. Carrying with them in the hold of the *Elizaveta* that summer, they took back to Russia perhaps the most valuable cargo that Baranov ever sent, comprising no fewer than 17,000 sea otters, worth well over a million roubles.

Then there was his profit-sharing agreement with the Bostonian ship, the *O'Cain*, under Joseph O'Cain and Jonathan Winship, which had recently come to a successful conclusion. That ship, with a good haul of otters, had returned in the spring of 1804. It was also around this time, by a small boat from Unalaska, that yet more gratifying news reached Baranov: it came in the form of a letter from none other than Tsar Alexander. The letter stated that he, Alexander Baranov, had been appointed by the tsar to the rank of collegiate councillor. Henceforth he would count as a minor nobleman, to be addressed as 'Your Excellency'. He was now on a level with the officers of the naval service who had looked down on him for so long.

After long years in the colonies, did he deserve any less? In fact, to judge by the slavishly humble letter he wrote back to the tsar, it was as if the common merchant from Kargopol could not have asked for more. 'Allow me, Mighty Sovereign', he wrote, 'the temerity to fall at your feet and express my supreme gratitude, from the bottom of my heart, for such an incomparable favour'. But perhaps such humility was a device for raising the question that was always on his mind: even to the tsar himself we now find Baranov explaining that 'my strength, health and ability have become exhausted during my fifteen-year stay here, and I am forced to seek retirement and quiet . . .'.

It was probably wishful thinking. For in early April 1804, he was about to embark on his most ambitious project yet. In the company of 800 Aleuts and 120 Russians, he set out from Kodiak with two ships *Ekaterina* and *Aleksandr*, and a fleet of baidarkas, heading south. If this sounded like a grand expedition, it was soon to get even grander. Arriving in Yakutat at the end of May, he was pleased to find that his friend Ivan Kuskov had two more brand new boats, the *Ermak* and the *Rostislav* waiting to join them.

Over the summer this veritable armada (by local standards) proceeded south. They had before them the twin goals of hunting for sea otters and hunting for enemies. As usual, unexpected hazards arose. First, the hunters were hit by sickness. According to Baranov, 'several died and many had to be returned home very ill'. Then several of the boats, including the *Ermak*, with Baranov aboard, found themselves caught in a rapid tidal-current, and swept against cliffs and icebergs. In Khlebnikov's words, 'between the huge walls of ice, the currant produced whirlpools where the vessels twirled together with the floating pack-ice, pressed on each side by this piece or that . . .'.

He and his two companion ships were eventually obliged to exit this strait via a passage through which the tide rushed so rapidly as to resemble 'going down a waterfall', in the view of Georg Von Langsdorff, who tried it himself a year later (in 200 paces, Langsdorff estimated, the water dropped here by five feet). Having escaped the ice, they spent much of August looking for old enemies in the vicinity of Sitka. 'They hid themselves', fumed Baranov, later; but the Russians 'made themselves felt' by burning their houses and harassing them whenever possible.

Not until September did Baranov, under darkening autumnal skies, finally round Sitka Island and sail into harbour. Above him, on a grassy knoll, loomed the formidable log-built fastness of the Tlingit natives; while down below, at anchor, stood his makeshift trio of home-built sloops, *Rostislav*, *Ekaterina* and *Aleksandr*. These were vessels to inspire neither confidence in their owners, nor fear in their opponents. But to the undoubted astonishment of every Russian and native on that entire coast, there also happened to be another ship at anchor here. Baranov's eyes must have boggled. This was a magnificent 370-ton frigate of the Russian Imperial Navy. With perfect timing, it seemed, had the *Neva*, under Iurii Fedorovich Lisianskii, arrived from Hawaii.

It is hard to imagine how the battle to regain Sitka could have proceeded without it. As it was, the Tlingit had no chance. Sixty of their toions, 'wearing armour and carrying rifles and spears', came in glum silence to hear Baranov's terms. He could afford now to be confident. He addressed them as a group, demanding that all Aleut hostages be handed over, and that the Tlingit withdraw entirely from the Sitka area, allowing the Russians to rebuild their city in peace. If they refused, they would be pulverised by cannon. In the words of Khlebnikov, 'the talks lasted about two hours, but the Kolosh refused these very moderate terms and, shouting three times, 'Oo! Oo! Oo!' they went away'.

After the toions had withdrawn into their stronghold, Lisianskii ordered a bombardment of a kind never before seen on this coast. Forays and skirmishes ensued, in one of which Baranov took a wound in the arm. Just days later, a silence fell over the last Tlingit redoubt on Sitka. When Lisianskii's landing party reached it, they found that the adults had fled, leaving behind the corpses of their children.

No sooner had he got the all clear, than Baranov began rebuilding his fort. This time it would be centered on a high rocky promontory and surrounded by an immense stockade of sharpened spikes. Russian power would not be so easily dislodged from this place again.

CHAPTER FIVE

How the Russians met the Spanish in San Francisco Bay

The west coast of the continent stretched away to the

south alluringly and astonishingly empty.

New Archangel, Baranov's new headquarters on the northwest coast, was just as rainy as Kodiak, food was no easier to come by, and relations with the indigenous peoples were considerably worse. And the impenetrable forests, reaching right to the shore, were almost impossible places in which to build. 'The forest is so dense that I think that until the Russians came, the sun never shone within it from the day of creation', was how Nicolai Rezanov later described it. 'Their wildness is frightening . . . one has to crawl and climb instead of walk. The open spaces are covered with moss and tundra, and there are holes filled with water that seems to have no bottom'.

But Sitka had one advantage over Kodiak: as a base from which to push Russian rule ever further south, in the direction of California, it was ideal. Between Sitka and Vancouver Island, along the sheltered passage between islands and mainland, lay no more than 800 miles of coast; from there to Spanish California, perhaps another thousand. In the context of the vastness of Russian America and Siberia, these distances were far from daunting.

By the summer following Iurii Lisianskii's providential intervention, the rebuilding of the new city was well underway. It had been a hard winter, with 110 Russians and 700 Aleuts at Sitka needing to be fed. Shortages had occurred. And as always, the work had been carried out at the expense of Baranov's ever-fragile emotional health. When he sat down to write to his friend Larionov, his thoughts promptly turned to death. 'I am tired from constant labours, and even the honours bestowed on me by my Monarch become a burden when I think that at my age, the end is near'. But he had been through all this before. And at the same time, he had to admit to 'fair success' with the work. 'With the exception of the fort and barracks, which is just started', he could add, 'we had built quarters for the administration, warehouse for the food supplies . . . a kitchen, brewery, bakery, bathhouse, blacksmith shop, locksmith's workshop, copper foundry and quarters for the skilled workers, which are now being completed'. As it turned out, Lisianskii had been helpful in more ways than one. He personally had not stayed for the winter, but he had left behind a memento of his visit: a handsome supply of vodka. 'Even if we drank it only at times', admitted Baranov, 'we were not very moderate as to quantity'.

There would be no shortages of alcohol over the coming year, 1805. Fresh supplies, with interesting company, were already on the way. First to arrive that summer was Captain John D'Wolf, from Rhode Island, on his ship *Juno*. D'Wolf comes across as one of the most open-minded and culturally curious of all the US fur traders on the northwest coast from this time. More than fifty years later, at the age of eighty, he would even publish a genial book of memoirs, in which he would leave a few personal recollections of Baranov. 'From the kind treatment received from the governor', he would write, 'I was induced to form a very favourable opinion of him. He was 65 years of age, and had spent the last eighteen years of his life at different stations on the coast . . . excluded, as it were, from all civilised society, except that of a few of his fellow adventurers. He possessed a strong mind, easy manners and deportment, and was apparently well fitted for the place he filled. He commanded the greatest respect from the Indians, who regarded him with mingled feelings of love and fear'.

But right now, having been at sea since the age of thirteen, D'Wolf would have been in his late twenties: perfect material, in other words, to captain a vessel around the Horn, to 'collect furs for the China market', departing in August 1804.

This amiable man, by May of the following year, had already arrived at Sitka, where Baranov had been delighted to take most of his cargo in exchange for furs. 'After exchanging the usual compliments', noted D'Wolf, they were ushered 'into an apartment where we found a table spread with all the luxuries the place afforded. While we regaled ourselves with the sumptuous fare, the conversation turned to the subject of my cargo . . .'.

During the summer the Bostonian had then traded up and down the coast; on his return in September, he and Baranov had begun negotiating a profit-share hunting agreement for the coming winter. But their talks had been nowhere near complete when yet more sails had been spotted on the horizon, this time coming from Siberia. It was now the height of summer and more supplies, it seemed, were about to arrive. As it turned out, the men guiding the *Maria Sv Magdalena* from Kamchatka that day, were those convivial young drinking partners, Davydov and Khvostov. But it was the identity of the principal passenger that would prompt the most serious celebratory toasting.

'The appearance of so distinguished a personage, whose authority was for a time to supersede even that of the governor', D'Wolf recalled, 'was an event of great moment . . .'. Baranov had never received such a visitor before. And yet here before him right now, stood a tall, blonde man with a fastidious expression on his face. It was His Excellency, Nicolai Petrovich Rezanov, Chamberlain and Knight of His Imperial Majesty's

Court at St Petersburg, Imperial Inspector of the colonies and Plenipotentiary of the Russian-American Company.

It must have been a startling moment for both men. One was aristocratic, elegant and refined; the other tatty, short and coarse. But until now, no personal friend of the tsar had ever crossed the ten thousand miles from St Petersburg to be a guest in Baranov's house. This was immensely flattering. It was a sign to the chief manager that he and his work mattered in Russia.

Rezanov was destined to remain here at New Archangel for six months, attended by his supercilious German physician Dr Georg Heinrich von Langsdorff. In terms of the material conditions, it was surely the most unpleasant winter of either of their lives. As a minor European aristocrat, marooned in St Petersburg's remotest imperial possession, Rezanov would now experience for himself the vile food, the drunkenness, the scurvy, the leaking roofs, the stench of pickled walrus hide and rotting marine animals, the dark skies, the gravel-grey beaches and the incessant chill rains and fogs of coastal Alaska. Both he and Langsdorff have left accounts of their stay in Baranov's northern capital: Rezanov in the form of lengthy letters to the directors of the company in St Petersburg, Langsdorff in a scathing chapter of his book, *Voyages and Travels*.

The relationship between these two men was a curious one. It seems to have been completely without warmth. In his book Langsdorff several times expresses views that are critical of the man who employed him. Moreover, he seems to have disliked Russians in general. 'It must be confessed', he wrote, concerning the society of New Archangel, 'that Christian love, sympathy, and participation in the sufferings of others, are ideas here completely unknown . . .'. Fortunately for him he was to share lodgings with Captain D'Wolf, the only other non-Russian in the colony, whom he later described as 'one of the most compassionate and benevolent of men'. The feeling was mutual. D'Wolf retained such fond memories of his German room-mate that, years later, he named his son 'Langsdorff'.

As for Rezanov—to judge by his recent experiences—he could hardly have been in a positive frame of mind either. He must have been close to mental exhaustion. 'After travels of two years' duration with immoral men', he would write from Alaska, 'I have become used to abominations of all kinds . . . I cannot say that I feel good, at a time when I am busy with reorganisation of American possessions and trade, to be disturbed almost every hour by abuse and turbulence . . .'.

First there had been his traumatic journey from St Petersburg to Kamchatka. Subsequent to that, in September 1804, he had been deposited at Nagasaki to take up his position as the tsar's ambassador in Japan. But there, instead of being received with honour, he had been horrified to find himself under house arrest. Six months later he had been humiliatingly expelled, still bearing the presents he had brought for the Mikado.

Next, he had endured the frightening experience of sailing to America on a ship built in Okhotsk. 'The ignorance of the shipbuilders there, and shameless robbery by company representatives', he later expostulated, 'produces worthless ships that cost more than ships built anywhere else!' It is not clear if he had expected anything else. But before long, in a letter to the Minister of Commerce, he would be writing of the 'calamitous' situation of the Russian American colonies, the 'starvation' and the 'disastrous conditions of the country'.

The fact was Rezanov was no longer a young man. He was now forty-two years old. His wife was dead and his children far away. 'Personal advancement and praise', he was soon writing, in a letter to a fellow Court Chamberlain, written from the drabness of an Alaskan winter, '. . . are powerless to fill the feeling of emptiness and loss, which perhaps only death can remedy, by reuniting the man with what was so dear to him . . . my children tell me that I left them, and I fly in my thoughts to St Petersburg to kiss them and the remains of the friend that I lost . . .'. Nevertheless, Rezanov's arrival in America was the climax of fifteen years of work. His journey had been a mortifying one, but now he would finally see for himself the enterprise pioneered by his wife's father twenty years before. And life in New Archangel was not all bad. Baranov's capacity to entertain visitors was becoming legendary on this coast. One man who already seemed to be enjoying himself immensely was Captain John D'Wolf, who recalled that, after Rezanov's arrival, 'several days . . . were passed in festivity and mirth, and business was entirely suspended'.

Rezanov himself prefers not to speak of festivities. One of the first things he wanted to do in New Archangel was establish a library in the chief manager's house. Many patrons of the company, including counts, admirals, ministers and high clergy, had contributed volumes, which had now been brought half way round the world in Rezanov's crates. The purpose of all this was to 'sow the seed of science in the breasts of the peoples so far outlying from the enlightenment of Europe'.

One difficulty with this was Baranov's attitude. Years later, he supposedly complained to Vasili Golovnin that the company should have sent a doctor ('because there is not one'), rather than so many fine pictures. Another problem was Baranov's house. 'He lives in a sort of plank yurt', Rezanov wrote, in apparent shock, to the directors of the company, 'which is so damp that the mildew has to be wiped off everyday. The shack is full of holes and with the continuous rains it leaks like a sieve . . . once I found his bed standing in water and asked him: "Perhaps the wind tore off a board somewhere?" "No", he replied calmly, "it seems to have run in under the floor", and went about his business'.

But this is not to say that Baranov and Rezanov had no personal chemistry. They had things in common, including a tendency to maudlin thoughts and manic mood-swings. To judge by his letters, Rezanov looked upon Baranov with intense admiration. 'I tell you Dear Sirs', he soon declared, to his fellow directors back in St Petersburg, 'that Baranov is a quite unique and happy creation of nature'.

The only upsetting thing was that this happy creation—'this honourable old man'—was constantly asking that his resignation be accepted. In an official ceremony Rezanov had presented Baranov with a gold medal, which he had received 'with tears of gratitude', but it had not been enough to tempt him to stay. The problem appeared to be the lack of appreciation that had been shown him over the years, in spite of his good work.

Among Baranov's complaints to the plenipotentiary, we hear, was the allegation that company employees had been stealing his private possessions in transit. These were not mere trifles. 'His brother shipped him from Okhotsk nine pails of French brandy and three pails of table wine', Rezanov gravely recorded. 'They never reached him'. In this uncivilised wilderness, it was almost more than any human could bear. 'Do not forget, my dear sirs', the plenipotentiary added, 'that he is almost sixty years old now and that in the last battle with the Americans he was shot in the arm. In my presence, two pieces of bone were taken out of his wound'. No wonder then, that in spite of the chief manager's 'strength of spirit', he 'very often becomes desperate from grief and sickness'.

In fact it would not take Rezanov long to detect more profound reasons for Baranov's misery. Quite simply, the Russian-American Company, as he saw it, suffered from a deeply flawed organisation. A very visible problem was the incessant bickering, and in particular the 'disdain toward the merchant class'. The government employees, it transpired, regarded the company employees as scum. Was this the kind of behaviour designed to bring glory to Russia in America? 'The contempt which the nobility feels towards traders makes them all bosses here', Rezanov once wrote, angrily. 'Even if there is a merchant who has a rank well merited, they [the titled officers] cannot forget that formerly he was a merchant . . . to obey his orders seems to them humiliating'.

The principal victim of this unruliness was Baranov himself, the small trader from Kargopol. His difficulty, as Rezanov described it, was that 'fear of the law is required, but the laws are lacking, and the authority of superiors is not upheld'. In short, Baranov had no instruments of power. Men could treat his orders with insolence, 'but because no punishment is provided for insubordination here, the manager cannot even think of doing anything about it'. Fresh from his own humiliating experiences on the *Nadezhda*, it was a problem with which Rezanov could well sympathise.

Another problem, as he saw it, was the shortage of *promyshlenniki*, the common Russian fur hunters, now settled as workers in the Alaskan colonies. True, most of the men already in the colony were 'depraved, drunk, violent and corrupted to such a degree that any society should consider it a great relief to get rid of them'. But this did not stop Rezanov from pleading for more convict-settlers to be sent from Russia. Two years earlier, by chance, during a brief stopover in England on his journey on the *Nadezhda*, he had seen at Newgate Prison, more than 400 convicts about to be shipped to Botany Bay. If the British were using convicts to settle new lands, Rezanov seems to have concluded, it was probably a good idea. Hence his desire for 'drunks' and 'idlers' to be brought over, as well as traders convicted of 'fraudulent bankruptcy'. 'Moscow alone could supply enough men for this country', he chuckled, 'and still have half of its idlers left over'.

It would probably be unreasonable to expect anything else from a nineteenth century Russian aristocrat, even in the case of a thinker like Rezanov. But Langsdorff had quite different views on the *promyshlenniki*. He worried about their welfare. Despite being forced to live and work 'exposed, scarcely half-clothed, to the cold, the rain, and the snow, with scarcely a roof to shelter them', he noted, 'the portion of food allowed them . . . was two or three dried fish *per diem*; or sometimes by way of change, they were indulged with the rancid fat of a whale which had been cast on shore, and was perhaps already half-putrid'.

Rezanov may have been liberal, but Langsdorff the Central European sounds positively leftwing. The reason why fresh fish was hardly ever obtained, in his view, was because the men were supposed to stick to their assigned jobs: building, not fishing. This was bad management.

Occasionally the Aleuts got in some halibut or sea lion, and the *promysh-lenniki*, lacking anything else to barter, exchanged them for their clothes. 'The consequence was', the doctor scoffed, 'that at last many of them went about with no other clothing than stinking sheepskin full of vermin'. The upshot of all of which had been 'obvious'. 'They sank, one after another, wholly exhausted, a prey to the scurvy, and all work was in danger of being stopped'.

By February, of the 150 workers, eight had died of scurvy and 60 could not move. While Rezanov was devising ethereal plans by which the Company could seize the trade of the Pacific, Dr Langsdorff was writing page after ghastly page on the sufferings of the sick. We read of men sleeping in wet sheepskins, of sickrooms warmed only by the pestilential breath of their fellow men. And for such misery, Langsdorff was inclined to attribute blame to Rezanov himself. As he saw things, the tireless Baranov—a mere manager—had been obliged, in view of rank, to defer to the plenipotentiary; responsibility for the workers had then thoughtlessly been delegated to the most brutish sub-officers who (in Langsdorff's words) included some 'of the most unfeeling men that ever existed, exceeding anything ever drawn by Shakespeare in any of his characters'.

The implication was that Rezanov overlooked these abuses. This may well have been true. Russian noblemen were not renowned for their sensitivity to the sufferings of workers. This is not to say that Rezanov was uncritical of officers or government employees who seemed to be bringing the motherland into disrepute. Of Lieutenant Aleksandr Gerasimovich Sukin for example, Rezanov wrote, in apparent incredulity, that, 'he sits eternally in his room. His recreation is drink and sleep . . . he has no work or exercise of any kind, visits nobody and nobody visits him. He lives so quietly, it is as if he did not exist at all'. And then there was Lieutenant Khvostov himself, the man who had brought him in here on the *Maria Sv Magdalena*, and who would later take him out of here on the *Juno*. Even Rezanov had to confess that he was 'a most useful and amiable man when in the right condition'. The problem was his drinking. After being appointed as captain of the *Juno*, Rezanov reported, this Khvostov 'began a drinking bout that lasted three months steady. He alone, as you will see from his store account, drank nine-and-a-half buckets of French brandy and two-and-a-half buckets of strong alcohol. . . . He made drunkards out of the ship's apprentices, pilots and officers'. Rezanov seems to have been appalled by the behaviour of such men. He wrote in detail of Khvostov's obnoxious antics when drunk, which included losing his ship's anchor and firing its cannons for fun. When Rezanov limited the men to 'only' one bottle of vodka each per day, the merry lieutenant was so outraged that he threatened 'to attack the fort and take me and Baranov'. At this point, even Khvostov's bosom friend Lieutenant Davydov seems to have abandoned him as a lost soul. Baranov and Kuskov got so angry that they both resigned their jobs on the spot and refused to take their salaries, forcing Rezanov 'to use the authority given to me by the emperor to order the manager to remain in his post'.

Later, this outbreak of emotional chaos was resolved in traditional Russian style. Khvostov repented. Rezanov reported that he 'came repeatedly to beg my pardon with tears in his eyes. I forgave him and will take him with me when I start on my voyage'. Davydov also forgave him, as did Baranov and Kuskov. (The contrary Dr Langsdorff on the other hand, never saw what the fuss was about. His own judgement on Khvostov and Davydov had always been that these 'excellent officers', of 'well-known courage, resolution and professional talent', were his 'greatest friends'.)

Rezanov's primary concern was the glory of Russia, but he was not entirely careless of human life. He pondered at length on the question of how Russians could stay alive on this coast. In one accusatory letter to the directors of the company, he reminded them that profit could not just be reckoned in terms of otter skins. Lisianskii on the *Neva* may have recently taken a huge cargo of furs to Canton worth half a million roubles. But Rezanov insisted: 'If somebody would count what these sea otters cost in human lives, perhaps then they would push their caps made of these same sea otters lower on their brows, to hide their faces in shame'.

The first step, in his view, to make life safer for the Russians here was for the Russian army send a proper garrison. The second was to settle the question of provisions. How *were* the American colonies to be fed? As the man on the spot, Rezanov now had a better sense of the urgency of this question. 'My ills, and the climate, remind me of those who thought only of gain and sea otter pelts, and who did not take precautions necessary to safeguard the health of humans' he wrote, with some bitterness, that winter. 'The men sent to work in pouring rain, which continued for days and nights, and wearing clothes rotten from dampness, became sick with scurvy . . . I ordered them given wheat, molasses and beer made from fir cones. We all drank this beer as an antidote to scurvy'. But soon everyone was ill. 'Men who looked better,' he complained, 'have sometimes been put in a coffin.'

By November the workers were under rations of one pound of bread per day, per man. And because hostile Tlingit Natives controlled the sound, it was extremely difficult to fish. Anyway, wrote Rezanov, the fishing would be over at the end of November and severe storms would then keep them from shooting seals. 'We gathered snails and clams during full moon, when they are edible', he added, with a touch of Baranovian self-pity. 'At other times we have shot eagles and crows. Occasionally we can get cuttlefish. Any kind of fish caught by accident was a tidbit . . .'.

Langsdorff did not disagree that the food situation was dire—for the workers. But what he professed to find outrageous was that, 'while so large a portion of the people lay in this state of wretchedness, the directors and under-overseers, the clerks and their friends, the officers and their hangers-on, of their own authority sent the Aleutians out to hunt or fish, and fed sumptuously upon wild ducks and geese, fresh fish and fish pasties, good bread, biscuit, sugar, rice, molasses, brandy, in short upon whatever was afforded, either by nature or the storehouses'.

Baranov and Rezanov did not see fit to discuss such things in their letters. But in truth Langsdorff himself does not escape the charge of hypocrisy, either. He did not refrain from feasting and drinking himself, as noted by the carefree John D'Wolf, the only man in New Archangel that winter able to enjoy himself without feeling ashamed. From D'Wolf's account, we even hear of balls held in log cabins, attended by the lieutenants and their wives. The lady Aleuts joined in, who 'when dressed in their finery . . . appeared quite respectably'. And we are left in no doubt as to the principal participants in this merry-making: 'His Excellency the plenipotentiary was always with us on these occasions, and would upon emergency take the fiddle, on which he was quite a good performer. Dr Langsdorff and my [servant] Parker took turns at the bow, and with plenty of good resin for the stomach as well as the bow, we made gay season of it'.

The upright Rezanov, to judge by his own letters, seems to have blanked out such entertainments. All he could recall of them was the sight of Baranov weeping 'bitter tears' over the fact that the foreign guests—Langsdorff and D'Wolf—should have found 'a drunken republic' in Russia's much-vaunted American colonies. Unlike many of his compatriots, including Baranov himself, Rezanov believed that drunken misery was bad for the Russian soul. But fortunately for him, his aristocratic self-confidence could always guide him. He rode above the petty affairs of day-to-day life. 'A fanciful scribbler, a great talker', was how Vasilii Golovnin criticised him years later. 'A fellow better able to build castles in the air than to realise a well-laid plan—in sum, a man completely lacking in the patience and ability to realise large, distant goals'.

Khlebnikov, too, later described him as over-optimistic, in wanting to increase the scale of the staff, set their salaries and organise institutions. He quoted Rezanov's thunderously grand intentions in full: 'The profits extracted from the Company should be firmly guaranteed; the cultivating and husbandry branches should flourish and crafts and manufactures should ease the need of the inhabitants; trading should be based on standard rules of conduct, the administration and the law should guarantee safety of person as well as property; sea travel with adequate vessels and men should be guaranteed, military forces in good order and discipline should offer everyone necessary protection from enemies; the duties of the inhabitants should be equal to their capabilities; and humanity should be respected to the full'.

But both of the aforementioned critics, Khlebnikov and Golovnin, were writing in an age when the empire had already become purely a government concern. They themselves were agents of the government. Rezanov, like Baranov and Shelikhov before him, was a different breed of man, who believed in the power of individual Russians. When not dancing and feasting himself, Rezanov remained busy in discussions with Baranov: what to do about immorality among the *promyshlenniki*; how to placate the savages; how to increase the population of the colonies; whether to import convicts from Russia. And when he had finished asking about those things, he would think about how to force open trade with Japan; how to obtain flour from the Philippines and Chile; how to conserve the supply of seals and sea otters; how to turn the Pacific into a Russian lake. Did Russian workers have to spend their winters dying of scurvy? Of course they did not. Which was why—he and Baranov were certain—they should now be thinking of settling at more benign, southern, latitudes.

The west coast of the continent stretched away to the south, alluringly and astonishingly empty. By February 1806, Rezanov had resolved on travelling down this coast in person. He would be the first Russian of any power or status to do so: the colony at New Archangel was close to starvation, and the question of provisions needed to be answered for once and for all. 'The equinox threatens storms', he declared; 'but staying here means famine'.

The first difficulty, of how to travel, had already been overcome. Rezanov was contemptuous of the locally built vessels. So his solution, during the previous October, had been to buy the first ship that came along. With a chutzpah (and a cheque-book) that must have astonished

Baranov, he had promptly made an offer of 68,000 piastres to Captain John D'Wolf, for his ship *Juno*. The deal had been sealed to mutual satisfaction. After so many years of risking their lives on dodgy sloops and galiots, the Russian-American Company was now suddenly in possession of a splendid, 250-ton, three-masted ship. Rezanov described it as a 'good new ship, with good sailing qualities, built of oak, sheathed with copper, purchased with all rigging, sails and armament'. And D'Wolf had in his pocket a large note of exchange, cashable in St Petersburg. This had been the deal that enabled him to spend his winter relaxing in New Archangel (his crew, meanwhile, had taken their cargo of furs and were now heading for Hawaii and Canton on the rickety *Ermak*, which Rezanov had been only too happy to throw in as part of the deal. 'May God help them' he wrote, dubiously, on their departure. In fact they made the journey safely).

For the fastidious Rezanov, getting on a ship again, even a sturdy ship like the *Juno*, was no pleasure. In his letters, he made much play of his heroism in agreeing to do this journey at all. 'I am entrusting myself to the waves again', he wrote in February 1806, 'either to save the people from starvation or to die with them . . .'. Perhaps he was not reassured at the sight of the men who would be sailing his ship, namely the drunks, lieutenants Khvostov and Davydov.

For Langsdorff on the other hand, his departure from Alaska, on 26 February 1806, did not come a minute too soon. Dismissing Rezanov's worries over the hazards of sailing a coast unknown to Russian seamen, he wrote, with unconcealed disdain, that all members of the expedition 'quitted with joyful hearts the miserable winter abode to which they had been doomed, and by means of a favourable wind, before night set in, the hated Norfolk Sound [Sitka] was no longer in view'. But even once they were under way, the question of what *exactly* the purpose of this voyage was, remained inside the whirling mind of Nicolai Rezanov. Giant plans had begun to mesmerize him. 'Development here, once begun', he had recently written, 'will not stop for centuries to come'. The idea was an awesome one. But as events would show, he was absolutely right.

On the one hand, this trip was about buying food to alleviate the urgent hunger-pangs of an isolated colony of men stuck on the northwest coast. But on the other, it was about settling the future of the continent. Baranov's next lunge to the south, he knew, was already overdue, and he and Baranov had just agreed on the ideal location for the next Russian settlement: at the mouth of the Columbia River.

This was the first place where Rezanov would try to acquire the provisions he needed. By all reports, the land around the river was fertile and had excellent agricultural possibilities. At present, it supported a significant native population—a potential workforce for the Russian farms. And then there was the question of imperial aggrandisement. By erecting a settlement on the Columbia River, the several hundred miles of coast north of that point to Sitka would automatically become Russian, ripe for exploitation. The otter-rich Strait of Juan de Fuca (by today's Vancouver Island) would be fully within Russian hands. 'And even after we have a settlement on the Columbia River', he explained, 'New Archangel will still be a centre from which it will be very convenient to take Kaigany [Prince of Wales] Island. There, close to the Charlotte Islands, new shipyards can be built'. And given that the people on Prince of Wales Island were 'afraid even of Baranov's name', this would not be difficult.

While Alexander Baranov certainly concurred with this plan, it must be admitted that Langsdorff was far more dubious. 'It appears as if the settlement of Sitcha, or New Archangel, would be the *ne plus ultra* of the Russian possessions on this coast', was his sceptical, and wrong view of the matter. 'I have been assured by persons deserving of credit that the tribes lying to the south and southeast of Sitcha are much more populous and bear such a determined hatred to the conqueror Nanok [the local name given to Baranov] and his hunting parties, that it is very probable a disastrous fate would await him and his whole company if he should ever seek to establish a settlement further south . . .'.

But to Rezanov, what was needed, was to 'build navy brigs quickly, to discourage the Bostonians from trading here, and at the same time build a settlement on the Columbia from which we can spread little by little further south, to the port of San Francisco, which is the boundary of California . . . I feel positive that we will attract settlers from various places to come to the Columbia and in ten years time our strength will increase so much that we will be able to keep an eye on the Californian coast, in order . . . to make it a Russian possession'.

Rezanov was also confident that the Bostonians could be dealt with. Baranov, in his view, was doing exactly the right thing in employing them to do his hunting. The main challenge was to disabuse them of the idea that they were entitled to trade with the natives. Instead, they should come straight to New Archangel, to trade with the Russians, thus avoiding any 'danger from the savages'. In doing so, they could keep Baranov constantly supplied with 'flour, goats, butter, oil, lard, vinegar, pitch and other products of their country . . .' not to mention coffee, molasses and rum from the West Indies. Any surplus could then be shipped to Okhotsk and Kamchatka.

Even while designing the future of the world, Rezanov was, one assumes, sniffing for the scent of pine trees and spring blossom, as the *Juno* eddied past the shores of what is now Canadian British Columbia, stretching down towards Vancouver Island. Beyond the Strait of Juan de Fuca, they soon found themselves passing the heavily wooded shores of the land then known as Oregon Country, now the US states of Washington and Oregon. It was around the area of 46 degrees north that the water began to take on a reddish appearance, indicating the outflow of a great river. Wild ducks and geese appeared about the ship. According to Langsdorff, Rezanov, gazing from deck, was so enthralled by the proximity of the river that he now began to enthuse wildly on the port that the Russians were destined to build here.

But as George Vancouver could have testified, the Columbia River was not an easy one to enter from the sea. Even as Khvostov and Davydov prepared the tricky passage over the sandbar into the river's mouth, destiny seemed to intervene. 'Our chief Von Resanoff [*sic*] had already sketched his plans for removing the settlement from Sitka to the Columbia River, and was busied with building ships there in the air', wrote Langsdorff, with no little *schadenfreude*, 'when all our hopes and schemes were frustrated by the wind shifting suddenly to the southeast, and becoming so squally . . . that it was impossible to think any longer of running into a strange harbour'.

Rezanov seems to have viewed this setback with the equanimity born of high confidence. To miss the Columbia River this time was disappointing, but not fatal. Hastily revising his plans, he ordered that they carry on their way, pushed by the helpful winds currently blowing to the south: in a fortnight they would be at the shores of Spanish California itself. Russians had already heard of the warm sunshine and agricultural potential of this land. In comparison to Alaska, let alone eastern Siberia, it must have sounded unimaginably beneficent. From here food could certainly be obtained.

That he would then be entering territory that technically belonged to Spanish America—from whose ports, by law, foreign traders were excluded—does not seem to have troubled Rezanov. On the contrary, he was convinced of Spanish weakness in the area, and now wished to see the evidence with his own eyes. He knew that their presence in Upper

California was recent and tenuous, which meant that it could be used to serve Russian interests. As for the challenge of how to persuade the residents of San Francisco to waive their strict rules forbidding colonies from trading with foreign ships, Rezanov felt he could rise to it. He would be carrying seductive articles of European manufacture in his ship. How could they resist? 'The Spanish in California buy everything avidly, like savages, even trifles, and pay with sea otter skins', was his disdainful view; 'they have no factories or trade'. He had also heard of ways of circumventing their prohibitions, such as the method employed by D'Wolf, who had talked his way into a Chilean port by feigning damage to his ship. Once inside the port of San Francisco, Rezanov believed, he would be able to talk the Spanish round.

He was certainly right to be sceptical of Spanish power over this land. Despite the opportunities available to them, from their rich colonies in Mexico, it had taken Spanish explorers two hundred years to discover even San Francisco Bay, the finest natural harbour on the whole Pacific coast of North America. In centuries long past, explorers of the calibre of Juan Rodríguez Cabrillo and Sebastián Vizcaíno had sailed past this bay (as had the Englishman, Sir Francis Drake) without even noticing its existence. It was still less than fifty years since, in 1769, a scouting party from an expedition led by the Spanish explorer Gaspar de Portolá had looked down from a neighbouring hilltop onto this region, and seen a bay the size of a small inland sea. On what is now San Pedro Point, de Portolá reported they had spent a night encamped, surrounded by reeds, brambles and roses. From that moment, another six years were to pass until the first European ship, the *San Carlos*, commanded by Lieutenant Juan Manuel de Ayala, turned eastward between the headlands of the bay-entrance, and dropped anchor just inside the harbour of San Francisco. And even now, at the time of Rezanov's visit, its potential as a global trading-port remained unexploited—seemingly unrecognised—by the Spanish themselves.

Nevertheless, it was true that of the various claims to sovereignty over the American northwest, the Spanish was the longest established, and the most extravagantly protested. For fifty years now, ever since King Carlos III of Spain had observed the reality that his country was losing its status as a great European power, the viceroys of Mexico had been sending occasional ships up the west coast of America. Thus had a nominal state of New (or Upper) California came into being, the counterpart to Old (or Lower) California. Franciscan missions and *presidios*, as the

Spanish called their military posts, had begun to be built, beginning with San Diego on 16 July 1769. Following this, from 1770 to 1782, eight more Californian missions had been founded, including Carmel, at Monterey in 1770 and San Antonio and San Gabriel, near present-day Los Angeles, in 1771. The Mission San Francisco de Asis (popularly called the Mission Dolores), accompanied by a tiny *presidio*, had finally arrived on the San Francisco peninsula in 1776—in the very same week, by a strange twist, that American Independence was being declared on the other side of the continent.

The king in Madrid and the viceroy in Mexico were by no means resigned to defeat in California. Indeed, where Spanish kings were concerned, the American littoral was Spanish as far as the North Pole. The well-publicised voyages of Captain James Cook, and the Comte de La Pérouse—not to mention less well-publicised but no less sinister movements on the part of the Russians—had caused much indignation in Madrid. Nor did the Spanish care for the name that the British had given to that coast, 'New Albion'.

Eighteen years earlier, in fact, in January 1788, just before his death, Carlos III had ordered a new expedition to travel up the coast north of San Francisco, determined to anticipate Russian, British or French claims on its sovereignty. The mission's captain, Esteban José Martinez, was to reconnoitre as far north as possible, investigating any foreign activities as he went. In keeping with current international practice, he was not to incite hostilities, but to 'reaffirm' Spanish possession of the mainland, including Alaska, which was (after all) merely an extension of the Spanish Californias. He should perform 'proper ceremonies' where necessary and leave iron marks in the earth, indicating Spanish sovereignty, as indeed he did, all the way to Alaska and the Aleutian Islands.

But what of that? Now it was 1806, and Rezanov, as a Russian, had reasons to be optimistic. He knew as well as anyone, that Spain's iron crosses in the earth would count for nothing in the conspicuous absence of a Spanish fleet much of which now lay at the bottom of the Atlantic, along with the French fleet, following their destruction at Trafalgar by the British Admiral Lord Nelson. And in the vanguard of the latest Spanish advance through New California were neither farmers nor traders nor soldiers—but tiny numbers of missionaries. 'The Spaniards are very weak in this country', he had written, a few months earlier, to the board of directors of the Russian-American Company. 'And if in 1798, when war was declared against Spain, our company had forces adequate to the size of our possessions, it would have been easy to occupy part of California down to the mission Santa Barbara, 34 degrees north latitude, and to hold this strip of land permanently . . . the Spaniards do not use this fertile soil themselves and have moved north only to protect their boundaries'.

Needless to say, nobody in America had yet heard about Napoleon Bonaparte's latest triumph, namely the thrashing of a combined Russian and Austrian army at the Battle of Austerlitz in December 1805. But what Rezanov did know, as he watched the coast of northern California slide slowly past, was that Napoleon's wars were of far more pressing concern to the Spanish, the British and the French themselves, than to the Russians. Spain was being reduced to a mere vassal of Napoleon, and Britain was in fear of losing its markets. Russia still had a free hand in the east, to take command in America.

Their journey south was not accomplished at any great speed. Up to half the crew—who had already been unwell at the time of embarkation—were now suffering from severe scurvy. 'Thanks to God', Rezanov later wrote, after the failure to enter the Columbia River, 'a change in the moon brought us a continuing and favourable wind, and with pallid, deathlike faces we at last reached the entrance to San Francisco Bay'.

On the afternoon of 4 April 1806, outside the bay, the *Juno* stood at anchor. Thick spring fog made entry into the harbour impossible: delaying succour, for a few more hours, for the fifteen crewmen below deck, who lay close to death from scurvy. But up above, Rezanov would have heard the roar of breakers on the headlands with relief and a growing sense of destiny. He would enter the harbour tomorrow. There, if the Spanish did not sink them first, he would finally set foot on the land that he believed to hold the key to the future glory of Russia. The following morning he decided to make straight into the harbour, rather than risk refusal by asking for permission first. As they swept between the famous headlands, now spanned by the Golden Gate Bridge, and neared the fort, they observed a great commotion. One Spanish soldier asked through a speaking-trumpet: 'What ship is that?' When they shouted an order to anchor, the Russians shouted back 'Si Señor, Si Señor!'

Meanwhile, the viability of New Archangel still hung in the balance. Its reconstruction from ruins had commenced less than two years ago. And until Rezanov could return with fresh provisions, Baranov would be faced with the challenge of feeding several hundred scurvy-ridden men on minimal rations. The natives whom he had so thoroughly trounced the year before would soon scent the possibility of vengeance. Fortunately for

Baranov, in this desperate season, he was not entirely without the possibility of external help.

Offshore, cruising the coast, as usual, were the Bostonian traders. Baranov knew they would be out there, selling guns and armaments to the Indians, in exchange for furs. This was a practice he had not yet managed to prevent. Which was not to say that he feared a repeat of the events of 1802, when the Bostonians had connived with the Native Americans to destroy New Archangel. The mutually advantageous arrangement by which he now employed Bostonians to do his hunting for him had been working well; by this means a deep and lasting respect was in the process of being formed.

And as it happened, Baranov was about to receive his first visitors of the season right now. These turned out to be people he knew and trusted: coming ashore from the *O'Cain* that day was the 26-year-old Jonathan Winship. He had already visited Baranov in the same ship three years earlier; this time he came accompanied by his younger brother Nathan, a boy not yet out of his teens. The appearance of a friendly ship off Sitka in May 1806 must have seemed like a godsend to Baranov and his long-suffering men. It comes as no surprise to hear that on seeing Jonathan Winship again, Baranov gave him 'a hearty welcome, to one whom he hailed as a friend'.

The Winships then gave their news. Their current voyage, again on the *O'Cain*, had been a typical one: from Boston around Cape Horn to Oahu, in the Hawaiian Islands, they had sailed a non-stop 173-day passage, covering 22,492 sea miles without touching land, and furthermore 'without a man on the sick-list'. On arrival in Hawaii, the crew had soon found themselves 'surrounded by natives who were anxious to sell hogs and vegetables'. To stock up on fresh food was after all the main purpose of their stopover. But then King Kamehameha and his wives had appeared, and the Winships had found themselves 'prohibited from sailing by the royal savage, until he had disposed of his own stock, all of which Captain Winship was obliged to purchase at extravagant prices'. Thus did the *O'Cain* lay in overpriced hogs, vegetables and fruit, before sailing for New Archangel.

Winship also explained to Baranov at this time the latest political situation on Hawaii, as he had observed it. King Kamehameha, it seemed, was deliberately attracting foreigners to his country, and permitting them to settle as they pleased. He was also letting his own subjects travel abroad on foreign ships, so that they could learn the arts of sailing. He had sent to Boston for a shipwright, had established an 'admiralty' and had already purchased numerous one-masted vessels for himself, as well as one three-masted vessel. In asserting his independence over the Bostonian merchants despite formidable disadvantages, the man some were calling the 'Napoleon of the Pacific' was playing exactly the same game as Baranov himself.

But right now, naturally enough, Baranov's immediate concern was to strike a new profit-sharing deal with the Winships, by which Winship would borrow one of Baranov's hunting parties, in exchange for returning him a share of the furs. And indeed, 'after several pleasant interchanges of dinners and social visits' arrangements for trade and hunting were concluded. In all, 150 Kodiak Islanders would accompany the Bostonians south, under the leadership of Baranov's representative, Sysoi Slobodchikov. Women would also be taken, to run the shore camp, while men were off hunting. The Winships undertook, in return, to care for the Aleuts and to return them to New Archangel when the job was done, as well as to give the Russians a cut of the furs obtained.

Altogether, the Winships stayed at Sitka for a month, during which time Jonathan reported that 'the attentions and hospitality of the governor and his officers were of the most agreeable kind. Presents of fish and game were daily sent to the ship, and every possibly assistance was freely rendered'. Considering that lots of men were suffering from scurvy—and that Rezanov had still not returned from California with his emergency provisions—it seems remarkable how much was being eaten and drunk during this time. Indeed, Winship's only stated objection about dealing with Russians, was that the managers at Sitka would not break up the farewell party until all were utterly incapacitated by drink.

'Having a most excellent wind from the north', Winship himself reported, on the day of his departure, 'I did not consider it advisable to weigh anchor, as our visitors, the governor and other dignitaries, being mostly in a state of intoxication, in number about fifty, were creating such confusion and disorder among two hundred persons in the ship, that I concluded it would be imprudent to put to sea. At 5pm our visitors had the goodness to depart, doubtless not one sober man among them . . .'.

In fact Baranov's reputation for putting his guests through ordeals by vodka was fast on the way to become part of the legend of the north Pacific. Washington Irving, writing in the 1830s, astutely observed that this had not been pure conviviality, but a kind of device for manipulating younger men. In his words, 'the old Russian potentate [ie Baranov] exerted a considerable sway over a numerous and irregular class of maritime traders, who looked to him for aid and munitions, and through whom he may be said to have, in some degree, extended his power along the whole northwest coast'.

Over these coasting captains, then, 'the veteran governor exerted some sort of sway, but it was of a peculiar and characteristic kind; it was tyranny of the table'. And any temperate captain who refused to drink 'stood no chance with the governor'. In fact this hardly happened. The Bostonians themselves were no faint-hearts. For the most part, they 'joined in his revels, they drank, and sang, and whooped and hiccoughed . . . and then affairs went on swimmingly'.

For those who were able to notice, it was clear what was happening. It has been remarked that if the fur trade on the northwest coast was a school for Bostonian shipping, the headmaster of the school was Alexander Baranov. It is impossible to overstate the subtle power that this belligerent old man could wreak over the young men of Boston, once they had begun drinking with him. The notion that he was the overlord—and they the vassals—was beginning to become entrenched.

When Rezanov's ship dropped anchor in San Francisco Bay in 1806 the whole Spanish population of California did not reach a thousand people. This was certainly larger than the Russian population of Alaska. But then again, California, with its balmy climate, its docile native population and its immense agricultural potential, was a vastly easier and more attractive place in which to live. If the Spanish could not fill *this* land with settlers—Rezanov must have told himself—then they hardly deserved to possess it at all. And the population was not only small; it was also new. Only in 1804 had an administrative separation been established between 'New' and 'Old' California; that is to say, between the northerly part of the region (corresponding to today's US state of California), and the southerly part (the Mexican state of Baja California). The 56-year-old, silver-headed Don José Joaquin Arrillaga had then been appointed as the first governor of New California, to be based at the provincial capital of Monterey. He arrived to take up his post in 1806, just weeks before the appearance of the first Russian ship at San Francisco.

It is hard now to conceive what remote and primitive backwaters these Californian settlements then were. And by the time of Rezanov's visit, what development there had been, was already in decay. At San Francisco itself, the Spanish occupied just two points: the military *presidio*, beside the ocean and the entrance to the harbour; and the

Mission Dolores, several miles away to the southeast across scrubby hills.

The *presidio*, that is to say, the tiny fort at the tip of the peninsula, right by the southern end of today's Golden Gate Bridge, was insignificant compared with its neighbour to the north, Baranov's New Archangel. George Vancouver, who had dropped by here fourteen years earlier, had expressed astonishment at its inadequacy. After waking up on his first morning to catch a pleasingly English glimpse of herds of cattle and flocks of sheep grazing, he had opined that this was 'as fine a port as the world affords'. But the *presidio* itself had impressed none of his men. 'What was pompously called by this name, had but a mean appearance', scoffed one. And Vancouver himself admitted that he had been expecting an actual city, before being shown instead 'a square area, two hundred yards in length, enclosed by a mud wall and resembling a pound for cattle'.

In fact the original *presidio* contained a church, royal offices, warehouses, a guardhouse and houses for soldiers and settlers. But the buildings and furniture, being 'of the rudest fashion and of the meanest kind', hardly accorded with the ideas Vancouver had conceived 'of the sumptuous manner in which the Spaniards live on this side of the globe'. And it was laughably ill-defended. In short, mused Vancouver, 'instead of finding a country tolerably well inhabited and far advanced in cultivation . . . there is not an object to indicate the most remote connection with any European or other civilised nation'.

If things had been rudimentary in the 1790s, now they were even worse. Severe storms right across the province had recently left many buildings in need of repair. San Francisco in particular had suffered much damage to its adobe walls and fortifications; as had Monterey and San Diego. Such troops as were still in California were badly fed, badly paid and lacking in any sense of political mission.

The problems faced by the Spanish in California, in short, looked almost insurmountable to any who saw them. Smallpox epidemics had been wreaking havoc on the native populations, including those at Monterey. Desertions were becoming frequent and full-blown uprisings were not unknown, such as had happened at San José in 1805, when Father Pedro Cuevas was attacked and several of his party killed while paying a visit to a tribe of natives (in revenge for this, at least a dozen of the same tribe were subsequently killed and many more captured).

And above all there were the illegal foreign traders, usually from Boston, often now accompanied by expert Aleut and Russian hunters. In utter defiance of the law, the Bostonians would come with their liquors and cutlery and cottons and guns, for bartering among the natives along the coast of California in exchange for otter and beaver skins—resources, that is to say, which the Spanish regarded as exclusively their own. Skirmishes had sometimes followed, for example in the case of the ship *Lelia Byrd*, under Captain William Shaler, which had landed secretly at San Diego in 1803 to buy furs: on that occasion, a cannon battle had ensued. But mostly the Bostonians and the Russian hunters simply got away with their predatory behaviour because the Spanish lacked the resources to oppose it.

Nicolai Rezanov, in ordering the *Juno*'s anchor to be dropped inside San Francisco Bay on 4 April 1806, was taking an undoubted risk. There was no procedure for entering a Spanish harbour in California for the purpose of trade. The Russians knew of the Spanish hostility to foreign traders; they faced possible arrest as soon as they disembarked. But what choice did they have? Half of the men, after all, were at death's door from scurvy.

As it turned out, a strange but potentially epoch-making encounter was in the offing. 'We had scarcely reached our destination', recalled Langsdorff, '. . . when we saw fifteen horsemen come out from the fort of St Francisco, and advance at full gallop to the shore where our vessel was lying. . . . By calling and by making signs they made us understand that they expected a boat from us to come on shore . . . Lieutenant Davidoff and myself went in it as emissaries from the ship'.

Seagulls and pelicans would have been visible in the shoreline marshes. But on the quayside, the two Russians introduced themselves to the youthful Don Luis de Arguello, son of the local commandant, and to a missionary, Father José de Uria, who received the visitors 'with great courtesy' despite the fact that (as Langsdorff casually admitted) the initial conversation took place in Latin, between himself and the Franciscan friar—'because not one of our party spoke Spanish'. Arguello was a 'well-looking' young man, with a 'very singular dress', comprising a mantle of striped woollen cloth over his uniform, with his head coming through a hole in the middle. According to Langsdorff this garment looked like a bed-cover. Arguello's boots, too, were exotic creations, 'embroidered after a particular fashion', and decorated with extravagantly large spurs. Thus eccentrically clad in his poncho and spurs, he seems to have made a quintessentially Californian impression on the visitors.

Their reception had been disarmingly friendly. But the Russians still felt the need to disguise their true purpose in coming here—to trade goods for corn—until they had thoroughly won the confidence of the Spanish. Fortunately for them, they had a ready-made pretext on hand, namely the fact that the Russian government in St Petersburg, three years earlier, had obtained permission from Madrid for the government-sponsored expedition on the *Nadezhda* and *Neva*, under Captains Kruzenstern and Lisianskii, to pay a courtesy-call at California during their journey across the Pacific. As it turned out, neither of those two ships had taken advantage of that facility. So Rezanov now felt entitled to do so instead.

Within hours, the plenipotentiary himself was ashore, explaining to the Spanish that he 'had been entrusted by the Emperor with the command over all the American territories . . . and had finally decided to visit the Governor of New California to confer with him as the chief of a neighbouring territory, as to our mutual interests'. Coming from the handsome Court Chamberlain in his full-dress imperial uniform, such grand words must have sounded flattering indeed to the impoverished, isolated Spanish. They told the Russians without hesitation that the governor of New California, Don José Joaquin Arrillaga, based at Monterey, would be on his way to confer with them as quickly as possible.

'The cordial reception by the hospitable family of the commandant overwhelmed us', Rezanov later admitted, with no apparent shame at his own lack of candour. The Spanish assured the Russians that they had indeed received an order from the King of Spain, ordering them to receive the Russian ships 'in the most friendly manner'. So while 'four fat oxen, two sheep, onions, garlick, salad, cabbages and several other sorts of vegetables and pulse' were being sent for the consumption of the sick men aboard ship, Rezanov and Langsdorff themselves promptly found themselves lodged in the house of the Arguello family, being regaled by unbelievable luxuries such as chocolate.

This generous, openhearted Spanish family was to form the core of the Russian experience of San Francisco over the coming weeks. Langsdorff's enthusiastic account of how the Spanish lived forms a conspicuous contrast to his earlier cynicism about the ungodly Russians of New Archangel. 'Friendship and harmony reigned in the whole behaviour of these worthy kind-hearted people . . .' he later recalled of the Arguellos; 'they have no amusements . . . but what proceed from family union and domestic cordiality'. Perhaps more interesting still, was that the fifteen children of the family included a grown-up unmarried daughter, Doña Concepción, who 'was lively and animated, had sparkling love-inspiring eyes, beautiful teeth, pleasing and expressive features, a fine form, and a thousand other charms, yet her manners were perfectly simple and artless . . . .'.

What kind of land was this, to produce such honest, selfless inhabitants? Rezanov, we can be sure, was already busy assessing its agricultural potential as a granary for Baranov's northern empire, even though the windswept, cloudy, barren area of drifting sand dunes immediately around the *presidio* could hardly have excited him. Fortunately the climate of northern California cannot be judged by coastal conditions alone. He would soon note that the Mission Dolores, a few miles inland, was a sunny, bountiful paradise. And on the very first day after their arrival in California, the mission was where Rezanov, Langsdorff, Khvostov and Davydov now found themselves invited.

The journey between San Francisco's two settlements, the *presidio* and the mission, took around an hour on horseback; for Vancouver, fifteen years earlier, the ride had been 'rendered unpleasant, by the soil being very loose and sandy, and by the road being much incommoded with low grovelling bushes'. For Langsdorff it was no better today. 'The road is bad either for horses or for walking, consisting almost everywhere of a loose sand', he complained. 'The surrounding country is in general naked and the hills, covered in some parts with low shrubs, afford but little variety'. (Langsdorff's scrubby hills, which today go by such names as Pacific Heights, Nob Hill and the Haight, contain some of the most expensive real estate in the world and are best crossed by cable car).

As for the mission, when the Russians got there an hour later, this was an extraordinary place. Today, the thick, whitewashed walls and heavy roof tiles of San Francisco's first building still present a startling eighteenth century vision of an alternative America. Its cool floor tiles, saints, candles and Mexican altars astonish visitors today, as they astonished George Vancouver 210 years ago, when he commented in awe on the chapel's 'magnitude, architecture and internal decorations'. The difference is that today's mission lurks in the midst of the urban jungle; then it commanded views over meandering streams, fields, hills, Indian reed huts, and a scattering of animals at pasture. What Rezanov would have noticed was that the Californian missions were the local centres of food production.

This Russian visit to the Mission Dolores seems to have been a memorable occasion on many levels. Having made a liberal distribution of presents to their hosts the monks, the four foreign visitors sat down to dine on soup, roasted fowls, leg of mutton, vegetable salad, pastries and preserved fruits. Langsdorff was astonished by the quality of the food, after his long months trapped at New Archangel. The wine and the tea, he then conceded, were only of middling quality; 'but that was succeeded by super-excellent chocolate'.

It was during the course of this abundant meal that the Russians now revealed their true hand for the first time. As Langsdorff put it, they now 'ventured to disclose the distresses of the settlement at Sitka, which was the real occasion of our visit, for a supply of corn, and other articles of the first necessity to us'. The idea was to seduce the monks by thoughts of trade, to a point where the *presidio*, and the law, would no longer be able to hold them back.

The plan seems to have been a good one. On the one hand the monks were candid in admitting that they would need to seek permission from higher authorities to engage in trade with the Russians. On the other, they were exceedingly keen on obtaining goods 'of which they were greatly in want'. Later the monks would be invited aboard the *Juno* to inspect the Russian goods, and would be 'much pleased with some coarse and fine linen cloths, Russian ticking, and English woollen cloth'. Other goods that they 'inquired very much after' included all iron and ironware, household utensils, sheep-shears, axes, large saws, and iron cooking vessels. Finally 'they were also keen on casks, bottles, glasses, plates, fine pocket and neck handkerchiefs and leather of all sorts . . . we had a number of shoes and boots ready made, and round hats, which were very acceptable to them'.

Word of the exciting trade goods in the hold of the *Juno* began to spread. The Spanish ladies of the *presidio* began to clamour for new cotton and muslin shawls. The Russians continued giving out presents to whet appetites. Don Luis Arguello got an English fowling-piece, and each of the fathers a piece of fine English cloth, as well as 'a piece of gold stuff for the ornament of their church'. As Rezanov frankly admitted in letters back to St Petersburg, these presents served the twin purpose of 'repaying them for our invitations, and hiding from them our own poverty and need'. Soon, Rezanov claimed, everybody was in love with the Russians.

To Rezanov's credit as a diplomat and a politician, a longing for trade does seem to have gripped the whole Spanish community. Soon everyone was waiting for approval to arrive from the viceroy in Mexico, granting the permits they needed to dive in. Father Pedro, from the mission of San José, at the south of the bay, journeyed to meet the Russians, specifically to enter into a wheat-for-cloth deal, subject to official approval.

The warm spring sunshine, the obliging people, the excellent food: life here in California was exceeding the wildest dreams of the average

Russian crew-member. This was indeed a kind of promised land; a land of pleasure and easy abundance; a kind of land that the vast majority of Russians had never imagined. Langsdorff spoke of the beneficence of this country 'in the 38th degree of latitude, where the original inhabitants live in a very mild and benignant climate, where they have no want of food, and little care about habitations or clothing, where without any irksome degree of toil they can procure flesh, fish, and vegetables of various kinds in great abundance'.

So pleasant in fact was the life, that before long, Rezanov found that his men were becoming insubordinate. 'The excellent climate of California', he recalled, 'the abundance of breadstuffs there as compared to our lack of them, and the prospect of facing starvation again in the future, were the hourly subject of conversation among our men'. The need arose to take measures against the threat of desertion, in spite of which, 'two very good men who were well cared for . . . ran away when they went to the creek to wash clothes, and disappeared without trace'.

Strange things were beginning to happen. It was as though the Russians were now so far from their heartlands they had become untethered from reality. And back in the Arguello household, something extraordinary was beginning to stir: Rezanov's own frozen heart. 'Of the lovely sisters of the acting commandant', we suddenly find him writing, in his subsequent report to the Company, 'Doña Concepción is the recognised beauty of New California, and Your Excellency will agree with me when I say that our past sufferings were requited, for our time passed joyfully. Pardon me, Gracious Sire, that in such a serious letter I mingle something of the romantic—but perhaps it is best to be very sincere'.

It was while this unlikely passion was beginning to take shape, that the governor of California Don José Joaquin Arillaga finally turned up from Monterey, eager to invite the visiting Russians to a banquet at the presidio. All was set fair, but for one consideration: along with the governor, had come news from Mexico of imminent war in Europe between Russia and Napoleon-controlled Spain. For a moment it seemed as though the Russians were about to be arrested after all.

But Rezanov, having been told of the news by the jovial Father Pedro, stayed cool. 'It seemed as if all the fear was on their side', he wrote later, 'and that they suspected our coming was with sinister intentions, expecting perhaps, that the other two ships would arrive soon'. So having put his men on standby, he put on his uniform and boldly went to dinner.

In the dark, accompanied by Langsdorff, Khvostov and Davydov and Father Pedro, he felt some tension. Was his whole mission about to be aborted? Would his plans to place Spain in thrall to Russia on this continent come to nothing? He had recently spent six months in detention at the pleasure of the Emperor of Japan; he did not wish the same to happen now in Spanish America. He need not have feared. 'Crossing the Plaza and seeing the smiling faces of the beautiful Spanish girls', recalled Rezanov, with relief, 'my suspicions vanished'. And indeed, there was the beaming governor in full uniform to greet the Russians. Intimacy and pleasure were destined to win the day. Even with their countries on the point of war with one another, the parties would find it hard to break the atmosphere of mutual politeness and respect. According to Khvostov's log, 'Rezanov, by his smooth manners, won the heart of Governor Arillaga. He seemed to like us even better than his own countrymen'. 'From this day on', added Rezanov himself, with great satisfaction, 'we were on intimate terms with the principal officers and officials of California'. Conversing in French with the governor, he quickly proposed that 'an intercourse might be established between the Russian settlements and this Spanish province, which would be a reciprocal benefit to them and that it might be carried on by vessels passing from the one to the other at stated periods'. The governor was anxious to agree, with the proviso, as always, that the plan would first have to be submitted to Madrid for approval.

In his power game with the Spanish, Rezanov seems to have been utterly dominant. Whereas he was at the height of his powers, the aging governor was diminutive and weak on his legs. From such a position of strength and worldliness, could Rezanov impress upon the governor the idea that he did not wish to wrest California from the Spanish, but merely to ensure that no other power could squeeze in between their lands. But there was clearly a threatening edge to his words too. 'I further explained to him', Rezanov later wrote, 'that His Catholic Majesty's possessions in the New World were of such vast extent that it was impossible to protect them, that seeing their weak means of defence, sooner or later they would become the victims of aggression . . .'. And when, in response to this, the governor 'frankly confessed that their court feared Russia more than anybody else', Rezanov affected astonishment. He told the governor to 'dismiss this erroneous idea from your mind'. The proof of his innocent intentions, he argued, lay in the fact that 'our monarch's possessions in the north have an inexhaustible source of wealth in furs . . . Russia's situation as well as its interests must convince you that we have no need of the southern parts of America. If it were otherwise, you must acknowledge that so strong a power [as Russia] would not disguise its intentions and you could never prevent it from carrying them out'.

With such a mix of charm, enticements, subliminal menace and sheer power, it seems, Rezanov would eventually wear the governor down. Initially, Don José Joaquin Arillaga had had no intention of permitting the Russians to fill his ship with Californian grain. Now he was beginning to yield.

And there was something else lending visible power to Rezanov right now, namely the lightness of his own mood. As a 42-year-old man, bereft of his wife, accustomed to Russian gloom and a pitiless physical environment, he was as susceptible to the unfamiliar pleasures of California as the lowest of his crew. By now he was learning Spanish at a furious pace, as well as 'associating daily with, and paying my compliments to, the beautiful Spanish señorita'. In short, he was falling in love, and as lovers do, constructing the personality of his beloved along lines that pleased him. 'I perceived her active, venturesome disposition and character', he wrote, 'and her unlimited ambition, which at her age of fifteen, made her alone among her family, dissatisfied with the land of her birth. She always referred to it, when we were joking, as a beautiful country, a warm climate, an abundance of grain and cattle—and nothing else. I described Russia to her as more severe as to climate, but still abounding in everything'.

As a matter of fact, his protestations to the governor of wishing to seal a pact of mutual benefit were entirely disingenuous. He had no intention of sharing the land that lay between New Archangel and San Francisco. What was to be lamented was that Russia had not followed through the policy of Peter the Great, in which case 'it is safe to say that New California would never have been a Spanish territory . . . but even now there still remains an unoccupied intervening territory fully as rich, and of much importance to us, and if we allow it to slip through our fingers, what will succeeding generations say? I at least will not be arraigned before them in judgement'. Even while courting the daughter of the commandant, and organising trade with the governor, he was also preparing to extend Baranov's empire to the very edge of existing Spanish dominions—in effect, to today's Marin County, and to the northern shore of San Francisco Bay.

One obvious reason for this was that San Francisco Bay was full of sea otter, a circumstance of which the Spanish seemed oblivious. Even

Dr Langsdorff seems to have seen this matter through the eyes of an imperialist. He spoke of his amazement, while on botanical or hunting expeditions, to see 'above all things, the valuable sea-otter swimming in numbers about the bay, nearly unheeded'.

Then there was the log of Lieutenant Khvostov, which was charmingly free of diplomatic subtlety or guile. 'Under the pretext of searching for two runaway sailors', he reported, one day, 'his Excellency [Rezanov] secured permission to send two rowboats round the bay'. Khvostov himself was appointed to lead this trip, which, to judge by his own log, was clearly intended to be a spying mission. Among other things along the way, he reported seeing wild wheat, peas and beans growing; more significantly, he noted the locations where Russian forts could be built. He spoke of locations that 'would be in a threatening position to the Spaniards, yet remaining entirely immune to any retaliatory shots, as this shore is much higher'. He also noted how, in its northerly extremities, the bay extended rather close towards Bodega Bay. 'I may boldly state that, once established at Bodega, the Russians could use this small isthmus to extend their settlement to the north shore of San Francisco Bay', he wrote, before adding the justification for such aggressive imperialism: 'The Spanish, being fanatics, are not interested in industries; they do not even have a rowboat'.

The Russians were playing an extraordinary double game. While plotting long-term aggression against the Spanish, they continued to enjoy their unlimited hospitality. Langsdorff refers to late night parties of singing and dancing, at which Russian and Spanish traditions were mingled. 'The favourite dance here is called the *barrego*' he noted. 'It is performed by two couples, who stand opposite each other. They hum a tune and stamp the measure with their feet . . .'. He also spoke of taking 'some pains to teach the ladies English country dances, and they liked them so much that we afterwards commonly danced them; they seemed particularly pleased that the whole party could be dancing at the same time. Some soldiers of the garrison, who would play on the violin and guitar, were our musicians'.

Lieutenant Khvostov, too, was coming into his own. 'We entertained the commandant Arguello and his wife, his three sons and four daughters at dinner aboard our ship', he recorded one day. 'The music during the dinner helped us to become better acquainted with the entire family'. Such banquets, accompanied no doubt by plentiful Russian liquor, began to become more frequent, and the revelry more intense; Khvostov began to sound once again like the Khvostov of old. 'During the dinner' he recorded on another occasion, 'we drank the health of Our Emperor and of His

Catholic Majesty and gave a thirteen-gun salute to which the fort responded with fifteen. For lasting friendship and trade relations between Spain and Russia, we shot nine guns and the fort responded with eleven guns . . .'.

From such an atmosphere, one result now seemed inevitable. 'Our constant friendly intercourse with the family of Arguello' wrote Langsdorff, 'the music, the singing, the sports, and the dancing, awakened in the mind of the Chamberlain von Rezanov some new and very important speculations, which gave rise to his forming a plan of a very different nature from the first, for establishing a commercial intercourse between the Russian and Spanish settlements . . .'. In other words, he had decided upon marriage with Doña Concepción.

Was it genuine love? Through the fog of the years it is hard to tell. In his report to the directors of the Company, he later claimed that the romance began 'under the influence of remnants of feelings that in the past were the source of happiness in my life'. Langsdorff was extremely sceptical as to his sincerity: 'He conceived that a nuptial union with the daughter of the commandant at San Francisco would be a vast step gained towards promoting the political objects he had so much at heart . . .'. We find him chuckling at Rezanov's resolve to 'sacrifice himself', by this marriage, to the welfare of his country.

Rezanov himself was also keen to correct any impression that he was putting his love for a woman before his love of Russia. Once married, he anticipated accumulating more knowledge 'as to their trade, their surplus and their needs'. He also foresaw the day when 'I shall be in a position to render new services to my country by personally examining the harbour of Vera Cruz, Mexico and by a trip through the interior part of America. Hardly anybody but me could do it, the suspicious Spanish government forbidding such investigations'. He now went to the girl's parents to inform them of his intention.

As he later admitted, the news came as a 'strike of lightning to them'. The difficulty was that their 'religious upbringing was fanatical'. They could not conceive that their daughter would marry a man of the Orthodox faith. Rezanov even noted, with private contempt, how the fathers 'took poor Concepción to church, made her confess, and tried to make her refuse me; but her determination finally quieted everybody down'.

As with everything else, Rezanov seems to have talked the Spanish into it. A betrothal was made, in secret, pending the permission of the heads of their respective churches, and total intimacy between Rezanov and the Arguello family established. 'Thereafter my position in the house of the commandant was that of a near relative and I managed the port of his Catholic Majesty as my interests required' boasted Rezanov. The governor himself, because of his long personal friendship with the Arguellos, 'now found himself to be in fact my guest'. And with his Spanish improving 'every hour' he could boast that, 'at length they did not keep the slightest secret from me'.

By now, the governor felt able to take Rezanov into all manner of confidence. He complained how the Spanish government never thought about economics or trade, but only about God and religion. For the King of Spain, it seemed, California was a giant and wasteful expense that brought in no revenue. Rezanov knew this. We sometimes find him bandying about the names of international ports—Manila, Canton, Bengal, Buenos Aires, Caracas, New Orleans—as if international trade were a trendy thing that backward people like the Spanish hadn't yet grasped.

The governor also complained about the smugglers on his coast, as Langsdorff noted, with apparent embarrassment. 'The governor one day complained, as if it had been a matter unknown to us' he recalled, 'that a certain Captain O'Cain had some years before come with thirty men and four women from Unalaska, secretly to catch these animals within the limits of his government'. We can imagine the Russian faces on hearing this, given that it was Baranov himself who had commissioned O'Cain to catch the otters. Rezanov however, undaunted, immediately responded by telling more lies. 'The Bostonians are doing even more harm to us than to you . . .' he told them. 'besides trading in our waters, this scoundrel of whom you speak seized a party of our Americans . . . he carried away about forty Kodiak Natives with their families'.

Only in one respect was the Spanish administration palpably superior to that of the Russians. One day, Rezanov was astonished to be handed a European newspaper just a few months old. Official papers, it transpired, were reaching the Spanish colonies once a month from Cadiz. 'I envied them this system' he sighed, 'and thought of our own poor possessions, for it seemed as if they were not in the New World but in the world of the dead'.

But with the agreement of his marriage, it seems, the last possible obstacle to a trade agreement had been lifted. The grain—4500 puds* of

---

* *Pud*, see above p 78.

it, along with a large quantity of flour, peas, beans and maize plus some salted meat, to the value of 24,000 Spanish piastres—had begun arriving on the shore beside the *Juno*, delivered from the missions in ox-drawn carts. Rezanov was immensely proud of what he had achieved. 'This, Gracious Sire' he later wrote to the main office of the company, 'is our first experiment in trade in California, which at a low estimate, might amount to a million roubles yearly'. He foresaw that this trade would soon supply not only Alaska with food, but also Okhotsk and Kamchatka. The price of grain in Irkutsk would fall, industry would be stimulated and 'Siberia will be awakened'. Looking even further into the future, to the day when Russia's own colonies had been established abutting those of Spain, he felt able to predict that, 'from the profits acquired by this trade, the company could construct granaries; by kind treatment of the many savages we could develop our own agriculture and cattle raising in the proposed southern colonies, and once our trade with Canton was fully organised, we could settle Chinese labourers there'.

Not everyone saw things this way. Behind his back as usual, Langsdorff was writing scornfully of Rezanov's plans. He found himself at a loss to imagine what goods could be produced in Siberia or Alaska, which the Spanish would want to trade for corn. But Rezanov was intoxicated. 'Everything was at my command. The soldiers of the garrison were hastening the delivery of grain, the people supplied us with water . . . I had nothing to do but give the necessary orders. Despite the many rumours of war, I entertained the Spanish with feasts and dinners, seeing to it that all who remained at the *presidio* after serving me had a good time. The governor . . . his weak legs notwithstanding, danced with us and we did not spare gunpowder on board the ship and in the fortress. The music of Spanish guitars was mixed with songs of Russian singers'.

With the crew of the *Juno* all now fully restored to health, they finally took their leave from the friendly, hospitable people of San Francisco. In his pocket, as he waved goodbye from the deck to his beloved Señorita, Rezanov was carrying two pieces of paper. One was a request for the tsar that he marry a woman of the Roman Catholic Church. The other was the draft of a trade arrangement with Spain, also to be signed by the tsar, by which Russia would gain exclusive and permanent rights to buy food from California in exchange for trade goods. This agreement, Rezanov was convinced, would not only feed Russia's north Pacific possessions, but would pave the way for Russia to move its border down to the confines of San Francisco itself. 'Present my plans to the Emperor' he begged the main office of the company; 'plans that will become immortal in centuries to come!'

The *O'Cain* was now heading south for California. But in the meantime, another of Winship's ships, the *Pearl*, under the captaincy of John Ebbets, was putting in at Sitka. On board was a mate by the name of George Clark, yet another of the Bostonians who had already enjoyed drinking sessions with Baranov on at least one previous visit. What marked him out this time was that he had recently been living on the Sandwich Islands; he even had a wife and children living there, as well as various business interests. More interesting still, was the news that during his residence on the islands, he had become a close confidant of Kamehameha.

At the beginning of the nineteenth century, it was on the basis of such chance encounters that trading relations between nations could emerge. Clark, it appears, had gone to the trouble of telling Kamehameha in detail about his northern neighbours. He had suggested to the king that Baranov could use regular supplies of Hawaiian food; and that he, Kamehameha, could use regular supplies of Russian shipbuilding materials.

So it was that the king had specifically asked Clark to travel to Sitka in the spring of 1806, to 'negotiate a commercial treaty' with Baranov, on his behalf. As Rezanov later reported it, the king 'proposes to send us taro, breadfruit, coconuts, yam, hogs, when there is a surplus, and cordage, receiving from us calico, linen cloth, iron and lumber for shipbuilding'. And Clark was able to tell Baranov one more thing. King Kamehameha, it appeared, had expressed a wish, in person, 'to come to New Archangel and lay the foundation for the trade, notwithstanding the distance'. Baranov's reaction to this rather astonishing proposal is not recorded; but he is unlikely to have opposed it. He and Kamehameha were, after all, the two most powerful and famous men in the north Pacific. There were each other's closest neighbours. They were both of a similar age, by now, well into their fifties. Both were anomalous rulers, both were mavericks, both were fiercely independent. So although they did not yet know it, the two men had a lot in common. For Baranov to cement some kind of relationship with the Hawaiian king would have been a foolproof way for him to acquire fresh food for his men, while holding off the growth of British and American sea power. From the Russian perspective, a foothold in Hawaii could form the third leg of an unbreakable triangle with Alaska and California. But what kind of relationship did Baranov want with Hawaii? Should he befriend the islands, or colonise them? The question of how to deal with Hawaii was one that would preoccupy Baranov for the rest of his life.

Meanwhile, on the *O'Cain*, his Russian and Aleut hunters, with the Winship brothers, were sailing south from Sitka. Over the summer they would reach the Queen Charlotte Islands, then the Farallone Islands, just outside San Francisco Bay; they bought some furs, and caught others as they went. Later, the hunting in the far south, south of today's Mexican border, proved to be so good that in three months they managed to catch furs worth $60,000 in Canton.

This particular hunt would turn into a marathon exercise lasting an entire year. Exactly as the Russians themselves had been doing, the Spanish of California protested vehemently at seeing so much peltry taken from territory they regarded as their own; but there was little that they could do, given the enfeebled state into which they had fallen. When the hunters finally returned to Sitka in October 1807, they were carrying 4820 sea otter furs to be divided equally between Russians and Bostonians. The Winships' portion of the cargo alone would bring in over $130,000, when they subsequently sold it in Canton.

Only one hitch spoiled the hunt unless it was part of the plan. For some unknown reason, Baranov's personal representative on the expedition, Sysoi Slobodchikov, fell out with the Winships late in the autumn of 1806. He was prompted to part company with them. So while the Winships were spending the 'extremely cold and stormy' winter of 1806–07 safely under Baranov's eye in Sitka, Slobodchikov himself got to spend a winter in Hawaii, chatting with Kamehameha under the palm trees. The king seems to have been delighted with the company of Baranov's own representative: so delighted in fact, that he presented Slobodchikov with one of his famous brightly coloured feather cloaks, to take back to his chief at New Archangel. 'The cape' wrote Khlebnikov later, 'was of shining red and yellow feathers, a mark of his respect and good wishes. From then on at various intervals, they would send each other gifts through American shipmasters'.

We have no record of whether Baranov ever wore the cloak. But given that this was his first ever gift from a foreign leader, it is hard to imagine that he did not hold it dear. Hawaii, in his imagination at least, now shimmered a little closer.

CHAPTER SIX

THE IMPACT OF INTERNATIONAL POLITICS

Russian claims over the northwest coast were now as close to being uncontested as they had ever been. Russian plans to exploit the Columbia River, northern California and Hawaii were looking more feasible by the day.

Apart from getting drunk with visiting sailors from Boston, Baranov found little to enjoy in life, as he grew older. He was a man still severely constrained by duty, despite the fact that he had got past sixty years of age (apparently to his own disbelief). He wrote of being afflicted by constant stress, while his repeated requests to return to Russia were being denied. And regarding his personal circumstances, all that can be said is that, by 1806, they were marginally improved. We know that news reached him this year of the death in Russia of his legal wife, a woman whom he had not seen since before 1790. For the grizzled old man of Alaska, whose friends and colleagues had been dying off for years, this melancholy news brought one positive consequence. Henceforth he was finally free to marry his long-standing mistress and housekeeper, the daughter of the Kenai toion, known to the Russians as Anna Grigorevna, by whom he had already had a son and a daughter.

The Church was pleased, though it is far from apparent that Baranov was bothered about legitimising his marital status. When Nicolai Rezanov made a brief stopover at New Archangel in June, on his journey from San Francisco back to Siberia, he found the old man dejected as usual. The two men spent time discussing detailed plans for annexing the whole coast as far south as California to the Russian Empire. And despite understanding the enormity of what was at stake—Russian hegemony in North America west of the Rockies—Baranov was still more interested in seeking permission to quit his job and retire back to Russia.

Rezanov regretted this greatly. 'I will tell you', he had already written to the company main office, 'that the loss of this man will not only be a loss to the company, but to all our country. And you may believe me, as one who puts his honour above all else, that with the loss of Baranov, you will be deprived of the means of executing all the vast projects toward which his labours have blazed a wide trail . . .'. Unfortunately for Baranov, however, quitting his post would never be a simple matter. Before he could leave, another manager had to be selected. And the problem was that the company did not regard any of those currently in America as having sufficient class. Now that the colonies mattered to the dignity of Russia, there was extreme reluctance to appoint another common merchant like Baranov.

Of the possible candidates, the man running Kodiak, Ivan Ivanovich Banner, was generally felt to be too humble and pleasant (according to Khlebnikov, this 'irrelevant pleasantness' had been the cause of 'various orders and instructions not being carried out'), and Baranov's esteemed old friend Emelian Grigorevich Larionov, on the island of Unalaska, had recently gone mad and died. Then there was the man of Baranov's own preference, his deputy, Ivan Kuskov. Twenty years younger than Baranov, Kuskov was now in his early forties. He was known as a reliable, dependable man whose 'aptitude, disinterest in personal gain and knowledge of local conditions make him very useful'. But to Baranov's annoyance, Rezanov had already written to the company main office ruling Kuskov out as a potential manager, 'because of his lack of knowledge of politics'.

One reason why Baranov so insistently wanted to retire was that Sitka still felt as though it were in imminent danger of attack from Tlingit Natives. It was a frightening environment for an old man to inhabit. Before sailing for Okhotsk, Rezanov had time to see this for himself. 'Now we dare not go for a walk very far', he noted, '. . . even though the shipyards are not farther than three hundred sazhens from the fort, we always had loaded guns with us'. Sentries kept constant anxious lookout, with cannons at the ready. At night there was fear that Tlingit might set fire to the ships.

The related problem, of Bostonians selling arms to the natives, was behind all this. It was a problem that Baranov had failed to solve, for all his efforts in cultivating the friendship of individual Bostonian seafarers, and in hiring them to do his hunting for him. As has been pointed out, the Tlingit Native Americans who threatened Sitka had been well armed by the men from the United States. 'They have supplied them with guns and powder to such an extent', noted Rezanov, 'that now they themselves do not dare to sail alone in a three-masted ship with eight cannons, and . . . two American ships are always together, not daring to separate'.

What role could crusty Baranov still play in surmounting these challenges, when the much younger men who had kept him company over the previous year were all now leaving? Rezanov, who had provided the support of the Russian state itself, was heading for the civilised sanctuary of St Petersburg, taking his companion, Dr Langsdorff, with him. To Baranov's regret, the irrepressible young drunkards Khvostov and Davydov were also abandoning him, off on a bizarre venture, initiated by Rezanov, to conduct a raid on Japan, in retaliation for the inhospitable treatment that the plenipotentiary had received during his own mission to that country the year before. Khlebnikov later referred to this as a shameful waste of valuable manpower, and 'a venture completely alien to Baranov', involving as it did 'the removal for two years of more than 60 of the best workers'. The raid, as it turned out, would end up as a comic-book farce.

Meanwhile, Rezanov was promising to return, to help in establishing permanent trade with San Francisco, as well as in building the first Russian settlements in northern California. But as Baranov watched his friends leave, this must have been a distant prospect. The exodus seems to have been the end for him, mentally. He no longer felt fit to oversee the massive project of expanding Russia's empire in America. Only one more job would detain him during the rest of that summer, namely to give his assent to a rash scheme by which his friend from Boston, Joseph O'Cain, would transport a group of shipwrecked Japanese sailors, currently in Hawaii, back to their homes in Nagasaki. The hope was—as O'Cain explained—that such a generous gesture might be the key to undoing Japanese resistance to permitting trade with foreigners.

Had it come off, Baranov could have claimed a Russian victory in an arena where Rezanov had conspicuously failed. But it was a long shot, and in Baranov's mind it seems to have been his last throw of the dice. Having entrusted a cargo of precious furs to O'Cain, he now announced that he too would be leaving New Archangel, and withdrawing to the relative peace and quiet of Kodiak. In fact the move may have been a miscalculation—Kodiak was no safer than Sitka. Rezanov had recently expressed his fear that the Bostonians might launch an attack there, remarking that he 'should not be surprised if a hundred riflemen, with several thousand Koloshes, would attack Kodiak and destroy everything down to the foundations. They have English rifles, while we have ones from Okhotsk, which have never been used since they were delivered, since they are good for nothing'.

But Baranov was not deterred by such worries. Kodiak was at least closer to Russia than Sitka. By all appearances, he was hoping that an appointed successor, perhaps dispatched by Rezanov from St Petersburg, would soon be arriving for him. When that happened, he would in a better position to take the first available transport to Siberia and Russia. Meanwhile, he was leaving Ivan Kuskov in charge of the ongoing building work at New Archangel. Perhaps he hoped that the added experience would finally qualify Kuskov to take over his job. It seemed unlikely that he would ever return to his duties.

In fact, Russian claims over the northwest coast were now as close to being uncontested as they had ever been. Russian plans to exploit the Columbia River, northern California and Hawaii, for food and secure bases, were looking more feasible by the day. Baranov may have felt that he personally was too decrepit to finish the job, but it must have been clear to him that the Russian-American Company would never get a better chance than it currently had, to establish itself as the dominant power in the north Pacific for decades, perhaps centuries, to come. After all, the number of foreign ships coming to the northwest coast had recently undergone another dramatic decline. Only three American ships and one British would reach the area in 1808, compared with what had been a steady flow of at least twenty ships per year ten years earlier. In the absence of competition, the occasional ship that did brave the risks of embargo or confiscation, such as the *Pearl* of Boston, could harvest record-breaking hauls of skins (6000 were supposedly taken during its voyage of 1808–09). Although otters were already on the way to being decimated, there was sufficient interest in beaver, elk, and other land animals to make up the shortfall.

The reasons behind this fortuitous disappearance of foreign ships from the northwest coast lay in international wars and politics. The concerns of daily life on the northwest coast of America were as remote from current European preoccupations as could be imagined. But even Baranov knew that the British Empire was still locked in an intractable power-struggle with Napoleon and his continental allies. And this was the struggle that was helping to put Russia in the ascendance in the North Pacific.

By the autumn of 1806, the French dictator was at the height of his powers. In October, he crushed the Prussians at Jena and Auerstädt, driving Kaiser Friedrich-Wilhelm III from Berlin. Just one month later, the so-called Berlin decree of the Continental Blockade was signed in the Potsdam palace, forbidding any trade between the European continent on the one hand, and Britain and her colonies on the other. The objective was to kill British power and prosperity at the roots.

Of all the continental powers, only Russia was still resisting Napoleon. But soon she too would be forced to join his war against Britain. During the summer of 1807, the Russian Tsar Alexander submitted to a treaty of peace and friendship with France, signing, at Tilsit, an agreement of offensive and defensive alliance. In the event of Britain refusing to submit to Napoleon's terms by 1 December 1807, Russia would be obliged to act as one with France, in declaring war and joining the continental blockade.

This was not a happy situation for the Tsar. He had not willingly entered into this alliance. To require his Russian merchants to cease trading with Britain was a serious sacrifice. In recent years, many of their biggest markets had been in Britain, including those for hemp, flax, lard, iron, wheat and linen. To be at war with Britain, furthermore, was extremely bad news for the country's shipping. After Tilsit, the threat from the ubiquitous and all-powerful British fleet would render further round-the-world journeys from Russia to the northwest coast dangerous and impractical. Although Captain Lieutenant Hagemeister did reach New Archangel in the *Neva* from St Petersburg in September 1807, the second half of his journey, via the Indian Ocean to the Atlantic, was considered too risky to be worth taking (Hagemeister would eventually return by land, over Siberia).

But one Russian, at least, did not fear in the least the inconvenience caused by Napoleon's wars: Alexander Baranov. *His* coast, after all, was sufficiently remote not to be bothered by either the British or the French. His own coastal vessels, plying the waters between New Archangel, Kodiak and Okhotsk, were not in danger of being stopped or plundered. His great rivals the Bostonians, on the other hand, were suffering very serious inconvenience indeed. In response to Napoleon's continental blockade, Britain, in November 1807, announced that American trade with Europe would henceforth only be tolerated through British ports. Any vessels caught attempting to trade with Britain's enemies (which now included Russia) would be deemed illegal, and regarded as enemies themselves. To which Napoleon's immediate response was to announce that ships from the United States would be regarded as British, and hence liable to confiscation. Anyone flying the stars and stripes from their masthead, in other words, now ran the double risk of being stopped by both the British *and* by the French. This left Baranov, safely ensconced on the northwest coast, at a considerable advantage.

One result of all this, meanwhile, was that Russia and the United States were being pushed by Napoleon's wars into enjoying an ever closer relationship. A striking parallel was beginning to emerge in the experience of the two countries. Both were being bullied, against their wishes, into taking sides in a European war not of their making. As a result, the President of the United States, Thomas Jefferson, and Tsar Alexander I of Russia, were coming to see one another as friends and allies.

The correspondence that had arisen between the two leaders is fascinating for being so improbable. In order to impress the president of the land of the free, the autocrat of all the Russias, it seemed, had taken advice from his old tutor, Frédéric La Harpe, who had discussed liberal reforms, political freedom and even a constitution with him. The Tsar, in these discussions (said La Harpe later) became accustomed to referring not to his 'subjects', but to his 'countrymen', even using the revolutionary term 'concitoyens'. Through diplomatic channels, Alexander's alleged interest in republican forms of government was brought to Jefferson's attention.

Thus did they begin writing to each other, in terms of effusive mutual appreciation. 'I have always felt a great esteem for your nation which knew how to make noble use of its independence by creating a free and wise Constitution assuring the well-being of each and all', declared Alexander, to which Jefferson replied by speaking of the 'exalted pleasure' he felt, at the 'manifestations of the virtue and wisdom' apparent in all the tsar's actions. In August 1806, Jefferson forwarded to the tsar a four-volume work on the *Life of Washington* and a copy of the Constitution of the United States. Alexander in turn sent back a bust of himself, which Jefferson later kept in his study at Monticello. In a letter to the tsar written at the same time, Jefferson emphasised the concurrence of the interests of the United States with those of Russia, in the development of maritime commerce among the neutral nations. This was aimed in particular at the hated British practice of stopping American ships at sea and plundering them of goods or men. In the years 1803 to 1812, the British would capture no fewer than 917 American vessels, insisting, among other things, on their 'right' to remove English deserters by force.

Russia, too, saw advantages in close relations with the United States. Right now, while forbidden to trade with Britain, she was in search of alternative markets. And looking to the future—to a time when the continental blockades were no longer in force—she was keen not to remain reliant on Great Britain for her trade, as in the past. In 1805 Count Nicolai Petrovich Rumiantsev, the minister of commerce, had expressed a fear that Great Britain 'could become the mistress of purchasing prices for our products'. He had also expressed a wish to 'try to engage the Americans in a rivalry with the English'.

On the northwest coast, citizens of Russia and the United States were rivals. The question of Bostonians selling arms to the natives had infuriated Baranov for years. But with close relations between their respective governments now developing, a more co-operative future beckoned.

In the meantime, to express his own outrage at British and French confiscations, President Jefferson was moved, on 22 December 1807, to pass his amazing Embargo Act. For the next year and a half, by law, American ships were required to stay in port, and to refrain from attempting foreign trade. It was the most isolationist measure in the whole history of the United States. It was also drastic and self-defeating: its principal victims would be the American merchants themselves, who could no longer legally ply the Pacific in search of markets. Its principal beneficiary, once again, would be Alexander Baranov.

We know little of Baranov's life on Kodiak during this time. As yet, no successor had been sent to relieve him. One man who did meet him here was the wandering Scotsman, Archibald Campbell. 'He gave us each a tumbler of brandy', recalled Campbell, later, of his arrival at Kodiak in December 1807, 'and sent us to the . . . barracks where the Russian convicts lodged'. Baranov may have been in semi-retirement, but his notions of hospitality do not seem to have changed. Campbell was one of the most open-minded and sympathetic men to have chronicled his adventures in northwest America from this time. He was also among the most unfortunate. He had been among the crew of Joseph O'Cain on the *Eclipse*, dispatched the previous year by Baranov to China and Japan to exchange furs for goods. O'Cain's hopes of prising open the Japanese market had not been realised. Nevertheless, he had succeeded in trading his furs at Canton for a valuable cargo of nankeens, silks, tea, rice and sugar. But at the moment of completing her return journey back to America, the *Eclipse* had met with disaster. Like so many ships before her in this region she had fallen victim to the storms and rocks of the very coast on which she was attempting to land. Campbell had been among the survivors, along with O'Cain himself, washed up on Sanak Island not far from Kodiak; but while attempting to retrieve the ship's cargo, he had fallen victim to severe frostbite in both feet.

Despite the wretchedness of his condition Campbell, after being rescued, found the time to observe and describe the settlement on Kodiak. 'The town consists of about fifty houses', he recalled later, 'built of logs, the seams of which are caulked with moss and roofs thatched with grass; they are . . . heated by stoves or ovens . . . the heated air then, diffusing itself through the room, renders it extremely uncomfortable . . . Windows, instead of being glazed, are covered with pieces of the gut of the seal, split up and sewed together; this after being well-oiled is stretched on a frame'.

But the main picture we get from Campbell is of his gratitude towards the Russians and their kindly governor. By now he was a helpless invalid, with feet so gangrenous that they needed to be amputated. Considering the atrocious prospect of going under the knife in Russian America, Campbell showed remarkable *sang-froid*. 'My case excited great compassion', he wrote, 'and a subscription was raised for me by Governor

Baranoff and the officers of the ships that lay in the harbour . . . which amounted to 180 roubles'. Given that he was destined to be a cripple for the rest of his life, he had no hope of finding productive work. So Baranov gave him a job on Kodiak, teaching English to native boys. Such, perhaps, was the life of a governor in retirement, tending to stranded sailors, and ensuring the educational welfare of the children.

Unfortunately for Baranov, greater duties than these still lay ahead of him.

The first evidence that Baranov's sojourn in Russian American might not yet be over, reached him some time late in the year of 1807. It came in the form of news of Nicolai Rezanov. In better circumstances, Rezanov should by now have been in St Petersburg, explaining his grand plans to the tsar. But since his departure from New Archangel, in the June of the previous year, Rezanov had set himself a punishing schedule. From Alaska he had first made the long sea journey via Kodiak to Okhotsk, reaching Siberia's eastern shores in September. He had then wasted no time in commencing a land journey across the continent. It had taken him five months, galloping on horseback in the depths of winter, to reach Irkutsk. But in his haste to reach St Petersburg, it seems that he had badly neglected his health. As it was, he had been travelling nearly non-stop for four years, experiencing emotional highs and lows in constant succession. And now, as he rode, he was subjecting his body daily to temperatures that could drop as low as -50° Celsius.

It was a month out of Irkutsk, by the ice-stricken Yenisei River in the frozen heart of Siberia, that he had fallen into his final sickness, as a result of a violent fall from his horse. In March 1807 the Plenipotentiary of the Russian-American colonies died in the snows of Krasnoyarsk, still three thousand miles short of his destination. The job of extending Russia's imperial frontier to the gates of San Francisco would now fall to others; Russian dreams of marrying the beautiful Dona Concepcion and cultivating fruit trees in the sunshine of California would now fall to no-one.

For Baranov personally, the news had startling implications. Rezanov had had no time to appoint a successor to replace the long-suffering governor. The giant jobs that had been ordered, but left undone—the settlement of the Columbia River, the extending of the imperial border into California, the establishment of a base on the islands of Hawaii—would now fall onto his aging shoulders, and his alone. Baranov had little choice, it now seems, but to return to New Archangel to resume his duties. By the summer of 1808 he was back, presumably in a bad mood.

Not that his circumstances were particularly bad. On arrival, he would soon have detected the eerie silence on this coast, caused by the helpful absence of foreign seafarers. And in New Archangel itself he would have been astonished to notice the building that had been continued in his absence. This was becoming a place where a governor of a vast colony might now feel proud to live. The governor's residence had now been transformed. It sat atop the rock in the centre of the town, two stories high, with living quarters, offices, reception halls and a banqueting hall. Finally, the items brought by Rezanov in 1804 could be housed in elegance. A couple of years later, Vasili Golovnin would be astonished to find in Baranov's house, 'ornaments and furniture in profusion, of masterly workmanship and costly price, brought from St Petersburg and from England, which corresponded with his position as the head official of a great company . . . an extensive library in nearly all European languages, and many pictures of remarkable merit . . . in the uncultivated wild border of America there would be none except Mr Baranov to value and understand them'. From the house it would have been possible to look down over a fortified settlement that now contained the homes of perhaps a thousand people.

Shipbuilding was also progressing well. Around the time of Baranov's return, the *Otkrytie*, a new 300-ton ship with three masts was launched. Perhaps, in such an atmosphere of progress, Baranov felt easier about applying himself to the task in hand. The threat of hostile Tlingit Natives to local hunting operations had not gone away. But now Baranov's response was not to retreat to Kodiak, but to think about moving his operations further south; to bypassing the Tlingit barrier, simultaneously advancing Russia's imperial frontier. His three main objectives remained the Columbia River, Hawaii and California. How could he add these three crucial areas permanently to his possessions, thus forming an unbreakable Russian hold over northwestern America?

The plan he came up with was to send men to all of them at once. So it was, in the autumn of 1808, that he prepared three expeditions to travel down the west coast of the continent. This was the first time he would be sending his own vessels on such journeys, hitherto having always relied on Bostonian ships to do so. The *Sv Nikolai* would aim for the Columbia River area, while the *Kodiak* headed for the area immediately to the north of San Francisco, as Rezanov had urged. A few weeks later, the *Neva* under Captain Lieutenant Ludwig von Hagemeister, would set out for Hawaii. All three expeditions were to identify sites for settlements. All would then return to Baranov, and await further orders.

Baranov would have appreciated the fact that he no longer had to make do with drunks and castaways from the wilds of Siberia to captain his vessels. For his expedition to Hawaii in 1808, he would have been glad that he could turn to a young man of the Russian navy, of German landed gentry by birth, who had worked under the British Lord Nelson among others, and who spoke six languages, including fluent English. Which is not to say that Ludwig von Hagemeister was a man who would have been comfortable in the environs of Russian America. Hagemeister, if anything, represented the aspirations of nineteenth century imperial Russia: arrogant, refined, stately, Germanic. One suspects that he would not have had time for drinking contests from Baranov's buckets of raspberry vodka. Nobody yet knew it, but this was the man who would eventually unseat the ramshackle, eighteenth century individualist of peasant origins, Baranov, from his job.

In the meantime, the ostensible purpose of his visit on the *Neva* to Hawaii, was to purchase a cargo of salt and other provisions from Kamehameha. But there is little doubt that the real purpose was to scout for possible locations for a settlement. The nineteenth century historian of the northwest coast Hubert Bancroft says Baranov 'certainly' intended founding a settlement at this time, citing a now-vanished document of instructions in the Sitka archives. One of the passengers on the ride to Hawaii was also witness to this intention. This was the brave Archibald Campbell, who had now lost both feet and was virtually immobile. 'On the return of the *Neva* from Sitka', he later recalled, 'she was ordered to be prepared for a voyage to the Sandwich Islands (as Hawaii was then known), and was provided with a supply of adzes, hatchets, teeth of the sea-horse and other articles suitable for that market. It would appear that the Russians had determined to form a settlement upon those islands; at least preparations were made for the purpose . . . the ship had a house in frame on board and intimation was given that volunteers would be received'.

More compelling still, was the evidence of what happened to Campbell when, having arrived, he mentioned to a fellow Scot residing in the islands that he 'understood the Russians had some intention of forming a settlement on the Sandwich Islands'. Once this had reached the captain's ears, Campbell reports, 'he gave me a severe reprimand for having, as he expressed it, betrayed their secrets'. It comes as no surprise to learn that, from then on, Campbell heard nothing more of the projected settlement. All Campbell could see was that the Russians seemed to be getting a friendly reception. They arrived at Honolulu on 29 January 1809, to find Kamehameha approaching 'in a large double canoe'. Captain Hagemeister went 'to receive his majesty, and shook hands with him when he came on deck. He was on this occasion dressed as a European, in a blue coat and grey pantaloons'. On board, the king asked if this was an English or American ship. Upon being told 'Russian', reports Campbell, he answered 'very good!' A handsome scarlet cloak, edged with ermine, was immediately presented to him with the compliments of Alexander Baranov.

Once on dry land, Campbell was impressed by Hawaii in the same way that anyone would have been, who had just arrived from New Archangel. 'I was much struck with the beauty and fertility of the country', he exclaimed, which looked 'so different' from barren Alaska. The surprising prosperity of Honolulu 'which consisted of several hundred houses' and was 'well-shaded with large coconut trees' was also evident. He later spoke in idyllic terms of the bountiful conditions, as he 'passed by footpaths winding through an extensive and fertile plain, the whole of which is in the highest state of cultivation. Every stream was carefully embanked, to supply water for the taro beds. Where there was no water, the land was under crops of yams and sweet potatoes. The roads and numerous houses are shaded by coconut trees, and the sides of the mountains covered with wood to a great height'. He continued to assume the probability that 'the Russians will in future derive from hence the principal supplies of provisions for their settlements on the Fox islands and northwest coast of America, and even Kamchatka'.

It is not clear exactly how the discussions between Lieutenant Captain Hagemeister and King Kamehameha unfolded. Russian plans to establish a settlement were, in fact, not to be realised on this occasion. Nevertheless, Hagemeister's own report to the directors of the Russian-American Company, written a year later, shows clearly the light in which the Russians continued to view these islands. He spoke boastfully of an English frigate *Cornwallis*, coming all the way from east India and purposely landing at Hawaii 'in order to find out whether we [Russians] had made any territorial claims'. In fact, the evidence was that, 'because of the climate, one of these islands with small harbours can produce foods in quantities sufficient to supply a large part of Asiatic Russia'.

On the question of exactly where to make a settlement, Hagemeister also had ideas. 'We should start it on the island of Molokai, which is more fertile than the others', he declared. It had a port for small boats, and good fisheries. 'The king would be willing to sell us either this, or some other island'. 'If we cannot occupy the whole island now', his report went on, 'it is possible to buy a part of the land from the king'. One or two towers with cannon would defend it, plus 'only about 20 Russians for defence and about the same number for agriculture'. It was true that Kamehameha had plenty of cannons, 'but they do not know how to use them; the king keeps them only for display'. In short, Hagemeister was 'sure' that the islands could be occupied by friendly methods. 'But if force is necessary' he concluded, 'then two ships would be sufficient'.

As far as Hagemeister could see, the only prior claim to the islands came from the British, by right of first discovery, in view of which he did wonder whether 'it would not be necessary first to take up that matter with the British government'. In fact this may have been something of an understatement: from Campbell we learn that the king's residence, built close upon the shore, 'was distinguished by the British colours and a battery of sixteen carriage-guns'. And Kamehameha was known to feel a close affinity for the British king (some months later, he gave a message to Archibald Campbell to pass on to George III 'to remind him of Captain Vancouver's promise that a man-of-war, armed with brass guns, should be sent to him' and to apologise for being 'so far away that he could not help him in his wars'.)

But what heartened Hagemeister beyond anything else were the absentees from these islands. He was able later to report to Baranov that he had hardly seen any American ships at all during his stay. The joint effects of war and embargo had, temporarily at least, cleared these waters of Russia's most credible rivals. The message for Baranov would have been clear: none was now better placed for obtaining a permanent foothold in Hawaii than he.

The other two ships now nosing their separate ways down the west coast of the continent, on Baranov's bidding, had also found themselves in relatively empty seas. Which was one more reason for the crew of the *Sv Nikolai*, that winter, to feel hopeful. Their ship was on a historic colonising mission. They had been charged with the job of investigating the region between today's Vancouver Island and the Columbia River, with a view to locating a site suitable for a Russian fort and settlement, in addition to buying otters from local Indians as they went along.

The two leading men of this expedition were unusually open-minded, sensitive individuals, by the standards of some of their vodka-swilling colleagues. The first of these was the ship's captain, Nikolai Isakovich Bulygin. In the year 1808 he would have been about 35 years old. We know that he had started life in the Russian navy, before being sent to work for the Russian-American Company. But what really distinguished him, among all the seafarers and hunters working for Baranov, was his devotion to his wife, Anna Petrovna. This brave woman was among those on board the *Sviatitelia Nikolai*, as she headed for the Columbia River.

The other remarkable character on board was the man in charge of dealing with the natives, one Timofei Osipovich Tarakanov. Tarakanov had been appointed the *prikashchik* on this voyage, entrusted with the jobs of managing the company's goods, conducting the trade with natives, directing the fur hunters and safeguarding the company's financial interests. He had been chosen for his resourcefulness and sobriety, and because he was one of the very few Russians in America whom Baranov could rely on to keep proper accounts. At the time of this voyage, he was only thirty years old, but from long experience, he was accustomed to dealing with natives, and seems to have spoken some of their languages. He may have been one of those who had survived the attack on Sitka in 1802. He had certainly been one of the very first Russians to sail to California, when Baranov, in 1803, had sent him aboard the Yankee ship *O'Cain* to supervise the hunting of sea otters.

Their ship the *Sv Nikolai* was described as a small schooner, specifically designed for charting the coastline. In theory, once they had done their work at the Columbia River, they were scheduled to rendezvous with the *Kodiak* at Grays Harbour, where Bulygin would report his results to Ivan Kuskov. According to circumstances at the time, the *Sv Nikolai* would then decide whether or not to join Kuskov's trip to California. In practice, the realisation of these plans depended on Bulygin and his men landing their ship safely in Oregon Country, with all their guns intact.

The problem for Bulygin's men was the nature of the stretch of coast to which they had been assigned. The agricultural potential of the land around the Columbia River was not in doubt, and the subsequent history of the United States has shown that these parts of Washington State and Oregon do indeed possess some of the best farmland in the country. Seen from the sea, however, this great promise was far from evident. The coast would have shown no visible change since the British sea captain John Meares had seen it twenty years earlier. 'The appearance of the land was wild in the extreme', Meares had then written. 'Immense forest covered the whole of it within our sight, down to the very beach, which was lofty and cragged, and against which the sea dashed with fearful rage. The shore was lined with rocks and rocky isles, nor could we perceive any bay or inlet that seemed to promise the least security to the smallest vessel . . .'.

Native to this land, furthermore, lived peoples who already had a reputation for ferocity: the Quileute and Hoh. These were people who lived much as all the coastal peoples lived, with a diet chiefly composed of salmon, berries and fern roots. But the life here was by no means one of peace and tranquillity. Intruders were regarded with great suspicion. A state of low-level war existed between these peoples, and the Makah, just to the north, and the Nootka, of Vancouver Island, who periodically came down in war canoes for the purpose of seizing men and goods. Those taken captive were then regarded as a kind of commodity, to be used as gifts or barter. He who owned captives, could call himself rich.

History had already shown that Europeans were as vulnerable to being kidnapped as anybody else. The very first ship to put in at this coast, the *Sonora*, from Spain in 1775, was ambushed and destroyed here when collecting fresh water. Some years later a British ship, the *Imperial Eagle*, lost a boat crew here at the mouth of the Hoh River. Much more recent had been the celebrated case of blacksmith John Jewett, survivor of a Nootka attack on the ship *Boston* in 1804, who had subsequently been held captive for about a year. The Russians knew of these hazards, but were willing to discount them. Bulygin, after all, was even bringing his wife.

Within a fortnight of leaving New Archangel, they had caught sight of the Cape of Juan de Fuca, by Vancouver Island. Tarakanov later wrote of being surrounded by crowds of natives here in small canoes. All were armed, he noted, with firearms and knives and spears. But this was to be anticipated. These Russians were accustomed to dealing with the natives, and knew how to take precautions. No more than two natives were allowed on board at the same time, for example. And their ship's guns were at the ready. Tarakanov was not overly afraid. Perhaps he should have been. What happened next was to be a story as ghastly as any in the annals of the white man's tribulations on the American continent.

For its details we are indebted to Tarakanov's humane account, which provides rich evidence of the difficulties still facing any power attempting to colonise this coast. After a few days of favourable weather, he reported, a giant storm of wind and rain blew in. When the storm ceased, three days later, the murk cleared to reveal that the *Sv Nicolai* was riding dangerously close to the shore, and being swept in. 'It seemed to us that the loss of the ship was inevitable', he recalled, soberly 'and we expected death at any moment'. The danger persisted. Their foreyard snapped off. Finally, on 1 November 'a swell cast us into the surf and then ashore at 47° 56' north latitude. Thus the brig met its fate'.

Amazingly, they were alive. But once they had got over the shock of being beached, the Russians realised, with cold fear, that they were isolated in a country of unremitting strangeness. In fact this was the western, seaward side of the Olympic Peninsula, a land of dense hemlock forest, inhabited by the Makah people. Thick tangles of vines and brush crawled about the forest floor; giant ferns filled the forest openings. Everything was dripping and sodden. Tarakanov was quick to see wherein lay the gravest danger. 'If captured', he speculated, 'we would live out a miserable life as slaves of the savages, a consequence a hundred times more horrible than death'. They needed to save their firearms. In fact, their ship had been cast up on dry land, and remained intact, at low tide. Thus was it possible to begin taking off the cannon, powder and other necessities, while some of the men removed topmasts, sails and rigging. After posting guards and sentries, they set up two tents made out of sails, then lit a big fire to dry themselves.

This had hardly been done 'when a large number of the natives . . . came close'.

The atmosphere was tense, but a hostile encounter was not yet inevitable. There on the beach, Tarakanov invited some of the Makah into his tent, and soon received an offer from one friendly young man to visit him at his 'residence'. With Tarakanov assuring the man of the peaceful intentions of the Russians, this latter 'promised friendship and declared he would attempt to bring his fellow countrymen round to the same attitude'.

But these moments of sanity soon degenerated into a much more familiar pattern of native-European relations. Outside Tarakanov's tent, with the natives crowding round in curiosity, things were already getting out of hand. First, it seems, a little 'thieving' took place. Then the Russians started driving the natives out of the camp, to which the latter responded by throwing rocks. Finally the *promyshlenniki* opened fire. 'I rushed out of the tent', reported a despairing Tarakanov 'only to be hit with a spear that wounded me in the chest'. A general battle had commenced. Virtually everyone would sustain injuries before the enemy was finally chased away.

By resorting so readily to firepower themselves, despite the presence of Bulygin's wife, the Russians had sealed their own fate. Hostility from the indigenous people of the region, and a fearful winter without food or shelter from the incessant rain, was now guaranteed. When the Russians looked for a place to fortify, they soon found the coast 'lacking in advantages for a party in our predicament'. The land was covered with dense forest 'which extended so near the water that large waves washed the trees'. A decision was made to leave the ship and its cargo for the Indians to plunder. They would walk to Grays Harbour, apparently 65 nautical miles distant, in the faint hope of meeting up with Ivan Kuskov on the *Kodiak*. They set off carrying their guns and ammunition, along the beach.

Progress was only made with difficulty. 'Tricksy' natives kept catching up with them, offering misleading advice. They found a cave, where they passed a night in a 'violent rain and snow storm'. Then, during the morning 'the miserable weather continued' and large rocks began falling about them, pushed from cliffs by the natives above. 'To them we were neither a threat nor a danger', mused Tarakanov, bitterly, 'but it seems they begrudged our very existence'. For two more days this went on, until they found themselves in the territory of another tribe, who seemed friendlier. These now agreed to help the Russians across a small river that ran into the sea at this point. They provided two boats, one large, and the other small, to convey all the Russians at once. In the small boat, steered by a native woman, was placed Anna Petrovna, and three others. The larger boat took nine of the best *promyshlenniki*, as well as Bulygin and Tarakanov. But it was a trick. In the middle of the river, wooden plugs were suddenly pulled from the bottom of the larger boat. The natives piloting it jumped in and swam. Spears and arrows came flying in from the shore. Miraculously enough, a cross current suddenly caught the holed boat and dragged it on to the far side of the river, before it could sink. But the men had no time to count their blessings. As they stumbled, drenched, to shore, they looked back and saw with horror that those in the smaller boat, including Anna Petrovna, had been taken hostage.

Again a battle was fought, but on this occasion the natives prevailed. One of the Russians was mortally wounded. The end of it would leave the survivors scrambling up river in bare feet, desperate to escape. 'Our situation seemed miserable' recalled Tarakanov. 'We felt terrified and in the depths of despair. But our unhappy commander suffered more than anyone else. For he had lost his wife, whom he loved more than himself, and knew nothing of her fate at the hands of the barbarians. Bulygin was tortured grievously. One could not look at him without being moved to the greatest sympathy and tears'.

Ivan Kuskov, in the *Kodiak*, had no idea of the suffering to which his colleagues had now been condemned. He was not even aware that the

Sv Nicolai had failed to appear for the rendezvous at Grays Harbour, for the simple reason that he too had been prevented from entering the harbour by unfavourable weather. But this would not have been a matter of enormous concern to him. Travel in these seas was always an unpredictable business. As it was, his journey down to California proved to be a smooth one. If we exclude Rezanov's exploratory trip of 1806, Kuskov's 1809 visit in the *Kodiak* can be described as the first independent Russian hunting trip to California. But Kuskov knew what he was doing. Baranov had always asked the *prikazshchiki* accompanying Bostonian seafarers on previous voyages to make detailed notes, in preparation for doing such trips themselves. As Langsdorff had noted, the waters of northern California were teeming with otter, and it was known that 'a very advantageous trade might be established'—even if it were also 'very questionable' whether the Spaniards would consent to such trade.

In fact the Spanish attitude had already been severely tested, ever since the time when Baranov had first started contracting Bostonians to carry his Aleut hunters to California. Governor Don José Joaquin Arrillaga, who had entertained such intimate relations with Rezanov, was furious about these hunting operations. He had written to the viceroy in Mexico, complaining that 'there is not an otter left from Mission Rosario to Santo Domingo'. His frustration with the Bostonian smugglers was almost identical to that felt by Baranov. 'There is no other way to prevent them except to tell them not to hunt' fumed the governor, 'and to this they pay no attention'.

Playing cat-and-mouse with the Spanish seems to have been part of the fun of trading on this coast. Confrontations were frequent, though violence rare. The main participants were the men whom Baranov had commissioned; familiar characters such as Joseph O'Cain and the Winship brothers. O'Cain for example, in the *Eclipse*, just two years before, had tried to wheedle his way into San Diego Bay, by telling a 'piteous tale' to Manuel Rodriguez, the port commander, about his need for emergency repairs and supplies. The Spanish had correctly seen this as a tactic, and barred him from entry, despatching a corporal and some soldiers to follow his progress along the shore. But just outside San Diego, O'Cain had turned the tables by coming ashore and taking the soldiers prisoner. He had held onto them for a time; then deigned to release them. The Spanish were furious. But the *Eclipse* continued its leisurely way, collecting otters at will.

In the years prior to Kuskov's arrival, such incidents had been plentiful. Oliver Kimball (Joseph O'Cain's brother-in-law) had been commissioned by Baranov to take his ship the *Peacock* down to California in the winter of 1806–07. In theory he had been requested to avoid Spanish settlements; in practice he had ended up hiding in Bodega bay for several months, from where he even dared to send boats through the Golden Gate into San Francisco Bay, defying the *presidial* cannon. Governor Arillaga seems to have been almost at his wits' end. Reports of Bostonian ships and Russian hunting canoes lurking off San Francisco, Santa Barbara, Santo Domingo, Los Angeles and San Diego had been coming in thick and fast, but, sadly for the old governor, there was little he could do about them.

When Kuskov arrived in California, the Spanish were in a particularly bad mood, having spent the previous months watching Captain George Ayres of the *Mercury*, also on commission from Baranov, hunt otters up and down their coast. Ayres would later receive a letter from the commandant of Los Angeles requesting that 'as soon as you see this, you retire from this coast with your frigate and people who accompany you'. Ayres would eventually head back north, but not before collecting more than 2000 precious skins.

It was on 15 December 1808 that the *Kodiak* reached the calm waters of Bodega Bay, just a few miles north of San Francisco. Kuskov began work at once. The first of the two jobs with which he had been entrusted was to hunt for otters. In the relatively mild coastal air of this latitude, the Russians and Aleuts alike can rarely have found this easier or more pleasant. After a few weeks, following the advice of Rezanov and Langsdorff, they decided to find a discreet way into San Francisco Bay itself. As had been suggested by Lieutenant Khvostov, to enter through the Golden Gate was an unnecessary risk. There was an easier way. Kuskov's men picked up their baidarkas and carried them overland, from Bodega over the Marin Peninsula, to reach the bay from the north.

By February 1809, about fifty Russian baidarkas were actively hunting on the waters of San Francisco Bay. They did not quite manage to pass without detection. One Aleut who landed on Angel Island was seized by the Spanish, and taken to the *presidio*. Then, some time at the end of March, a group of about twenty baidarkas were reported by the Spanish to have landed on the southern fringes of the bay; a Spanish sergeant and eight soldiers hurried to challenge them. Firing occurred, and four Aleuts were killed. Given the relatively casual regard that the Russians had for the lives of their native hunters, even this did not deter them. The *Kodiak* would not leave Bodega until August, by which time it would be carrying in its hold 2000 skins for Alexander Baranov. It would be one of the most profitable hunts the Russians had ever conducted.

But Kuskov would not leave Bodega until he had accomplished the second of his two jobs: that of identifying a suitable location for a permanent Russian settlement in the area. The spot he chose lay some 18 miles north of Bodega Bay. It was a strip of grassy tableland, perched a hundred feet above the ocean, securely ensconced between the ocean and the mountains. Behind it, sky-high redwood trees covered rolling foothills; before it, high bluffs overlooked two small bays, enclosing beaches strewn with driftwood. A small dockyard could be constructed there, from the plentiful timber. In early summer Kuskov would have found long grass rippling in mild winds and buzzards wheeling in the up-draughts. This beautiful place, he could hope and believe, would soon represent the front line in the expanding frontier of imperial Russia.

No such hopes attended the crew of the *Sv Nicolai*, wandering, lost, some hundreds of miles to the north, in the late autumn of 1808. Their adventure had now become entirely irrelevant to Baranov's dreams of imperial expansion. Their only possible goal now was survival. 'Without knowing where to go', wrote Tarakanov, 'we wandered in the forest and mountains, trying only to escape from the savages'. For days rain fell. Worse still, they had nothing to eat. No edible mushrooms or wild food could be found; they resorted to eating tree fungus and even their own clothes, including their raincoats, the soles of their shoes, and their gun-covers. Finally, on a day when they had 'not even a speck of food', they agreed to butcher 'our steadfast friend, our unfailing sentinel, our faithful dog'.

It was now that Bulygin decided to resign his command to Tarakanov, on the grounds—as he himself put it—that he had almost lost his mind. This move seems to have given the party a boost. They now succeeded in stealing 25 fish from a native village, despite having to endure another battle to do so. They also agreed on a realistic plan, to continue walking upriver to a place where fish would be available, where they could build a fort and spend the winter. On they went, despite 'terrible rain' impeding their march. From time to time, they bullied natives into selling them fish. 'By necessity we were forced to take strong measures', explained Tarakanov, 'measures which our conscience completely justified'.

Then one day something extraordinary happened. An Indian appeared and asked whether they wanted to buy from him a person whom he seemed to know by name—Anna Petrovna. 'This astonishing proposition brought cheer to us all, but Bulygin, hearing his words, was beside himself with joy'. Bulygin promptly offered his last greatcoat as payment and Tarakanov his new nankeen cotton dressing gown. Everyone, even the Aleuts, offered some part of their clothing. A soggy pile of tunics and baggy trousers began to accumulate. But then the Indian showed his hand. He was not interested in clothes. To Tarakanov's displeasure, he wanted only guns. 'We did not refuse him, but stated that before concluding the deal we wanted to see Anna Petrovna'. This request was accepted, and a short while later, another group of Indians could be seen bringing the unfortunate woman to the far bank of the river. After the Russians had 'implored them to bring her to our side', they set her in a canoe and brought her to the middle of the river, halting at a distance of about forty yards. Thus did negotiations begin.

Deep in the gloomy rainforest, the atmosphere was one of agony and drama. 'I could not even imagine what the unhappy couple felt during this meeting', recalled Tarakanov. 'Anna Petrovna and her spouse each melted into tears, sobbed, and could scarcely talk. Looking at them, we too wept bitterly. Only the savages remained unmoved by this pathetic spectacle. She tried to calm her husband, assuring him that they kept her well and now were staying near the mouth of the river . . .'.

The negotiations proceeded, hesitantly. Tarakanov now offered all the clothes, plus one broken musket. The natives stuck insistently to their original demand of four guns. When the Russians hesitated, the natives made as if to carry Anna Petrovna away again. 'At that point' continued Tarakanov, 'Bulygin, again taking the attitude of commander, ordered me to pay the savages all they demanded. I pointed out to him that we had only one good musket for each man, that we had no tools for repairing them, and that these guns were the only things that could save us. To give away such a number of muskets would be foolish . . . to obey his order, I insisted, would ruin us. Hence I asked him to forgive me, but concluded that I must venture to disobey him'.

It was a hideous situation. Bulygin, overwhelmed by tears and emotion, pleaded his case. But all the men stood by Tarakanov. 'We knew this refusal would be a shock to our distraught commander, but what else could we do?' So it was that Anna Petrovna was abandoned. She was once again removed from sight to the far side of the river, and the Russians went on their way without her.

The walk upriver was taking them into colder and colder lands. Eventually they reached a point where heavy snows prevented them from going any further. It was here that they elected to build their cabin, having obtained a large amount of fish, plus a boat, by seizing one native and holding him to ransom. Finally, they had come to a place where they would be left alone for the winter. There they remained, 'for a long time the sole inhabitant of our realm of land and water'. Which was not to say that their nightmare was over. Come the spring of 1809, it resumed again. But this time they planned to continue going upriver, before crossing the mountains to the Columbia River, where lived a people 'less barbarous than here'.

Only one man, for obvious reasons, was interested in going back down again. This was the tearful Bulygin. And as the snows began to melt, so he announced that he was ready to resume command of the party. He was determined to go back to the place where they had last seen his wife. Tarakanov agreed to risk it, rather than 'drive him to despair by opposing his plan'.

So they made their way down river, putting their faith in the services of a 'guide' of uncertain trustworthiness. Later, when he proved to be honest, they gave him, among other presents, a medal stamped out of pewter. 'On one side we depicted an eagle of sorts, which represented Russia, and on the other the year, month and day when this savage, Liutliuliuk by name, received it'. Before long, they found themselves back in the terrain of the Makah people, where they had suffered so grievously the year before. They began passing people on the path—recognisable people. Among them was one woman whom Bulygin remembered instantly as having participated in the seizure of Anna Petrovna. Bulygin took his chance and seized her, along with another young man. The game of hostage-taking had been joined. The Russians now informed the local Indians, that they would not let them go 'until our own hostages were received'. In response to which, the husband of the woman 'begged us not to hurt her, but said he would try to find our captives, who now belonged to another tribe'.

A few days later, fifty Makah came to the opposite bank of the river under the command of 'an elderly man dressed in a European jacket, trousers and a beaver hat'. Tarakanov went to hold discussions with them, leaving Bulygin behind, apparently in fear that he would be unable to control his emotions again. On reaching the river, he recalled—'to our great joy'—they saw Anna Petrovna.

It must have been a curious meeting, to say the least. Some six months had passed, since their last encounter. Nevertheless, Anna Petrovna greeted the men in Russian in the normal way. To the surprise of

Tarakanov, she then expressed her concern for the welfare of the hostages being held by the Russians. She declared that these two were 'very fine people who had rendered her many services and had treated her very well, and she demanded that we free the woman at once'. This gave the Russians the first inkling of what was to come. Tarakanov continued: 'When I told her that her spouse would free the captives only on condition of an exchange for herself, Mrs Bulygin gave us an answer that struck us like a clap of thunder, an answer we could not believe for several minutes, taking it all for a dream. In horror, distress, and anger, we heard her say firmly that she was satisfied with her condition, did not want to join us, and that she advised us to surrender ourselves to this people. The toion, she explained, was an upright and virtuous man, widely known along this coast. He honestly would free us and send us to the two European ships then trading in the Strait of Juan de Fuca'.

So it is that we come to the man who was really at the centre of this drama: the chief in the jacket, trousers and beaver hat. We learn from Tarakanov that his name was Yutramaki. By coincidence, a detailed description of this same chief has also come down to us from the pen of John Jewitt, the survivor of a Nootka attack on the *Boston* in 1804, who had also spent a long period marooned on this shore.

'This chief, who could speak tolerable English', Jewitt had written, 'had much more the appearance of a civilised man than any of the savages that I saw. He appeared to be about thirty, was rather small in person but extremely well formed with a skin almost as fair as an European, good features and a countenance expressive of candour and amiableness and which was almost always brightened by a smile. He was much neater both in dress and person than any of the other chiefs, seldom wearing paint, except upon his eyebrows . . . he always treated me with much kindness, was fond of conversing with me in English and in his own language, asking me many questions relative to my country, its manners, customs etc, and appeared to take a strong interest in my fate . . .'. Later, Yutramaki had conveyed a letter from Jewett to a Yankee trading ship, the brig *Lydia*, enabling its crew to rescue their missing compatriot. It was into the hands of this enigmatic but benign toion that Anna Petrovna had now fallen. Nevertheless, to Bulygin, 'who loved his wife passionately', it would be impossible to explain any of this. Tarakanov now attempted to persuade Anna Petrovna 'to come to her senses and take pity on her unhappy spouse, to whom she was indebted for everything'. She remained adamant that she would not.

After returning to Bulygin, Tarakanov 'for a long time' hesitated to reveal what he had heard. 'Yet nothing could be done. It was impossible to hide the truth. I had to disclose everything to our anguished commander . . . he heard me out, but apparently did not believe me at first, assuming that I was joking. But after reflecting a few moments, he suddenly fell into a frenzy, grabbed a gun and ran towards the riverbank intending to shoot his wife. After several steps, however, he stopped short, and began to weep, then ordered me to go along to argue with her'. Tarakanov went to give it another try, but he could see that Anna Petrovna had crossed that thin line separating 'civilisation' from what the Russians saw as 'savagery'. In this environment, it would have been clear to a perceptive person that the advantages of the latter far outweighed those of the former. 'Now I am living with kind and humane people', she told Tarakanov, again. 'Tell my husband that I scorn his threats'. Bulygin listened carefully to Tarakanov's latest report. 'For a long time he was silent, like a man who has lost his memory. At last he gave a sudden cry and fell to the ground as though dead. When he came to his senses we had laid him on a greatcoat, and he began to sob bitterly and said not a word to us'.

By now, the last phase of their suffering was about to begin. Tarakanov possessed the strength of mind to conclude that Anna Petrovna might be right. He calculated that she was better qualified than they were to judge the natives, having spent the best part of a year living with them. So he now announced to his exhausted colleagues his intention to surrender to the natives, without further delay, rather than to 'wander about in the forest, continually struggling with hunger and against the elements, fighting the savages, exhausting ourselves'.

It took a few hours for the men to make up their minds. To submit to slavery, after so many months on the run, would have felt like a crushing defeat. There was no knowing, furthermore, who would become the property of which chief. They ran the risk of being scattered or sold off to yet remoter tribes. But eventually several of them, including Bulygin, assented. They gave themselves up, while the remaining comrades (soon to be captured by another tribe) departed by themselves.

Thus were Baranov's attempts to settle the Columbia River area ending in apparent disaster. No one yet knew how costly this misfortune would be, when history came to pass its final judgement. But there was no question that the establishment of Russian farms in Oregon Country would have solved the problems of provisioning the Alaskan colonies, not to mention Kamchatka and Okhotsk. The sailing time from Sitka was just a couple of weeks; and the growing conditions by the Columbia River were vastly superior. As yet Baranov had no news of the *Sv Nicolai* at all. But it certainly appeared as though he had lost a valuable ship, as well as several of his best men.

Worse still was the evidence that others were already moving to exploit the gap left by Baranov's failure. What was now happening was that the political establishment in Washington DC was coming to its senses. Thomas Jefferson's expensive, self-destructive Embargo Act would be repealed in the summer of 1809. Almost immediately, Jonathan and Nathan Winship, in the *O'Cain* and the *Albatross* respectively, prepared to set off on a new, highly ambitious voyage out of Boston. It was said that they 'hoped to plant a Garden of Eden on the shores of the Pacific'; more specifically, they were set on establishing the first trading post on the Columbia River—a site that they, as compatriots of Robert Gray, felt entitled to claim, by right of first discovery. Their departure took place at almost exactly the moment that Anna Petrovna, on the other side of the continent, was telling her husband that she did not wish him to rescue her.

The Winships, travelling separately, were old hands at doubling the Horn by now, which is not to say that the going was ever easy. Nathan Winship, in the *Albatross*, had a particularly arduous journey. 'The passage of Cape Horn was effected after severe toil and hardship' wrote William Dane Phelps, a contemporary chronicler of Bostonian sea voyages, 'encountering a series of heavy gales, mountainous seas, hail, snow and icebergs'. The *Albatross* had endured 200 unbroken days at sea before she made her first stop, at Easter Island; in which time 'grass had ample time to grow on her bare planks'.

Once in the Pacific, the world turned highly colourful, as usual. At Easter Island they were beset by cunning thieves and rogues. On the Marquesas Islands, several of the crew tried to desert. Then at Hawaii, after meeting Kamehameha's Prime Minister, 'Billy Pitt', Nathan was presented with a letter from his brother Jonathan, advising him to 'proceed with all possible dispatch to the Columbia River, to anticipate any movement of the Russians in that direction'.

The news of Baranov's imperial intentions, it seemed, had finally riled the men of Boston into taking up imperial attitudes of their own. In May 1810, with supplies and livestock on board, the *Albatross* sailed into the mouth of the great river that had proved such a singular challenge to both Bulygin and Rezanov before him, and came to anchor beside an oak grove. Their aim, as they freely admitted, was to build a fortified agricultural base. If citizens of Russia could maintain forts on this coast—then so, surely, could they. On 4 June 1810, they broke ground, planted a garden, and began work on a log house, the very first structural evidence of the presence of the United States on this coast.

The project did not get far. After just one week, a group of natives appeared to inform them that their presence was not welcome. Vastly outnumbered, and with no will to fight, Winship and his men did not hesitate. 'Much to our chagrin we find it is impossible to prosecute the business as we intended', wrote one of the men. Surprisingly enough, these native claims were recognised by some contemporary Americans as reasonable. 'The country was theirs', admitted Phelps. 'They had an undisputed right to resist the attempts of any person or persons who should endeavour to dispossess them of the country where God and nature had planted them'. For this reason (according to Phelps), Winship did not wish to see blood shed, and withdrew.

But the Russians could not afford to relax. The experiment of Nathan Winship was but the precursor to a more concerted Bostonian invasion of the Columbia River. Just months later, in September 1810, another ship called the *Tonquin* sailed from New York, bound for the northwest coast. Financing this expedition was the most formidable rival whom the Russians would yet have to face.

So brilliantly chronicled by Washington Irving in his book *Astoria*, the attempt of John Jacob Astor to build the USA's first permanent settlement on the Pacific coast of the continent has entered American legend and popular history as surely as Baranov's exploits have been forgotten. Like his rival Alexander Baranov, Astor had been born into a poor family on the continent of Europe; but otherwise the destiny of the two men was as different as can possibly be imagined. Astor was among the first of America's great capitalists. He had been born in 1763 in Waldorf, Germany, and reached New York as a penniless immigrant at the age of 21. But within 15 years of his arrival in the United States, his personal fortune had grown to exceed a quarter of a million dollars.

The basis for his success was fur, or 'cold gold', as the Americans liked to call it. In this sense, the Russian whom Astor closely mirrored was not Baranov but Grigori Shelikhov; and like his Russian counterpart, Astor was no angel. He paid low wages to his *voyageurs* (the North American equivalent to *promyshlenniki*) and then charged them high prices to buy the supplies they needed to survive while in his employ. He forced his subordinate traders to mortgage their lands to his company. He also sold opium to China, liquor to the native Americans and guns and ammunition to practically everyone. No wonder he eventually became a multimillionaire. Years later, his operations would come to encompass the interior, the west and east coasts of North America, the west coast of South America, Hawaii, Canton, England and the Mediterranean. By 1833, he would be the dominant figure in the American fur trade, hold a commanding position in London, and virtually control Canton. At his death in 1848 (aged over eighty), he would be worth between $20 and $30 million, much of which had been acquired not through fur but through Manhattan real estate. And yet through his whole life, it seems, no single project would sear his imagination as deeply as his attempt to plant the US flag on the northwest coast.

The seeds of this interest had been sown during Astor's early years of trading, in the 1790s, when the Canadians had still had a monopoly on the North American fur trade. Restrictive trade agreements at that time had prohibited direct trade between Canada and America. But in 1794, when Britain had finally agreed to permit trade between its Canadian colonies and the United States, this situation had changed. It had been from that time that Astor began expanding his fur activities out from the northeast, west towards the Great Lakes. Another big expansion in his empire had taken place in 1800, when he entered the China trade for the first time, obtaining a share in a ship sailing for Canton with furs and ginseng, and returning with teas, silks, spices and chinaware. Given that his rivals in Canada were forbidden from trading directly with China (rules of the East India Company decreed that Canada was only permitted to sell furs in America and England), Astor's discovery of the Canton market was a huge step forward. So it was that he decided to put all his energy into the trade. By 1803, he was already sending all his best furs to Canton, getting valuable silks and teas in return, and sending them to Europe where they were able to generate still more profit. Before long, he had become the first millionaire in the history of the United States.

But like most millionaires, he was hard to satisfy. The Canadians still seemed to be trapping and exporting the lion's share of the furs on the North American continent. Even in the aftermath of the Louisiana Purchase, and the acquisition of the Mississippi and Missouri Rivers for the United States, the Canadians were continuing to collect three-quarters of all the furs taken west of the Mississippi river.

The US government did not like this, and neither did Astor. He began to formulate plans to wrest the fur trade from the Canadians. His first big idea had been to set up a headquarters in New York, to which he would gather furs from right across the continent. But being the creative individual that he was, he soon saw the limitations of this. In the end, the solution he had settled on would be truly radical: he would build his headquarters not on the Atlantic, but on the *Pacific*.

The Pacific coast of America in those days was still a wild, dangerous place that lay not only beyond the United States, but beyond the civilised world itself. And yet Astor's plan had had several advantages. One was that the most pristine hunting grounds lay far to the west, beyond the reach of other hunters. Another was that the west coast harboured the most valuable fur-bearing creature of all, namely the sea otter. Then there was the matter of transporting his furs to their natural market in China. From a port on the Pacific coast, journey times would be a fraction of what they would be from New York.

He would not be without rivals for possession of this region. The Russians were known to be encroaching here, from their headquarters in the wintry north, as were the British Canadians, in the form of the Northwest Company, coming overland from the east. The Canadians, who were in the same position of weakness as Astor himself, had to be beaten in a straightforward trial of strength and will. But regarding the Russians, who were already entrenched, something subtler might be required. 'As, in extending the American trade along the coast to the northward', Irving explains, 'it might be brought into the vicinity of the Russian Fur Company, and produce a hostile rivalry, it was part of the plan of Mr Astor to conciliate the good will of that company by the most amicable and beneficial arrangements . . .'.

But just as he had been on the point of launching his scheme, Thomas Jefferson's annoying Embargo Act had been introduced. For a couple of years, Astor had been forced to bide his time. In the long run, this quiet period may have been to his advantage: it was now that he settled on some of the finer details of his plan, in particular, on the location for his trading post. He would place it at the mouth of the Columbia River, where it would constitute the terminus of a giant area stretching from the Great Lakes along the Mississippi to St Louis, west along the Missouri to the Rockies, then down the Columbia to the ocean. And unlike Alexander Baranov, who had chosen to give his capital the patriotic but unspectacular Russian name of New Archangel, Astor planned to cast aside all personal modesty in naming his settlement after himself. A town called Astoria, he hoped, would one day become the great western equivalent to

New York or Boston. In the inimitable language of Irving, Astor foresaw his establishment at the mouth of the Columbia as 'the emporium to an immense commerce; as a colony that would form the germ of a wide civilisation; that would in fact, carry the American population across the Rocky Mountains and spread it along the shores of the Pacific, as it already animated the shores of the Atlantic'.

By February 1808, Astor had already persuaded President Jefferson of the virtues of his scheme, insofar as it 'should assist in ousting British influence from the trans-Mississippi area'. In April of the same year, he obtained a charter for the American Fur Company, which was intended to be the parent of the intended settlement. It had a capital of one million dollars; 'the capital was furnished by himself' commented Washington Irving. 'He in fact constituted the company'.

Shortly after the repeal of the Embargo Act, Astor's first ship the *Enterprise* had then sailed from New York in November 1809, bound for the Pacific, under the captaincy of John Ebbets.

This was where Astor's 'amicable and beneficial arrangements', for placating the Russians on the northwest coast, came into play. As everyone knew, the Russians in America had two big anxieties. One was that they had a problem in feeding themselves, and had often relied on Bostonian seafarers to provide them with adequate supplies of basic foods and other goods. With Russia at war with Great Britain, and round-the-world transport from St Petersburg much reduced, this problem had lately become more acute. The other difficulty was that they lived in fear of the native Americans using firearms against them—firearms conveniently provided for them by seafarers from Boston. With these issues in mind, the *Enterprise* carried supplies and plans to the Pacific, specifically for the delectation of Alexander Baranov.

Astor's tactic, of appeasing the Russians through friendship, rather than of confronting them with aggression, fitted well with the mood of the times. It was precisely now that relations between Tsar Alexander and President Jefferson had been turning so cordial. Indeed, the governments of the two countries had just agreed to exchange ambassadors for the very first time. From St Petersburg, Count Feodor von der Pahlen was travelling as Envoy Extraordinary and Minister Plenipotentiary to the United States, and coming the other way, from Washington to St Petersburg, was John Quincy Adams, the former senator and Harvard Professor, and future President of the United States. Warmth and good feeling was in the air as he arrived, to plead with Russia to defend the rights of his weak and faraway republic against encroachments from the world's mightiest powers, France and Great Britain.

On seeing St Petersburg, Adams would describe it as the 'city of princes' and the 'most magnificent city of Europe or of the world'. In such an atmosphere, the conflict of interests on the northwest coast was a mere trifle: and Astor, it seemed, was offering a simple solution.

Whether Astor's offers of help would satisfy Alexander Baranov himself was less clear. Yes, the problem of US traders selling arms to the coastal American natives was an issue that had been depriving him of sleep for more than twenty years. He, more than anyone alive, would have been glad to see an end to this nuisance. But would he also have accepted Astor's plans to settle in the middle of a coast that he had, for so long, hoped to claim for himself? To do business with Astor would be to accept defeat on the Columbia River.

But in the current diplomatic environment, Baranov would have had little choice but to welcome Astor's friendly overtures. As Irving explained, the US was extremely keen 'to remedy the evil' from which Russia had been suffering at the hands of its citizens. In fact, this 'evil' was already being discussed at the highest levels, precisely in response to Baranov's prior complaints. In the spring of 1808, the company directors had sent a protest to Count Rumiantsev, now heading the ministries of both Commerce and Foreign Affairs. They had spoken of 'the damage inflicted on the company by Bostonians' and requested the 'gracious assistance of the highest authority in forbidding foreigners, especially North American republicans, to trade with the savages, such being the custom in other European colonies in both Indies, and induce them to trade only with the company and nowhere else but on Kodiak as the main local Russian trading post'.

Count Rumiantsev had listened sympathetically, before making his own report on the matter to Tsar Alexander in May 1808, informing him of the situation by which Bostonian seafarers were inciting the natives 'not to respect the Russians', and explaining that, 'to support this corruption, they barter to them all sorts of firearms'.

This was the problem to which Astor was now proposing a grand remedy. His idea was to supply Baranov with food at New Archangel by means of regular deliveries from his own projected headquarters on the Columbia River. Such a trade, once established, would exclude the casual traders who had been supplying weapons to Indians. Once Astor, in other words, had won a monopoly on taking furs and trading with the Russians, freelance American seafarers would cease bothering with this coast at all.

Prominent Russians were impressed by the plan, including Ambassador Pahlen, who had just arrived in Washington. Astor, as he saw it, was proposing 'to implement effectively the aims of our court, without interference from the United States government'. And the Russian Consul-General in Philadelphia, AI Dashkov, also wrote to Rumiantsev at this time, explaining that he had begun negotiations 'between the main office of the Russian-American settlements and a certain merchant from New York who is already familiar with this trade'. By such means, he declared, he was in hopes of 'reaching the desired object . . .'.

In fact, a deal between Astor and Baranov would also have affected both sides in other respects. As mentioned earlier, one of Astor's motives in settling the Pacific was that he hoped to weaken the positions of his rivals the Northwest Company and the Hudson Bay Company of Canada. So it was that he now offered a 'project of agreement with the RAC and American Fur Company for the purpose of excluding all outsiders from commerce', as well as for 'preventing the import of firearms for the local population'. More controversially, Astor was also keen on dividing the area up into distinct national regions. The region he wished to reserve for himself was that part of the coast lying between 44° and 55° north; the Russian area would thus be confined to the coast north of 55°. According to these proposals, his American Company, along with the Russian-American Company, would bind itself not to supply firearms to natives in the other's area. The Russians would undertake to deal exclusively with the American Fur Company. Within two or three years private traders would thus be compelled to leave the area, to the advantage of both parties.

It took time for Astor's proposals to be negotiated into a formal agreement. When the discussions eventually took place in St Petersburg, the Russians were certainly pleased to consider means of preventing the sale of firearms to the natives. They were also pleased to discuss means of curtailing the growing power of the British in North America. The growth in recent years of the British-Canadian Northwest Company had disturbed them as much as it had disturbed Astor—according to Pahlen, its employ- ees already reached 3000 in number, and its operations stretched so far north and west from Lake Superior that 'it already has a station on the northernmost tributary of the Columbia River and hopes to reach the coast'. A deal with Astor would prevent, among other things, the appear- ance of 'these undesirable neighbours' near Russian territory. Only the ter- ritorial issue was bound to cause disagreement. Some Americans already saw Astor's projected colony as the precursor to a general invasion of the

Pacific region. Thomas Jefferson, for one, was looking forward to the day when the descendents of Astor's settlers on America's west coast 'should have spread themselves through the whole length of that coast, covering it with free and independent Americans unconnected with us but by the ties of blood and interest, enjoying like us the rights of self-government'.

But there was a big snag to this: the presence of Alexander Baranov and the Russian-American Company. Dashkov had received a memo from the company directors at the time of his appointment, explaining that the Company had not as yet extended its possessions further south than New Archangel, because of a 'lack of time, chance, and especially, of a sufficient number of fur traders'. But, it went on, 'as soon as the times and chances will allow, the company's industrial activity will advance to the Charlotte Islands, and further to the Columbia River'. They had also called Dashkov's attention to 'some rivalry' with the United States as regards discoveries and ambitions, especially in the Columbia River area.

Evasive discussions about borders had been rumbling on ever since then. But from the time of his arrival in America, Dashkov had been under clear instructions not to commit himself to a southern border for the Russian territories. This created certain difficulties when it came to discussions with President Madison. 'Having learned that I am not authorised to define the southern border of our possessions to serve as a demarcation line for the American vessels trading there', Dashkov pointed out, in a dispatch to St Petersburg, 'Mr President finds it difficult to introduce a definite law forbidding the contraband trade'. So the Americans had some cards to play. But the fact was that Baranov was still in the driving seat on this coast. The Russian settlements here had already survived for three decades, giving their owners intimate knowledge of the climate, the natives and the waters.

Astor could try settling here if he liked, but Baranov was not ready to accept permanent limits to his own territorial ambitions which was why the company directors, in St Petersburg, now rejected Astor's proposed border. They announced that they could not discuss the issue, on the grounds that borders were governmental issues. Thus they secured agreement that the area between 44° and 55° should remain a jointly owned territory, in which neither side would 'interfere with each other's trading and hunting grounds, nor furnish arms and ammunition to the Indians'.

Not even an incredulous John Quincy Adams would be able to argue the Russians out of this one, despite being under orders to establish a Russian border in such a way that 'the limit should be as little advanced southwardly as may be' and despite his personal conviction, as expressed in a letter to his mother from the time, that the US was 'a nation coextensive with the North American continent, destined by God and nature to be the most populous and most powerful people ever combined under one social compact'.

The final, detailed agreement with Astor would not be settled until late in 1811. But long before then, the Russian consul Dashkov was writing to Baranov, recommending Astor to him as an active New York merchant who 'wishes to enter into an agreement with you' and 'proposes the use of his vessels for transporting your goods to Canton'. Astor himself also wrote directly to Baranov around the same time, informing him that he was giving Ebbets authority not only to sell his cargo to the Russians, but to negotiate a permanent deal by which his ships would supply Baranov's needs into the future.

When Ebbets finally arrived at New Archangel in the *Enterprise* in July 1810, carrying Astor's letter, Baranov regarded him in a friendly light. He agreed to buy 54,000 roubles of goods from him. And the two men did indeed sign a contract, in which Baranov commissioned Ebbets to take a cargo of furs to Canton, wherewith to buy Chinese goods. Baranov now knew of Astor's bold plans, but trusted the honesty of the American captain, it was said, 'through the special respect of and confidence in the esteemed Mr Astor'. This trust was well-placed: in the event, Ebbets would return from China in May 1811 bringing with him 100 cases of lump sugar, 1000 pikuls of wheat, 8000 bolts of cotton, 520 chests of tea, 100 cases of tea, 14 cases of table china and 1200 bolts of various silks. When Baranov saw, moreover, the accurate accounts, he would be 'certain of Ebbet's sense of honour and justice and was very pleased with the trading deal which had brought much profit to the company'.

But there was one area that Baranov refused to discuss with Ebbets: the future. According to Khlebnikov, he 'refrained from concluding a contract for the future', on the grounds that his current reliance on American supplies would be temporary. Once Russia's current state of war with Great Britain had ended, then 'the Main Office would send everything he needed from St Petersburg'. And as usual, Baranov was also thinking of his own mortality. In his own letter to Astor, he could not help mentioning 'that at his own request he hoped soon to be relieved of his duties and could not therefore conclude any permanent obligations'.

By now the *Tonquin*, with its crew of settlers, would already have departed New York, bound for the Columbia River. At the same time, a group of fur hunters and dealers, under the leadership of William P Hunt, was beginning the long overland expedition from the United States to the Pacific Coast. If all went well, the two groups would meet in Astoria, some time during 1811.

Baranov was now fully informed of Astor's plans to settle the region. He would not have been pleased, but he had no need to panic as he would have also known, better than anyone, the difficulties that Astor's men would soon be facing.

It is hard to guess whether Baranov would have celebrated the twentieth anniversary of his arrival in Russia. He now lived in comfort, with all manner of provisions in good supply. When Captain-Lieutenant VM Golovnin arrived in 1810 to inspect the colonies, he found that thanks to deliveries by Bostonian seafarers, 'such as wheat flour, rusks, rice, salted beef and pork etc . . . all of the storehouses of Sitka were filled with the necessities of life', and that the rye flour he had brought from Russia was entirely superfluous.

Other things never seemed to change for Baranov. Back in 1809, for example, some of his employees, under the influence of drink, had tried to launch a rebellion against him. Khlebnikov refers to them as 'stormy and deluded spirits, stupid ignoramuses who had no basic understanding of anything'. We can assume that they were fed up, cold and hungry, and in the manner of the mutineers on the Bounty twenty years earlier, had entertained dreams of a better life in the South Seas. Their plan was to steal a stock of furs, and sail off over the horizon on the *Otkrytie*, which was armed and ready to sail.

But in the manner of nearly all Russian mutineers in history, this group betrayed themselves by drunkenness and incompetence. Their plot was uncovered and the ringleaders arrested. But all the same, it would have been depressing for Baranov that in the very small community of New Archangel there were those who wished to kill him. According to Khlebnikov, Baranov was also afraid that 'there was a chance that some suspicions, however slight, might fall on him'. Had he been abusing his men? Was he applying excessive discipline?

'With advancing years', reported Khlebnikov, 'he longed for the peace which should accompany age, and regularly each year he besought the company directors to send him a successor. . . . He had long wished for rest from his ceaseless cares and arduous labours, and longed only for peace in his homeland amongst those near and dear to him. Nevertheless in spite of all his representations, he was persuaded by the Directors to take up his burden yet again, in these familiar but harsh surroundings'.

In June 1810 the latest round-the-world transport from St Petersburg arrived, braving the risk of capture by the British. Aboard was the energetic and haughty Captain-Lieutenant VM Golovnin. From his extensive writings we know something of Golovnin's views on the management of the company in New Archangel: he despised it. He expressed astonishment at the nature of the man in charge. As he later wrote, with the utmost disdain, Baranov had become famous 'on account of his long residence among the savages, and still more so because while enlightening them, he grew wild himself and sank to a degree below the savage'. For men newly arriving from the court of St Petersburg, this was how Baranov now appeared: savage, old-fashioned, unchristian and just a little mad.

Golovnin was the kind of man who felt that naval men, rather than rascally merchants, should be running the company at all costs. His view would later be transmitted to the main office in St Petersburg, which was now actively seeking a successor to Baranov. Partly on Golovnin's imperious advice, they would this time seek someone more reliable; more predictable; more in their own mould. Their choice would settle on Ivan Koch, the old commandant of Okhotsk, who had maintained long-distance communications with Baranov for the past twenty years. As soon as possible, Koch would sail for America.

Baranov was used to arrogant navy men turning up at New Archangel and picking over his premises. But nothing could have prepared him, psychologically, for the next arrival. It was a double-masted brig from the United States, under one Captain Brown. On board he had a handful of strange looking passengers with familiar faces. It must have required a double take, on Baranov's part, to recognise them, because here, after an absence of more than two years, were the last survivors from the wreck of the *Sv Nicolai*.

Chief among them was Timofei Osipovich Tarakanov. Conspicuously absent were the ship's former captain, Nicolai Bulygin, and his wife Anna Petrovna. Once ashore, Tarakanov told Baranov and Golovnin the whole horrifying story. He told of the desperate attempts of the survivors to survive a winter without food, in the most atrocious weather. And he told of their ultimate decision to surrender to the Native Americans, in the hope of lenient treatment at the hands of the sympathetic Yutramaki himself, the toion in the beaver hat, jacket and trousers.

But in the event—Tarakanov could now reveal—these hopes had soon been dashed. While he himself had indeed become the property of Yutramaki, only misery had lain in store for the Bulygin family. That ill-starred couple had found themselves as chattels, passed from one chief to another, sometimes briefly reunited, sometimes inexplicably separated. In these circumstances, their doom had been certain. 'Nicolai Isaakovich and his Anna Petrovna suffered a most bitter fate', Tarakanov reported. 'At times they were together, at times separated, and they lived in continual fear that they would be parted forever. Death finally ended the misery of the unfortunate pair'.

Mrs Bulygin had died in August 1809, alone, and far from her husband. 'When she died' said Tarakanov, 'she was in the hands of such an abominable barbarian that he did not even permit her body to be buried, but ordered it thrown into the forest'. When her husband had heard the news, he too had pined away, finally dying six months later.

It need not have turned out so. Tarakanov himself had been having a better time of things with the kindly Yutramaki, who treated him 'as a friend, not as a prisoner'. The captive Russian had managed to keep his master happy, by building him toys such as kites and rattles. By the time autumn had come round again, he was living independently in his own hut, shooting birds, carving wooden dishes and forging iron knives for his master. In the light of his resourcefulness, he had found himself and his master 'invited everywhere as equals'. During the winter he had then used his new position to protect the other surviving Russians, before in March 1810 moving to a new summer residence, where he built 'another earth-covered lodge more spacious than the first, and fortified it with gun ports'. The fame of this building had spread far and wide.

It had been two months later that Yutramaki finally took him to the ocean and showed him the ship that would take him back to his own country. The two men, we assume, must have become very close during their time together. Aboard, to Tarakanov's surprise, was another survivor from the *Sv Nicolai*, whom Brown had already picked up. Over the coming days, as word spread, several more of these, long-thought to be dead, were brought to the shore and bartered.

Thus did thirteen half-starved survivors finally make it back to New Archangel, and Tarakanov was able to provide Alexander Baranov with many details as to life on the Oregon coast. But these can have been of little comfort to the old governor in what he believed to be his last year of service. Finally, it seemed, he had suffered an irreversible defeat. Astor's *Tonquin* was already heading for the Columbia River, while his overland expedition was battling across the plains. Baranov's erstwhile hopes of leaving behind as his legacy an empire that extended unbroken from Siberia to Spanish Mexico seemed to be on the point of failure.

And as if this were not bad enough, he would have more bad news the following year. In October 1811, a ship called the *Maria* came into view off Sitka. Ivan Koch, the old commandant of Okhotsk, on his way to take over Baranov's job, was to have been on board. But from the quayside, Baranov would have scanned the decks of the approaching ship in vain. Old Koch, it turned out, had died in Kamchatka, *en route* for America. For a while longer, it seemed, Baranov's desire to abandon the rigours of New Archangel and return to Russia would remain unfulfilled.

---- CHAPTER SEVEN ----

THE EUROPEAN WARS AND NORTHWEST AMERICA

With the Americans and the British at war with one
another, the way would be open, once more, for the
Russians to claim the whole coast for themselves.

T he Hawaiian Islands, in the three decades since their discovery by Captain Cook, had continued to grow ever more alluring for visitors to the Pacific. Their convenient location, the friendly reception they provided, the fabulous climate and the facility of obtaining provisions there, all contributed to this. And as the value of the trans-Pacific trade increased, so this allure—for a permanent, exclusive footing on the islands—continued to increase with it.

All knew that King Kamehameha was a formidable ruler. It was plain that he could not simply be duped or intimidated, as had been done, and would be done, to so many other 'savage' chiefs in the New World. Contemporary visitors had described him not only as 'a great warrior and politician', but as 'a very acute trader, and a match for any European in driving a bargain'. He had also made himself rich beyond the dreams of men such as Alexander Baranov. Campbell in 1809 mentioned that 'he has amassed a considerable treasure in dollars, and possesses a large stock of European articles of every description'. A few years later VM Golovnin would estimate his wealth at 200,000 Spanish silver dollars. His warehouses at Kailua bulged with sandalwood, copper, iron, fishing nets, navigation instruments, liquor, gunpowder, cloth and 'other precious merchandise'. In spite of this, or perhaps because of it, the agents of foreign powers were now encircling his islands like hungry sharks.

Nominally, Kamehameha had sworn his allegiance to King George III of Great Britain, at the time of George Vancouver's visit to these islands over fifteen years before. In practice, the Hawaiian king enjoyed warm relations with the citizens of various nations, including the United States and Russia, both of whom felt entitled to a place of special esteem in the King's heart. The United States could boast that the majority of all seafarers visiting Hawaii were its nationals. Russia, on the other hand, could point to the proximity of its settlements on the northwest coast; as well as to a certain spiritual kinship between Kamehameha and Baranov.

Everyone wanted to court the king's favour in the hope of establishing exclusive relations with him; everyone watched with vigilance and jealousy, lest their rivals should do so first. In such an atmosphere of intrigue and competition, it was unclear for how much longer the king would be able to sustain the delicate combination of diplomacy and strength that was the key to keeping his predators at bay.

Among the predators bound for Hawaii in the spring of 1811 was Astor's ship *Tonquin*. It was clear that Astor's men had designs on Hawaii in exactly the same way that Baranov did. 'It was part of the wide and comprehensive plan of Mr Astor', noted Irving, 'to establish a friendly intercourse between these islands and his intended colony'. But that was not all: Astor also, in Irving's view, had plans for 'getting possession of one of their islands as a rendezvous for his ships and link in the chain of his commercial establishments'. The *Tonquin* was sailing under the leadership of Captain Thorn, a dull, dictatorial and suspicious man, who constantly wanted to hurry his crew along, even threatening to leave them behind on remote islands rather than waiting for them to complete their tasks. Also on board were a number of partners of the company, under the leadership of Duncan MacDougall, a Scot (according to Irving) of doubtful courage and uncertain allegiance. The other partners were also mainly Scottish, and their habit of speaking among themselves in Gaelic did not endear them to their captain.

Having taken the usual route from Boston round the Horn, they finally reached Hawaii in March 1811. From Irving's account of how they spent their time on the islands, we glean more examples of the diplomatic manoeuvring that characterised life at the court of King Kamehameha during these years. First we hear of an audience with his British adviser John Young, a 'dignitary' who, in Irving's words, 'after being tossed about the seas like another Sinbad had, by one of the whimsical freaks of fortune, been elevated to the government of a savage island'. Young, by now, was occupying the role of something like a freelance prime minister. He was the king's confidante, and had taken on himself the task of screening out undesirable guests. Irving analysed him as a person who found it preferable 'to rule among savages than serve among white men; to be a feathered chief than a tarpauling boatswain'.

But as usual, it was Kamehameha himself, not his advisors, whom the Astorians wished to meet. Fortunately for them their wishes would soon be coming true. Irving leaves a detailed description of the arrival of the king aboard the *Tonquin*: he appeared, 'between fifty and sixty years of age, above the middle size, large and well made, though somewhat corpulent. He was dressed in an old suit of regimentals, with a sword by his side, and seemed somewhat embarrassed by his magnificent attire'.

The unctuous MacDougall, in a scarlet coat, now saw to it that US flags were displayed, and guns fired, to impress his 'illustrious guests'. Although Captain Thorn would find the experience of chatting with the Hawaiians to be a 'bitter trial', MacDougall and the partners escorted the king to the captain's cabin, and regaled him with wine. In their discussions 'the partners endeavoured to impress the monarch with a sense of their importance and of the importance of the association to which they belonged'. They let him know that they were chiefs of a great company, set on establishing itself on the northwest coast. They told of their hopes to open trade with him and send him ships. 'All this', declared Irving, 'was gratifying and interesting to him, for he was aware of the advantages of trade'.

Relations had been established. The next day, MacDougall and his partners reciprocated the visit that the king had made to them, some even going out in Highland plaids and kilts to impress the natives. Thus did the Astoria-project enter the complex network that Hawaiian politics already comprised. By the time Captain Thorn finally cajoled his crew back into the *Tonquin*, so that they could resume their journey to the Columbia River, Kamehameha had added the names of MacDougall, and perhaps Astor, to his contact book.

Nor would the Astorians be his last interesting guests of the season. In the autumn of the same year, 1811, Kamehameha also had the pleasure of receiving his old friends the Winship brothers, *en route* from America to China.

During the course of the previous year, the Winships had been on a fabulous winning streak. Since abandoning the attempt to build his own post on the Columbia River in July 1810, Nathan, on the *Albatross*, had then embarked on one of the most successful fur hunting trips of all time. After spending the best of a year charging up and down the coast between San Diego and New Archangel collecting skins, he had found his vessel so full of furs that the hemp cables had to be carried on deck and the water casks broken. By now he had accumulated no fewer than 74,000 prime fur seals, plus 600 sea otters and various other items. The load was valued at more than $150,000.

Once Nathan had teemed up with his brother Jonathan, on the *O'Cain*, in September 1811, the two brothers had then set sail for China to unload their cargo, and it was during their regular stopover in Hawaii that a new idea presented itself to them. In the offing was one of those exclusive deals with Kamehameha which other sailors would be watching out so jealously to prevent. The new Winship plan was to enter the trade in sandalwood, a yellowish aromatic timber called 'fragrant wood' by Hawaiians, and used locally for carving the bows of instruments, and for perfuming clothes. The Winships had no hesitation in identifying this precious hard wood as something that the Chinese would clamour for (and they were right: the trade in sandalwood would eventually rival that for fur). With this new money-spinning idea evolving in their minds, the brothers hurried on to Canton to sell their furs, reaching it in record time.

So experienced had they become in these Pacific crossings, that the work was now beginning to seem truly easy. After a stopover in Canton of just two months, they were off again, back to Hawaii, loaded down with Chinese products for the Hawaiian king. This time a third trader accompanied them, and once again the trip was painless. 'During a passage of fifty-two days', wrote Phelps, 'the three ships were scarcely out of sight of each other, and when the weather permitted, the Captains always dined together. They all arrived at Oahu the same day'.

Alexander Baranov would have hated to hear of the facility with which Bostonian seafarers were now crossing and re-crossing this ocean. His own Russian vessels, after all, were still not permitted into Chinese ports. Other than sending his furs on the laborious overland route to Kiakhta, his only choice was still to sell furs to people like the Winships.

Other nations too, envied the Bostonians. British seafarers from the Northwest Company were forbidden to trade with China by East India Company rules. As for the Spanish, they were simply not up to it: according to Phelps, in one of his more chauvinistic moments, the huge number of fur seal skins now being taken to China by the Winships contrasted 'Spanish indolence and imbecility with the activity and enterprise of "Boston Men"'. No wonder the direct trade between America and China had now fallen almost wholly into the hands of US citizens.

Having arrived once again back in Hawaii, the Winships now proceeded to strike their exclusive sandalwood deal with Kamehameha. Thus it was on 12 July 1812, that the king promised to sell sandalwood to the Winship brothers and their partners exclusively for ten years. In return he would receive one quarter of all net sales. Kamehameha had never before risked staking so much in a single relationship. Finally, it seemed he had come down from the fence. For both parties it was a major deal, which threatened to seal US dominance of the Pacific trade, perhaps forever. All of which must have been depressing news for Alexander Baranov when it reached him a few months later. Kamehameha's affections were turning towards the United States. Russian hopes of placing Hawaii at the heart of their own Pacific empire were close to being dashed.

Captain Thorn and his Astorians finally arrived at the mouth of the Columbia River in March 1811. Their intention was to found the first settlement on the Pacific coast under the flag of the United States. But as many a seafarer could testify, entering the mouth of this river was no easy task. It was on this coast that Nicolai Bulygin had met with disaster in 1809; it was also here, in 1806, that bad weather and awkward tides had prevented Nicolai Rezanov in the *Juno* from landing. The crew of the *Tonquin* must have been aware of the difficulties, and as their anxiety grew, so the suspicion began to arise in some of them that Captain Thorn was driving them to disaster.

According to Irving, relations between the Scottish company partners and the paranoid American captain had been poor from the start. Thorn even seemed to be afraid that MacDougall and his colleagues were hatching a plot against him; a suspicion justified, as he thought, by their constant use of the Gaelic language within his earshot. He later wrote to complain to Astor of being subjected to these conversations of such a 'mysterious and unwarrantable nature'.

But now, with the *Tonquin* standing off the stormy, roaring coast within sight of the great Columbia River, conditions were found to be exactly as dangerous as the men had feared. 'A fresh wind from the northwest', wrote Irving, 'sent a rough tumbling sea upon the coast, which broke upon the bar in furious surges, and extended a sheet of foam almost across the mouth of the river'. In spite of the evident danger, Captain Thorn now shouted for the chief mate, Mr Fox, to go out in the whaleboat with a few men, to sound the bar and the channel. Bobbing there on the swell, with the wind and the roar of the surf in their ears, the atmosphere must have been icy in more ways than one. Fox, it comes as no surprise to learn, regarded this mission as suicidal. He now began pleading with the partners to save him from the captain's folly. To go near those breakers in a small boat, he pointed out, would mean certain death. But the tiresome Captain Thorn had no doubts. He and his men had a job to do, and that was that. So the men got into the whaleboat, and it was lowered. Off it went towards the shore 'until it entered, a mere speck, among the foaming breakers, and was soon lost to view'. A day later, when it had not returned, Captain Thorn obdurately insisted on sending off the pinnace with another group of men on the same mission. But from the moment of its launch it too, on the current, 'was hurried away, the crew crying out piteously for assistance'.

Such were the disasters and mishaps that heralded the founding of Astoria. When the *Tonquin* had finally found a safe berth, a little outside the actual river mouth, search parties were sent to find the missing crews of men. But of these, just two individuals (both from the pinnace) were found alive, thrown up by chance on the beach. The others, including the chief mate, were missing, presumed dead. 'Thus eight men were lost on the first approach to the coast', noted Irving, in sombre tone, 'a commencement that cast a gloom over the spirits of the whole party, and was regarded by some of the superstitious as an omen that boded no good to the enterprise'. Although the *Tonquin* had succeeded in landing her men at the treacherous mouth of the Columbia, it had done so at a terrible price.

Not that Astor, back in New York, would necessarily have worried about the price, as long as the profit still looked promising. And the project still looked feasible, in spite of these early losses. Work was ready to begin. 'The surrounding country was in all the freshness of spring', declared Irving, 'the trees were in young leaf, the weather was superb and everything looked delightful to men just emancipated from long confinement on shipboard'. And after a site with a good harbour had been selected on the southern shore of the estuary, and friendly overtures made to the local Chinook people, the men set about clearing thickets and marking out a place for residences, a storehouse and a powder magazine. Conditions seemed promising, given the fecundity of the local soil, and the tolerant mood of the local tribes. While Captain Thorn now took the *Tonquin* off to cruise the nearby coasts, exploring and hunting for furs, Duncan MacDougall's craftsmen and builders were actualising a dream by the Columbia River. Astoria had been born.

Not that anything on this coast would be easy or straightforward. MacDougall was expecting at any moment the arrival of William P Hunt, leading his overland expedition and reinforcements from the United States. Instead, no sooner had they laid the first foundations of their future homes, than the Astorians began to hear rumours from the local natives that a group of white men might be operating in the interior, between the Rockies and the ocean. What was more, these bizarre rumours shortly afterwards turned out to be true: MacDougall was astonished one day to see nine white men paddling towards them in a canoe. One of the nine cheerfully introduced himself as Mr David Thompson, an astronomer and partner of the Northwest Company. Thompson now explained, no doubt with malicious pleasure, how he and a group of British fur traders, from the Northwest Company, had already erected a trading house a few hundred miles upriver to the east, and were thus threatening to block Astoria's hoped-for land links with the United States. And just as this information was arriving to unsettle the security of the fledgling settlement, worse was about to arrive regarding the fortunes of the *Tonquin*. In the view of

Irving, the curmudgeonly temperament of Thorn was once again to blame for this new tragedy. While scouting the coves and inlets of the coast, it seemed, the prickly captain had been growing steadily more irritable at the local native practice of demanding extortionate prices for their furs. One day his temper had boiled over, and in a fit of rage he had kicked a crowd of native traders off his ship, throwing their skins after them. In doing so, he had entirely ignored their dignity.

The native Americans had begun preparing a ghastly revenge. It was inevitable. Once Thorn's temper had calmed sufficiently to permit fresh trading, a large group of them, in pretence of contrition, had crowded the *Tonquin*'s decks. At a given signal, these had then fallen on Thorn and his crew, commencing a general slaughter. The natives were already in control of the boat, when the last man alive, the ship's clerk, wounded and disabled, down below with the magazine, had decided to choose death over capitulation. He lit the powder, thus engineering what may have been one of the first suicide bombings in history. While the natives were 'in the midst of their eagerness and exultation', reports Irving, 'the ship blew up with a tremendous explosion. Arms, legs and mutilated bodies were blown into the air, and dreadful havoc was made in the surrounding canoes'. The sole survivor from this disaster—the interpreter—was able to relay the news, some weeks later, to the horrified builders of Astoria.

With the loss of the *Tonquin* and its contents, as well as the deaths of so many valuable men, the men of Astoria now really were in trouble. They suddenly faced the possibility of ruin during their very first year. MacDougall, as the leading partner in the settlement, could now sympathise with what his counterpart Alexander Baranov had endured arriving on the northwest coast twenty years before. In Irving's view the loss was a 'grievous blow to the infant establishment of Astoria, and one that threatened to bring after it a train of disasters'. Was the first attempt to plant the flag of the United States on this coast already doomed?

As rainy autumnal weather came in, their hopes cannot have risen. Of William Hunt's men there was still no sign. And Irving, on the shocking climate of the Pacific seaboard, was soon reporting that 'the tempests of wind and rain are terrible. The sun is sometimes obscured for weeks, the brooks swell into roaring torrents and the country is threatened with deluge . . .'. Nevertheless, by the beginning of October 1811 a 'commodious mansion' had been completed of stone and clay. A small schooner, the *Dolly* had also been finished. It would be the first American vessel launched on this coast. A precarious toehold had been established. To only one straw of hope were the Astorians still clinging, as the old year gave way to the new: that 1812 might bring them better luck. For a while this hope seemed to bear fruit. Early in the new year, nearly 18 months after setting out by land from the other side of the continent, William P Hunt finally brought his men into Astoria.

Hunt is a difficult character to reassemble from the records. Through Russian eyes he was a swindler who sold guns to natives and abused Baranov's hospitality. But through the eyes of Washington Irving, he was an honest American hero who fought harder to safeguard the property and the good name of Astoria than any other man. As Astor's chief agent, he would take charge of the colony from Duncan MacDougall the moment he arrived. Whichever way we see Hunt, the overland expedition that he had led from the United States had turned into one of history's great travel nightmares. His men had had to contend with broiling plains, impenetrable mountains, hostile natives, floods and blizzards. Their accomplishment, if nothing else, had been to confirm that crossing the American continent by land from east to west was still one of the most arduous journeys on the planet, far harder than the equivalent journey from Europe through Siberia to the Pacific. On the afternoon of 15 February 1812 their canoes had finally swept round the last bend of the last cape of the Columbia River and come in sight of the infant settlement of Astoria. For over a year they had been wandering in the wilderness, 'a great part of the time over trackless wastes where the sight of a savage wigwam was a rarity'. In the circumstances, declared Irving, it was not hard to imagine 'the delight of the poor weather-beaten travellers at beholding the embryo establishment, with its magazines, habitations and picketed bulwarks, seated on a high point of land dominating a beautiful little bay . . .'.

It was certainly a crucial moment in the life of the colony. Might Hunt's arrival enable the Astorians to survive the disasters that had already befallen them? A few months later, in May 1812, the men's hopes would be boosted again by the arrival of a new ship dispatched by Astor from New York, the *Beaver*, bringing badly needed supplies. In this atmosphere of faintly reviving optimism, Hunt could now turn his thoughts to the matters that most urgently required his attention. First among these was the question of relations with the neighbours: above all, it was now time for him to pay a call on that legendary doyen of the northwest coast, Alexander Baranov himself.

It was in August that Hunt set sail for New Archangel in the *Beaver*. Back at Astoria, Duncan MacDougall once more was left in charge. Enemy tribes were known to be prowling around, but the Chinook Indians who occupied the immediate environs of Astoria seemed to be friendly and protective. News of war with Britain had not yet reached these shores. Danger for Astoria, it was thought, was not imminent.

No news of Napoleon's attack on Russia had yet reached the northwest coast. But by a strange irony the foundation of Russia's furthest flung colony would occur at precisely the moment of the nation's greatest peril at home. Baranov's worthy assistant, Ivan Kuskov, would dedicate his Californian fort in the same week that Napoleon was entering Russia's old capital, the now-abandoned city of Moscow. While Mother Russia was being consumed in the hell and fire of September 1812, the Russian flag was being raised in California.

The Spanish would call it Fuerto de los Rusos; the English would call it 'Fort Ross'. But for the Russians themselves, it would simply be 'Ross', or 'Rus'. In the Russian language, the Rus was the name that had been given to the earliest Russians; the first people from whom the culture and power and greatness of Muscovy had subsequently derived.

Fort Ross would be seen as a place of small beginnings, but a great destiny. Such were the hopes that Alexander Baranov could invest in a projected settlement on the wild coast of northern California. He had not been deterred by the news of John Jacob Astor's schemes for planting the US flag on the northwest coast. Nor had he forgotten the injunction of his old boss Nicolai Rezanov, who had so strongly advised the establishment of a colony, abutting San Francisco Bay. All the while the lands of northern California had remained unoccupied his own aspirations for territorial expansion in America had remained intact. There were good reasons for this. If a Russian settlement could be placed as far south as San Francisco, there was a strong likelihood that all the intervening land south of Sitka would become Russian by default. Just as citizens of the United States were pushing their border ever further west, so Baranov could feel that he was pushing his border ever further south. The question was: who could push faster? And unlike the Americans, who had the impenetrable barrier of the Rocky Mountains to contend with, Baranov faced no particular obstacles that he had not already overcome. True, Astor's men had managed to break the Russian monopoly on the northwest coast, with their settlement at the mouth of the Columbia River. But Baranov, with his hard-earned experience of America, was still in an excellent position to outflank them. So he had called for his dependable assistant once more, the man who had chosen the likely site for a Californian settlement two years earlier. None was in a better position to be sent south again, finally to plant the flag of the Russian-American Company in Californian soil, than Ivan Kuskov.

Kuskov must have been delighted at his commission. By the harsh standards of the northwest coast, let alone of Russia itself, California would have seemed like an amazingly comfortable place for him to build a settlement. Down there below the 40th parallel, he would face none of the difficulties that Astor's men were currently enduring on the Columbia River, or indeed that Baranov himself had already endured in Alaska. California was not that kind of place. The climate was warm and food abundant. Winter, in the Russian sense, never visited this part of the world.

For his historic journey in the late summer of 1812, Ivan Kuskov had simply retraced his journey to the same protected coves, just north of Bodega that had caught his fancy in 1808. Nothing had changed: the surrounding oak and redwood forests, the tall bluffs from which to watch for enemy ships, the mountains immediately behind the coast, to deter enemies from attacking by land, and the platform of grassy, flat land, above the bluffs, on which to build his stockade. It was an idyll of peace and beauty, and must have resembled, as it still can in summertime, a little corner of Russian heaven. Kuskov's choice had been a good one.

Even the local people, comprising perhaps 1500 people along a 50-mile strip of coast, were amenable, far more so than the fierce tribes around Sitka or the Columbia River. In peace and quiet, without fear of attack, the first settlers, comprising 95 Russians and about 80 Aleut hunters, soon set to work chopping wood and erecting a stockade. Before long bastions in the stockade were beginning to arise from the virgin soil, along with a chapel, the commandant's house, soldiers' and officers' barracks, a kitchen, warehouses and a jail. The structure of the main fort would be completed by 1814. And outside the stockade, something of a Russian village began to materialise. Eventually this would feature a blacksmith's shop, a tannery, a boathouse, a cooper's shop, a bakery, a carpenter's shop, a mill for grinding flour, threshing floors, a well, a stable, a sheepcote, a dairy house, cow stables, a hog pen, as well as baths, kitchens, and houses for the Aleuts.

At least one report from the directors of the Russian-American Company at this time suggests that Fort Ross was being seen as a possible future headquarters of Russian America. 'Baranov sent an expedition to the coast of New Albion in search of a better spot for settlement than Kodiak or Sitka', ran the report, 'and this expedition, headed by adviser-in-commerce Kuskov, did find one near the California port of San Francisco . . .'. But that eventuality was for the future. In the meantime, having founded his redoubt, and having laid the ground for agriculture and cattle breeding, Kuskov's instructions from Baranov were to establish trade relations with the Spanish of San Francisco. To do this, he would need to clarify the attitude of Spanish authorities, and then to enter into negotiations with the local commandant for receiving provisions. None of this would be straightforward. Spain's refusal to let its colonies trade with foreigners was a tradition as old as the hills. As recently as the spring of 1812 Baranov had passed on a message via a Bostonian seafarer to the commandant of San Vicente, requesting that trade relations be opened, only to be told that the Spanish were 'pleased to consider the Russians as friends', but that the viceroy in Mexico did 'not wish to permit such free trade'.

And then there was the problem of the sea otters: the Spanish were astonished and furious to find Aleut hunters, under the supervision of Russians, invading San Francisco Bay. When Kuskov arrived, apparently planning to settle permanently in the area, this problem threatened to spill out of hand. The number of Aleut canoes in San Francisco Bay on any one day was sometimes well in excess of a hundred, taking into account Kuskov's own Aleuts, as well as others in the company of various Bostonian traders. The Spanish did their best to stop this, stationing sentries at all the wells and springs round the bay where Aleuts obtained water. But this did not prevent Kuskov from obtaining huge numbers of skins during his first years at Ross. In March 1814, one of Astor's vessels purchased no fewer than 3400 immensely valuable otter skins from him. The Spanish themselves could only dream of getting involved in such fabulous trade deals. But even if they had been able to hunt otters, they would not have been permitted to sell them. They had no ships to speak of. As it was, impoverished and impotent, in threadbare uniforms, from storm-damaged forts, they could do little more than scuttle about their own shores in the wake of their invaders.

Offshore, the Russians found that they could move virtually unchallenged. In the same year that he founded Ross, Kuskov also decided to take over the Farallone Islands, a few miles out to sea from San Francisco, and make them a permanent base for his hunters. For years to come

Baranov's seamen would hold these islands as the remotest outpost of Russia's Pacific empire; not only would its immense colonies of seals remain a valuable source of income, but its sea lions would provide the Aleuts with meat blubber and oil, as well as material for their baidarkas and clothing.

It was a humiliating situation for the Spanish. Their claims to sovereignty over California were being rudely ignored. Perhaps in recognition of their own pitiful weakness, they did not at first raise any formal complaint that the Russians were building at Fort Ross. Instead, Don Luis Arguello, the commandant of San Francisco, sent an envoy, Lieutenant Gabriel Moraga, to chat with the Russians.

Moraga's visit seems to have been entirely amiable. Kuskov showed him round the fort with apparent pride. The visiting Spaniard had no authority himself to grant Kuskov's wish and initiate trade relations, but he did tell the Russians, before leaving, that he would try to help them. In fact he was profoundly impressed by what they had achieved. 'They are in earnest and are many and valiant', he later wrote to Arguello. 'In a short time they have discovered the place, constructed buildings and the place is different from one day to the next . . .'. A few months later he made a return visit, apparently taking with him gifts of cattle and horses. Around the same time, Kuskov also had no difficulty in exchanging with the Spanish a cargo of supplies for one of foodstuffs valued at tens of thousands of dollars.

Nothing formal had been agreed, but early in 1813 Kuskov seems to have received verbal permission from Jose Arillaga, the ageing governor of California and erstwhile friend of Rezanov, to engage in some informal trade. For a while relations would proceed on this basis. Kuskov is known to have made visits to San Francisco, exchanging wheat, lard and flour for products such as fabrics, ironware and candles. In August 1815, the Russian round-the-world transport *Suvorov*, under Lieutenant Lazarev, also arrived here and one of the crew noted that 'we supplemented our provisions with the usual provisions . . . we bought several bulls, each between 18 and 20 poods* in weight, for not more than two Spanish thalers each, and put up excellent provisions of corned beef; the wheat which we also bought from the monks was quite cheap too'.

To an extent, friendly relations were in the interests of both sides. The Russians could use them to win trading concessions from the Spanish, and

* *Pood*, presumably the Russian measure of weight usually spelt *pud*, see above p 78.

the Spanish could persuade the Russians to cease hunting in San Francisco Bay. As Khlebnikov noted, later, 'at the harbour to San Francisco, the Spaniards kept a strict watch . . . and in order to retain their friendship we had to abstain from all attempts to visit that place for the purpose of hunting . . .'. But as awareness of their own weakness sank in, waves of insecurity began afflicting the Spanish in San Francisco. Their mood swung back and forth between acquiescence and outrage at the Russian invasion. When the viceroy in Mexico heard that Baranov had had the effrontery to build a fort in northern California he sent an immediate protest, which Lieutenant Moraga conveyed in person to Fort Ross in 1814. Kuskov told Moraga innocently that he had no authority to remove the fort, but that he would inform Baranov of the Spanish position and await orders. Such polite prevarication would serve him well on this, as on several future occasions.

There was little, in the meantime, the Spanish could do. In 1816, the governor of California admitted to the viceroy that it would be 'difficult' to expel intruders; in 1818 he was in fact ordered to expel them, but refused, on the grounds of inadequate soldiery. In short, Alexander Baranov had every right to feel proud of what Kuskov had achieved.

Ross was at the forefront of Russia's expansion into the new world. Before long its stockade would contain the house of the manager, the quarters of other officials, barracks for Russian employees, and various storehouses. Some of the buildings would have two storeys; the manager's house would have glass in the windows and be comfortably furnished. Outside the stockade, factories such as windmills, bakehouses, tanneries and brickworks continued to rise.

Relations between the Russians and the native Californians were also relatively good. The treaty that the Russian-American Company and the Californian natives eventually signed in 1817 would be the first between Europeans and natives anywhere on this coast. In the meantime, they traded happily between one another, the natives supplying grain and other foods in exchange for Russian manufactured products, such as cloth, tools, gunpowder, needles, thread, coffee, tea and sugar.

True, the climate was not quite as good as Kuskov had hoped, suffering from coastal fogs and unexpectedly cool weather in summer. Nevertheless, for most of the year it was vastly better than in any part of the Russian Empire. And eventually, all manner of fruit and vegetable would be grown here. The naval officer Golovnin would write, after his visit in 1818, that 'cabbage, lettuce, pumpkins, horse-radishes, carrots, turnips, beets, onions and potatoes grow in Ivan Kuskov's gardens; watermelons, musk melons, and grapes which he has recently cultivated, even ripen in open air. The garden vegetables are very pleasant in taste . . .'. Peter Corney, a British sailor who also came by in the early years of Fort Ross, was similarly enthusiastic about the crops. 'I have seen radishes that weighed from one pound to 28 pounds', he wrote, 'and much thicker than a stout man's thigh, and quite good all through, without being the least spongy'.

Fruit trees too were destined to prosper here, including varieties unknown in any part of Russia. 'The first peach tree was brought from San Francisco in 1814 on the schooner *Chirikoff* by Mr Benzeman' wrote Khlebnikov, 'and in 1820 fruit was already gathered from it. LA Hagemeister brought grapevines from Lima in 1817 and peaches from Monterey in 1818. In 1820 we planted there one hundred trees—apple, pear, cherry, peach and bergamot, and though they were small when they were planted, they bore fruit in 1828. Roses were brought from San Francisco and Palma Christi in the Sandwich Islands. The grapes were good and began to bear in 1813 . . .'.

Herds of livestock also began to flourish, including cattle, horses, sheep, goats and pigs, most of which had been procured initially from the Spanish. Eventually, three quite large ranches, with dwellings, storehouses, baths and corrals, would be farmed in and around the region of Fort Ross, Bodega Bay and Russian River. Slowly, Californian potatoes, wheat, fruits, tobacco, butter, leather and dried salt beef began to find their way up to Sitka and Kodiak.

By comparison to the disastrous founding of Astoria, the omens at Fort Ross, in short, seemed to be excellent. A century later, in the mid-1920s, a traveller in this part of northern California would note that the apple trees planted by the Russians at Fort Ross had 'brought a crop regularly every year for 113 years'. In the view of the writer, the fact that these trees had escaped all the blights of California owed itself to the good fortune that 'a Russian Priest sprinkled them with holy water when he planted them'. With the foundation of Fort Ross, the tide was turning once again in the favour of Russia. Alexander Baranov could congratulate himself that his American colonies had become self-sustaining at last. In some moods he might have been tempted to think of himself as the Tsar of California.

Back in his grand house at New Archangel, Baranov was playing host to Astor's agent William Hunt. The New Yorker had arrived offering terms. The two men began discussing a deal by which the Astorians might solve the Russian food shortages, and put an end to the problem of arms being sold to the natives. The talk would have touched on the cordial relations between their respective governments. Hunt seems to have found Baranov in vintage form at this time. He referred to the Russian's habit of constantly 'giving entertainments'. He also complained that 'if you do not drink raw rum and boiling punch as strong as sulphur, he [Baranov] will insult you as soon as he gets drunk, which is very shortly after sitting down to table'. But no matter how much Baranov personally drank, 'the old grizzled bear' seemed to Hunt to be 'as keen, not to say crafty, at a bargain, as the most arrant water drinker'. The fact was that Baranov viewed Hunt with great suspicion. According to a subsequent Company report, Hunt was responsible for 'most cunning and base harassments' during his joint trading ventures with Baranov in 1812.

True, Hunt had come as a guest, to close a deal with the Russians. But he was also the agent of a rival power. It is hard to conceive the significance of international relations from Baranov's perspective during these years. News from abroad, even from home, must have held a strangely ethereal and irrelevant character for him. Since 1790, the year of his arrival on these shores, Russia had been in alliance with Great Britain against France; then in alliance with France against Great Britain; now she was at war with France again. But news of great wars and shifting alliances was still taking at least a year to seep round the planet to this sodden corner of northwest America. In the manner of stars that had long ago ceased to exist, yet which continued to twinkle in the sky, so news arriving on the northwest coast from Europe often concerned events that had already passed into history.

For this reason, prior to 1812, it can be assumed that Baranov would have paid little attention to the vagaries of global circumstances. That situation was about to change. In general, these were years in which international commerce was being ravaged by the Napoleonic wars. Baranov would certainly have noticed the decline in the number of foreign seafarers to his shores. He would also have known of the predatory behaviour of the British navy on the high seas, harassing and threatening the transport of non-British goods. Whether he understood the international politics that lay behind the ebb and flow of foreign shipping is unclear. If nothing else, he would certainly have noticed the impact it had on his social life. And above all, this concerned the shipping of the United States. Baranov could not have failed to see that his old drinking partners the

Bostonians had gone missing during this period. Great Britain was seizing American ships that were not transporting British goods; France was seizing American ships that were transporting British goods.

It would have been a confusing situation. Seafarers from the United States had been hunting and transporting most of Baranov's otters for him, and as individuals some of them were among his oldest friends and confidants. But characters like William Hunt, newly arrived from Astoria, were also his most formidable rivals. In February 1812, the Russian-American Company main office was still issuing long letters decrying their habit of selling firearms to natives. And now Astor had even dared to build an American settlement on the northwest coast. On balance, Baranov did not trust men like Hunt and would not have been sorry to see the back of the American ships—on condition that Russian ships could be found to replace them.

Not that this was the official Russian position in 1812. On the contrary, in distant St Petersburg, the talk was only of friendship and solidarity between Russia and the United States. True, Russia had consented to take part in Napoleon's 'continental blockade', by which British goods could not be landed or sold on the European mainland. But on one crucial point she had disagreed with Napoleon: namely, on his insistence that American ships should be banned as well.

Russian fondness of the United States was more than just a matter of Tsar Alexander's bust gracing Thomas Jefferson's desk at Monticello. By the summer of 1812, Russia had not only placed her first ambassador in Washington, but had sent consular agents to cities such as Norfolk, Providence, Portland, Salem, Charleston and New Orleans. And Russia had become the one country on the European continent where American seafarers were still welcome to land merchandise. In 1810, over a hundred American ships got into St Petersburg despite the continental blockade. Tsar Alexander was even willing to inflame the wrath of France on this issue. Napoleon had written him angry letters, pointing out that US ships were carrying British colonial goods, whose further import had to be stopped forthwith. The tsar's reply had been that he was happy to ensure the prohibition on importing British goods, but that he would insist on his right to import goods from 'neutrals' such as the United States. Unlike other continental monarchs, the tsar was not ready to be Napoleon's stooge.

The United States, meanwhile, was furious at the situation in which they found themselves. In their eyes, the main fault lay with Great Britain, whose harassment of US shipping had been relentless. Nor was this harassment limited solely to trade issues: the boarding of American ships to seize alleged deserters from the British navy was also becoming a common practice. And having been forced into Britain's trading block, the United States had now become an unwilling victim of Napoleon's continental blockade.

Russia's friendship, in these difficult times, was deeply appreciated in Washington. But not even the best intentions of the tsar could prevent some US ships from falling prey to Napoleon's embargo. This was most likely to occur at the narrow entrance of the Baltic where ships to St Petersburg pass the narrow strait separating Denmark and Sweden. If news broke that an American ship had been seized in the strait, John Quincy Adams, the American ambassador in St Petersburg, would protest to the tsar that he should intercede; the French Ambassador, the Marquis de Caulaincourt, would then remind the tsar of his pledge of alliance with France.

Inevitably, Russia's allegiances were torn. But it was John Quincy Adams, not De Caulaincourt, who was winning the battle for the tsar's attention. Early in 1811, we find the tsar writing of how the United States of America had given him 'ample proof of its great desire to cultivate good relations with Russia and to establish continuing contacts with her . . .'. In the same year, President Madison, in his annual message to Congress, spoke of relations between his country and Russia being 'on the best footing of friendship'. In St Petersburg, John Quincy Adams had effectively become the American representative to the European continent at large. By 1812, Russia was the United States' best friend of all the Old World powers.

As has been said, close relations between America and Russia had already brought advantages to Alexander Baranov. The two countries now had an incentive to deal with the issues that had been annoying him. But events were about to take on a whole new character. On the seafarers' grapevine, rumours had begun to erupt that would ensure that Baranov could never again view the complexities of international politics as remote and irrelevant. The world was going to war.

For a start there was the startling news from Russia herself. On 23 June 1812, the first units of Napoleon's troops had crossed to the right bank of the River Niman, followed by the bulk of the 640,000 men of his *Grande Armée*. Mother Russia was suddenly caught in a fight for her very survival. Tsar Alexander was informed of the news the very next day while attending a ball held for the Lithuanian aristocracy in Vilnius.

But even that epic struggle would be less significant to Baranov than a conflict now unfolding in another part of the world. Because at the very moment that Russia was being attacked by one of the world's two greatest powers, the United States was going to war with the other. It was in the same month as Napoleon's attack on Russia, that President Madison sent a message to congress recommending an immediate declaration of war against Great Britain. He cited the unceasing insults that had been heaped on the flag of the United States, the illegal impressments of US sailors and the violation by British military ships of the tranquillity of the coast and the safety of US commerce. Before the end of the month, both Houses of Congress had fully approved the declaration.

Just like Thomas Jefferson's embargo of 1809 their decision looked heroic but self-defeating. The balance of power was wholly in the British favour. Great Britain at the time had a population approaching twenty million. Its economy was industrialised to a degree unmatched in the world and its vast navy comprised more than 1000 ships, of which, in June 1812, at least 700 were at sea. This huge force included 260 frigates and ships-of-the-line. By contrast, the United States had a population less than half that of Britain. But more to the point, its armed forces were virtually non-existent. Its navy comprised a derisory seventeen vessels, including eight frigates, of which three were unseaworthy. It also had one 20-gun ship, and eight small guard ships and brigs. How was this feeble force to protect America's courageous young merchants in their trading forays across the north Pacific?

As usual, the details of the conflict would be slow to reach New Archangel. But when they began trickling in, Baranov would have known what they meant. With the Americans and the British at war with one another, the way would be open once more for the Russians to claim this whole coast for themselves.

Insofar as war was bad news for the Americans trading on this coast, it was good news for the Russians. While William Hunt was still in New Archangel, drinking and sparring with Alexander Baranov, the colony at the mouth of the Columbia River was suddenly facing collapse. Hunt himself seems to have been in no hurry to get back to Astoria. After his long sojourn with the Russians he was now on the point of sailing to Hawaii, where he would spend several more months as Kamehameha's guest. But since the autumn of 1812, in Astoria itself, Hunt had been expected at any moment. And, mindful of the fate of the *Tonquin*, Duncan MacDougall and the other Astorians could only assume the worst. By January 1813 it was supposed that Hunt's ship, the *Beaver*, had been wrecked somewhere off the wilds of Alaska.

It was around this time that a freelance trapper arrived in Astoria, bearing still more alarming news. Just up-river, it appeared, he had bumped into some partners of the British Northwest Company, including a certain John McTavish. McTavish, with undoubted relish, had told the trapper the news of war between Britain and the United States. He had then explained that the Northwest Company was planning a 'vigorous opposition' to the American Fur Company. This would start with the arrival of a ship from Britain, the *Isaac Todd*, due at the mouth of the Columbia as soon as March, to 'get possession of the trade of the river'.

The North Pacific may have been a remote part of the world, but no place could hope to remain untouched by the effects of the new conflict. The United States and Britain had already begun attacking each other's merchant shipping. But given the overwhelming superiority of the British at sea, ships flying the US flag had found themselves at a hopeless disadvantage; ships such as the *O'Cain*, *Isabella* and *Albatross*, which had been merrily criss-crossing the Pacific for years, suddenly found themselves under blockade, desperately seeking refuge in ports such as New Archangel, Hawaii or Canton.

For the Americans, dire economic consequences seemed to be looming. Just one of the casualties of the new blockade on shipping, were the Winships' carefully cultivated relations with Kamehameha. Having sold their first cargo of sandalwood in Canton, they found themselves unable to transport the $80,000 they owed to Kamehameha back to Hawaii. As a result of this, the Winships would be 'placed in an awkward position' with the king. And given that Kamehameha's chief confidante was the Englishman John Young, it comes as no surprise to learn that the king's affection for the Bostonians now took a serious dip. For this and other reasons, the situation for US seafarers soon became desperate. No American skipper in any part of the Pacific could feel himself safe. In their fear of British cruisers, many of them simply retreated to the nearest friendly harbour for the duration of the war. Alexander Baranov, for one, would eventually find himself hosting a number of such refugees.

Duncan MacDougall, meanwhile, in Astoria, was thrown into fear and uncertainty by the very idea of war. According to Irving, the news 'seemed to produce a complete confusion of the mind' in him. At this moment, he assumed that Hunt on the *Beaver* would not be coming back. He could also assume that no more help would be coming from the United

States, given that the ports there would be blockaded. If the British were indeed sending their battleship *Phoebe*, the game seemed to be up. 'It was determined therefore' wrote Irving, 'to abandon the establishment in the course of the following spring and return across the Rocky Mountains'.

Big question marks hung over MacDougall's loyalty. Irving clearly believed him to be a British sympathiser, and his own partners were indeed astonished at the friendly attitude he was to show his rivals. When McTavish and a party of Northwest Company traders finally turned up in Astoria, MacDougall treated them with 'uncalled for hospitality, as though they were friends and allies'. In fact, MacDougall seems to have been an eccentric character all round: it was around this time that he also announced his engagement to the daughter of a Chinook chief. Irving refers delicately to the 'dismay' excited by the girl's bridal garments, given that she had 'painted and anointed herself for the occasion according to the Chinook toilette'.

Nevertheless, all the partners had come to agree with MacDougall's proposal to abandon Astoria by 1 June 1814, unless new supplies had arrived by then. They went so far as to sign a formal manifesto outlining the causes of their distress. These included the non-arrival of the latest supply ship; the apparent loss of the *Beaver*; their lack of goods; the ignorance of the coast; and their disappointment as to the interior trade, which they pronounced 'incompetent to stand against the powerful opposition of the North West Company'. Bizarrely, this manifesto was then entrusted to their enemy, John George McTavish, who promised to send it to Astor 'by the usual winter express', that is to say, by the postal service of the self-same Northwest Company.

Meanwhile, back in New York, Astor himself had been frantic with worry. He had already heard that the Northwest Company was asking the British government to help seize Astoria, on the grounds that 'unless nipped in the bud, it would effect the downfall of their trade'. The British navy, in response it seemed, had ordered the frigate *Phoebe* to accompany the *Isaac Todd*. They were to sail together to the northwest coast, capture or destroy Astoria and plant the British flag there. Hearing of this threat to his pet project, Astor had made urgent appeals for help to his own government. In response, the US navy had grudgingly agreed to send a little firepower of their own, in the shape of a frigate the *Adams*.

For a few months, the fate of Astoria thus seemed to hang in the balance. In June, Astor had received a belated letter containing 'the most flattering accounts of the prosperity of the enterprise'. But no sooner had this good news arrived, than the bad news followed: the order of the US government to send a frigate to Astoria had been countermanded (the *Adams* was needed for action closer to home). And anyway, a British blockade had now begun right down the Atlantic coast of America. From now on, it was clear that no help would be reaching Astoria until the end of the war. In the event, nothing could now save Astoria: not even the unexpected and belated return of William Hunt, after an absence of one whole year loafing around first in the Russian colonies and then in the Sandwich Islands. When he finally sailed into Astoria for a brief visit, he was astonished to learn that his deputy MacDougall had authorised its abandonment.

In fact it was shortly after this that McTavish and 75 of his British friends from the Northwest Company reappeared, cheerfully paddling down the Columbia. After explaining that they had come to wait for the British ships *Phoebe* and the *Isaac Todd* to arrive, they promptly raised a British flag and set up camp under the guns of the fort. In Irving's words, the men of the Northwest Company men now regarded the 'hampered and harassed Astorians as a conquered people'.

Such was the atmosphere in which McTavish now proposed to buy all the furs and merchandise of Astoria for a third of its real value: a proposal that the 'craven' MacDougall accepted with very little hesitation. 'Had our place and our property been fairly captured', Astor is supposed to have remarked bitterly, years later, 'I should have preferred it. I should not feel as if I were disgraced'.

On 12 December 1814, when the British navy arrived off Astoria, they were furious to see what a miserable little place it was. 'From all the talk that had been made by the North West Company of the strength of the place, and the armament they had required to assist in its reduction, he [the British commander] expected to find a fortress of some importance. When he beheld nothing but stockades and bastions calculated for defence against naked savages, he felt an emotion of indignant surprise, mingled with something of the ludicrous'. Nevertheless, the British entered the fort, raised the Union Jack, broke a bottle of wine and declared in loud voices that they were taking possession of the establishment and of the country in the name of the king. In doing so, they changed its name from Astoria to Fort George. Thus did Astoria—the 'germ' of American civilisation on the Pacific coast, the settlement 'that would . . . carry the American population across the Rocky Mountains'—come to its ignominious end, a bare two years after being founded.

The natives attending the ceremony saw it as 'an act of subjugation of their ancient allies'. William Hunt, when he heard of what had happened, was outraged. But the Russians, who were not present, could only have expressed quiet and cautious optimism. While their own settlement in California continued to thrive, that of their great rivals from the United States had been extinguished.

Now that Fort Ross had been established, Baranov's thoughts seem once again to have turned to retirement. 'Having spent twenty-three years in the colonies, in the 67th year of his active life', wrote Khlebnikov '[Baranov] awaited daily for a replacement to release him, to at last lift the burden of responsibility he had borne for so long . . .'. The task of governing the colonies had already, it seemed, become too much for this 'feeble old man'. It was time for him to go home.

At last Baranov and the company seem to have been of one mind. In the middle of 1812, the directors even went so far as to appoint a new assistant for him, Tertii Stepanovich Bornovolokov, an administrator and a self-taught scientist. By all accounts Bornovolokov was well qualified for the job. He was said to be honest and therefore somewhat poor. He had recently been appointed a member of the Russian Academy of Science and had published papers on subjects ranging from bituminous schist to the economics of the fur trade. He had ideas on improving the organisation of Russian mercantile companies. It was assumed that once in America, he would soon take over the job of chief manager in view of Baranov's age and infirmity.

Bornovolokov set sail from Okhotsk in August 1812, in the *Neva*. But as always, as if for the specific benefit of newcomers, the ocean was keeping some tricks up its sleeve. The voyage should have taken a month, but the ship was beaten back by savage winds blowing from the east. The commander became exhausted and had to yield his post to another. Having reached the mainland they eventually, in mid-November, managed to take refuge at Resurrection Bay on the Kenai Peninsula, but this was no place to spend the winter. So they set out once again in the hope of reaching Sitka quickly. Instead they met more storms and finally, in January 1813, almost within sight of Sitka, the vessel ran onto rocks and broke up in the boiling surf. There were only ten survivors, and Bornovolokov was not among them. Once again Baranov's appointed successor had failed even to reach his post. According to Khlebnikov, Baranov 'raged against the cruel destiny of it'. But there was little he could do. Providence, it seemed, did not yet favour his departure from America.

At least conditions in Baranov's colonies were continuing to improve. Fewer vessels were calling on him to offer food and goods for sale, but he had plenty of staples to live on now anyway. This was partly thanks to annual round-the-world transports from St Petersburg, partly thanks to the burgeoning agriculture of Fort Ross, and partly thanks to the trade-share agreements he had been making for so long with Bostonian seafarers. According to an 1811 report from the main office of the company, 'the Governor of the colonies, Baranov, had stored various staples of livelihood, bartered from Boston seamen and delivered via Okhotsk, in such abundance that they will be sufficient for all settlements for three or four years . . .'.

Given this, in fact, the Russian-American Company saw no requirement for Baranov to maintain contacts with foreign traders. 'We do not need Mr Astor sending goods for us here' they declared, in the autumn of 1815, while pointing out that goods from the latest transport from St Petersburg, together with those delivered earlier on the *Suvorov*, would suffice for several years.

So it was concluded that Alexander Baranov could now afford to stand aloof from his foreign rivals. In the view of the Company 'harmful competition' had already occurred as a result of Baranov paying Americans for their goods in furs. There had been cases of enterprising American captains taking furs from New Archangel to Okhotsk and selling them straight back to the company for vastly more than they had bought them for. Baranov began to limit his ventures with foreigners, and to save the skins for the Kiakhta trade. In 1816, fifteen foreign ships docked at New Archangel, but Baranov bought only a small quantity of provisions from them, and refused to deal with most.

The ongoing war between the United States and Great Britain created what must have been a strange atmosphere at New Archangel. Various captains of US ships were effectively stranded here, living uneasily off Baranov's hospitality. Tensions arose, not least with Astor's old agent, William Hunt, who was back again, having returned to Sitka for the duration of the war, a time in which 'he received all possible aid from Mr Baranov'. Hunt, still smarting from the ignominious collapse of the Astoria project, seems to have cut a rebellious figure. An increasingly bad-tempered Baranov suspected him of trading with the natives, right under his nose, in a manner 'harmful for the Russians in all respects'. Relations between the two were soon in a downward spiral.

Meanwhile several of the other captains, fearing that their vessels would be seized, tried selling them off, on the cheap. In 1813, Baranov was thus able to purchase a couple of fully-armed ships from Captain James Bennett on highly advantageous terms. The two ships, the three-masted *Atahualpa*, and the brig *Lydia*, were renamed the *Bering* and *Il'mena* respectively. For the first time in all his long years of service, Baranov now found that he had a surfeit of ships at his disposal. These were promising times for the Russians. In April 1814 Baranov dispatched the *Bering*, under the captaincy of her former owner James Bennett, to Hawaii, to purchase a cargo of 'taro root, tutui nuts for extracting oil, salt and other supplies'.

The journey was a straightforward one. Bennett stopped at Oahu, and also at Kauai, where he met the lachrymose renegade, King Kaumualii. Since the meeting between Captain Lisianskii's crew and Kaumualii back in 1804, the king of Kauai had been treading a delicate path of autonomy. His more powerful rival, King Kamehameha, had long since abandoned attempts to invade and subdue Kauai. Instead of seeking to destroy the renegade king, Kamehameha had resigned himself to accepting his tribute and vassalage. In recent years gifts had been going back and forth between the two men.

This did not mean that Kaumualii had become complacent. In 1809, when Lieutenant Ludwig von Hagemeister had visited Kauai, the king once again showed a tearful aspect, begging for Russian protection, and explaining his reluctance to accept Kamehameha's repeated invitations to visit him on Oahu. These fears were not without foundation, given that the last renegade chief to have done the same thing, back in 1790, had been murdered while Kamehameha looked on.

Nevertheless, in 1810, Kaumualii had finally plucked up the courage to go to Honolulu, having accepted the reassurances of the Bostonian skipper who agreed to carry him. Celebrations and peaceful declarations on all sides had followed, and Kaumualii, after agreeing to accept Kamehameha as his overlord, had been permitted to return to Kauai in peace. And yet at some level, it seems, Kaumualii could not forget the kind attention that Russians like Lisianskii and Hagemeister had given him in years gone by. He was still suffering from an inferiority complex in relation to Kamehameha, and still harboured private hopes of acquiring a powerful foreign sponsor and ally. With such support, might he recover his dignity, and perhaps even his kingdom? We have a glimpse of these lingering aspirations from an extraordinary pleading letter written by Kaumualii to Baranov in December 1814, to be delivered via Captain James Bennett. In it we find Kaumualii once again begging for arms and assistance, to defend himself against his enemies.

Written in English, without punctuation, the letter reads a little like a child's Christmas wish-list. 'I should like to have 200 muskets', Kaumualii informed Baranov, 'and one hundred kegs of powder and 40 boxes of musket balls and 20 from cannon of different sizes and two long brass *ditto* and 20 brass muskets and please to send the cannon in good order with carriages rammers springer ladles and worms and I want four more such stills as I got the last time but rather bigger and I want ten pieces of blue broad cloth and five pieces of red *ditto* and five pieces of blue duffel and four pieces of green cloth and two forges and two anvils and two pr of bellowses with the tools fit for blacksmiths use and some carpenter tools such as saws and gimbles of different sizes . . .'. In exchange for which, Kaumualii then pledged, he could supply the Russians with large quantities of food, or—if Baranov preferred—sandalwood (though if he wanted the latter, Baranov would also have to supply a 100-ton, coppered brig). Kaumualii's professed reason for his keen desire to trade with the Russians, in his words, was that 'I take you as a friend if you will accept me as one and I should like to see you down to the island once as I have heard tell of you a great many times'. Signing off, he added that his wife 'sends her best regards to you'.

In the event, we have no idea how Baranov would have responded to these requests, because the matter was about to be overtaken by events. Captain James Bennett in the *Bering* had spent three months trading in the islands. On board he was now carrying an extremely valuable cargo, the property of the Russian-American Company. But while resting over at Waimea Bay on Kauai one day in January 1815, he seems to have misjudged the weather: that night, a strong wind sprang up and drove the ship ashore and wrecked it. All of a sudden, thousands of dollars of Baranov's goods were strewn over the beaches of Kauai.

When Kaumualii heard the news, he seems to have been quite overcome by greed. It was as though he could realise his requests for foreign goods all at once. In the words of Khlebnikov, he promptly 'gathered on the shore with his suite' and told Bennett that he had given orders to salvage the cargo. Once this had been done, the king then announced that 'according to their custom, everything washed up on the shore belonged to him'. Bennett and five Russians, unable to dissuade Kaumualii from this 'injustice', were forced to remain on Kauai until April, living off 'the king's pleasure'. It was said of them that when their clothes wore out, they walked around 'like the islanders'. Not until Captain William Smith on the *Albatross* picked them up were they given new clothes and transported safely to Sitka.

Bringing bad news to the cantankerous Baranov can never have been much fun at the best of times. Furthermore, when Bennett arrived at Sitka to break the news that a Hawaiian King had appropriated the entire cargo of his ship, he found Baranov in the middle of a domestic drama.

William Price Hunt, the former Astorian, was at the bottom of it. As has already been mentioned, Hunt, forced to seek sanctuary with Baranov for the course of the war between Britain and the United States, seems to have been in a resentful mood. In fact Baranov later told the company that Hunt's sole purpose in remaining at Sitka was to engage in 'smuggling with the islanders'. Through Hunt, it seems, arms and weapons were being sold to the local Tlingit—a particularly sensitive issue where Baranov was concerned. 'He even went on the trails over which the Indians brought their furs for trade with the Russians', noted one witness, '. . . finally he even pitched a tent where not only Mr Baranov himself but I, and also many of the Russians, could see the Indians going each day with transports of furs'.

After this, and other examples of brazen misbehaviour, a furious Baranov decided to confront Hunt, seizing his powder and his small weapons to prevent them from being sold to the natives. He might have thought he could rely on the support of friends and colleagues: until men like James Bennett and, most astonishing of all, Lieutenant Mikhail Petrovich Lazarev, the commander of the round-the-world ship *Suvorov* which happened then to be stationed in Sitka, began taking Hunt's side.

The dispute that followed, between Baranov and Lazarev, was one of the most bizarre events of Baranov's whole residence on the northwest coast. 'Even Lieutenant Lazarev told Mr Baranov, "You're a fool!"' noted the surgeon from the *Suvorov*; '. . . Lazarev and Bennett abused this honourable old man with the very lowest expressions'.

We have to picture Lazarev, now aged 27, having emerged from a highly privileged background, first in the naval cadet corps in St Petersburg, then on secondment to the British navy for five years. To have been placed in command of a round-the-world vessel at so young an age was a sign of exceptional ability. The man on whom he was now showering abuse had little formal education, was aged nearly 70, and had been living on the savage northwest coast of America for a quarter of a century. Agreement, in short, was impossible. Baranov no longer seemed to care about his image or indeed his dignity. On legally dubious grounds he threatened to remove Lazarev from his command, unless the lieutenant backed down at once.

Of the character of Lazarev we have little independent evidence. Years later he was characterised by the Decembrist Dmitrii Irinarkhovich Zavalishin as a man of outstanding ability, but also of a 'positive lack of principal' and a 'conditional' honesty. 'All human worth, in his view', Zavalishin noted, 'revolved around being an excellent seaman'. Perhaps it is unsurprising that Lazarev and Baranov clashed. In the event, rather than submit to Baranov's angry demands, Lazarev decided to take unauthorised leave, taking a stack of furs with him. As he sailed out of New Archangel one July night in 1815, furtively and hurriedly, he was astonished to find himself coming under fire from the fort's cannon. Baranov seemed to have lost his head, to the point that he had dared to open fire on a ship of the Russian imperial government. On Lazarev's return to St Petersburg a year later, he would deliver a particularly critical report on the behaviour and state of mind of the incumbent manager of the colonies.

Of Lazarev's crew, nearly all had sided with their captain. There was one conspicuous exception to this: the *Suvorov*'s surgeon, a man by the name of Dr Georg Anton Schäffer. After the *Suvorov*'s sudden departure, Schäffer had been glad, it seems, to remain behind; he and Lazarev had not got on. Baranov, likewise, had been glad to keep him. Doctors of medicine were few and far between in the north Pacific. And anyway, James Bennett's new problem now had to be dealt with: the wrecked *Bering* and its stolen cargo on the island of Kauai. Bennett, in Sitka, was demanding it be reclaimed by force. But as Khlebnikov explained, Baranov 'would not countenance hostilities against Kamehameha, the King of the Sandwich Islands, whose vassal was Kaumualii'. Instead, the old manager conceived an idea for sending an envoy to hold delicate discussions with the Sandwich Islanders. To Baranov, the incident seems to have looked like an opportunity. And Schäffer was simply 'the right man to make an expedition to the Sandwich Isles to investigate the wreck of the *Bering*'.

March 1814, in many ways, represented the culmination of a century of non-stop Russian expansion. Following the utter rout and destruction of Napoleon's *Grande Armée*, Tsar Alexander had become the most powerful sovereign in Europe and the arbiter of its destiny. As well as being by far the largest, Russia was now easily the most populous of any European country, with over 40 million souls. For the first time, it had become obvious to all that her power was destined to be commensurate with her huge size and population.

Alexander entered Paris in triumph, after the abdication of Napoleon, to accept the restoration of the Bourbons, taking care to impose a constitutional charter on them first. He could now act the magnanimous statesman, protesting that he had made war on Napoleon and not on the French people. His plan was to convene the greatest international congress in history, at Vienna, in the autumn of 1814. The tsar's allies, all of whom he had saved from the French yoke, now awaited his decisions with fear. In this atmosphere, there was no longer anything strange in the notion that Russia might be entitled to a nice slice of the North American continent. Her standing in the eyes of her rivals had been enhanced in obvious ways. But Napoleon's defeat also helped Russia in other less obvious ways, relating to the war still being fought between the United States and Great Britain.

Until now, the British had been doing surprisingly badly in the fighting. The tiny US fleet had even managed to poke them in the eye with some naval successes. The main reason for this was that Britain's economy had been wilting under the twin pressures of Napoleon's war and the continental blockade. Her best troops, under Wellington, had been tied up in the Pyrenees. And over in North America, her Canadian territories contained a population of just 500,000, up against the 8,000,000 or so citizens of the United States.

But in 1814, as Napoleon rapidly collapsed, the people of New England were once again looking out across the Atlantic with fear. During the course of the summer, alarming news began reaching them of the occupation of Paris by allied troops. This could mean only one thing: that Britain was suddenly free to concentrate all its power on North America. Astoria was to become just one victim of the newly enhanced British position. By August, there may have been as many as 40,000 British troops on American soil. Their approach to the war became much tougher.

Inevitably, the first British tactic was to enforce a strict naval blockade. Soon the whole of the east coast of the United States was closed off to merchant shipping and American privateers had effectively been swept off the ocean. In August, more radically, British troops went so far as to land at Washington DC, where they burned the Capitol, the White House and other government buildings, before retiring to their ships. Meanwhile, the details of Russia's victory over Napoleon had stimulated much amazement and awe in the United States. Much was being written of the 'liberty' of Europe having been defended and rescued by the 'deliverer' Tsar Alexander. The Russian Ambassador, for one, wrote of the 'incredible' effect of the news on the Americans. 'I have letters from Boston, New York, and Philadelphia', he exclaimed, 'informing me joyfully that people congratulate each other on Russian victories, as if they were their own!'

Special church services and banquets were held, as far apart as Georgetown and Boston. John Quincy Adams, in a dispatch from St Petersburg to his Secretary of State in February 1813, spoke reverentially of Russian behaviour: 'The spirit of patriotism has burst with the purest and most vivid flame in every class of the community. The exertions of the nations have been almost unparalleled, the greatest sacrifices have been made cheerfully and spontaneously . . .'.

But there was also another aspect to American thinking that could now be detected. For the very first time, some were writing of an early hint of the 'Russian menace'. One Robert Walsh of Baltimore, a Francophile by family connections, highly regarded as a journalist and writer, declared that 'there is no government or peoples, on record, whose history is more atrocious in almost every stage'. He wrote of the 'barbarism' of the Russians, their eastern despotism and lack of civilisation. He worried about their boundless schemes of conquest.

Over the coming century and a half there would be many more reflections on this theme. In the meantime, with Russia all-conquering and America on her knees, Alexander Baranov knew that he had one more chance to accomplish his dream.

CHAPTER EIGHT

HAWAII

Hawaii, clearly, was the key. It could be seen as the third corner of a triangle, with Alaska and California representing the other two corners.

Russia now had the upper hand on the northwest coast of America as far south as California. For the first time, she had food enough to feed her settlers in America. But her position was not yet secure. In September 1815 a schooner sailed into New Archangel bringing news that the war between Britain and the United States had ended eight months earlier. Finally, William Hunt and his friends would leave their unwanted Russian haven and get back to work.

For Baranov this must have been a disconcerting idea. On the trans-Pacific routes, merchant-sailors from the United States would once again reassert their dominance. Once again the sale of furs from the northwest coast and of sandalwood from Hawaii would fall into their hands. Once again men like the Winships would be speeding back and forth across the ocean and enjoying intimate relations with King Kamehameha.

And all the while American seamen enjoyed this uncontested freedom of the seas, so the enthusiasm of men like Astor to establish outposts of the United States on America's Pacific coast would continue to grow.

What could Baranov now do to counter this tendency? Having settled as far south as San Francisco, what could he do to secure his position?

Hawaii, clearly, was the key. The kingdom of Kamehameha lay on any trans-Pacific route to China and Japan, whether from New Archangel or from Fort Ross. It could be seen as the third corner of a triangle, with Alaska and California representing the other two corners. Baranov would always remain vulnerable unless the third corner of his triangle could also be settled. Hawaii was, moreover, an unrivalled source of food and other provisions, of which the Russians in New Archangel had been in such dire need when they had first landed there.

In 1815, Hawaii could still be the lynchpin to Baranov's whole project. If Russia's position in the islands could be made unassailable, so could Russia's position in America. Baranov had been deeply envious of the Winships' close relations with Kamehameha, with regard to the trade in sandalwood. He would have loved to oust the Americans, and secure a similar place of intimacy with the old king. It was already evident that Kamehameha would never prostrate himself before any foreign ruler. Nevertheless, through guile and diplomacy, an exclusive position was still up for grabs in Hawaii. And where the American sailors were little better than merchants and freebooters, Baranov was a representative of his imperial majesty in St Petersburg. Right now, moreover, Baranov had a handy excuse for inveigling his way into Kamehameha's confidence, namely that the cargo of the *Bering* was still in the hands of Kaumualii, the renegade king. This gave him a pretext for bringing pressure to bear on Kamehameha and enticing him into concessions. All he needed was a suitable envoy.

As usual, Baranov lacked sophisticated, reliable Russians for diplomatic jobs of this nature. It had been his plan to send Lazarev in the *Suvorov*, until his unscheduled and bad-tempered departure. James Bennett had also ruled himself out by his unruly behaviour during the same dispute. One person who seemed to be available was a man who had stood resolutely behind him during his recent difficulties: namely, the itinerant Bavarian surgeon, Dr Georg Anton Schäffer.

Of all the players in the North Pacific during these years, few convey such an eccentric impression as Schäffer. He had been born in Germany thirty-six years before, as the son of a lowly miller. From the start of his career he had displayed a love of exotic places, accepting work in locations as far apart as Hungary and Galicia. In 1808 he had then been invited to Russia to serve as an army doctor. During the war of 1812 his brief contribution had been to join an unsuccessful project to use hot air balloons to combat Napoleon. Subsequently he had signed up with the Russian-American Company as the ship's doctor on *Suvorov*. In spite of this unusual background, in Baranov's eyes the doctor had undoubted advantages. He was German and therefore carried a plausible veneer of sophistication. He was educated, well travelled and spoke good English. His only apparent shortcoming was that he seemed to have a quarrelsome side—as Baranov himself noted, it appeared that 'he had left the ship *Suvorov* because of personal differences with the officers, and dissatisfaction that the ship did not put in everywhere that he had wanted to collect foreign specimens'.

Of Schäffer's other shortcomings, Baranov was unlikely to be aware. It could not have been known, for example, that during his medical training Schäffer had suffered expulsion for unspecified disciplinary offences. Nor would it have been obvious that he was ashamed of his social status, endowing himself with imaginary titles by signing his name variously as 'de Sheffer' or 'von Schäffer'. In fact, as events would show, the doctor suffered from something of a persecution complex, as well as from an uncanny ability to delude himself as to his own greatness. Moreover, he did not seem to be very personable: a man as sober and tolerant as Timofei Tarakanov, in his report of the subsequent events in Hawaii, would complain that the doctor had 'treated me like a stranger—never talked with me, never asked me anything'. The strain of working for Schäffer later drove Tarakanov to drink. And yet the importance of the mission that Baranov had now decided to entrust to Schäffer cannot be overstated.

The instructions that Baranov devised were careful and manipulative to the point of deviousness. 'From the very beginning', Baranov told him, 'try to win his [Kamehameha's] favour and to make him a friend. Not until you have done so are you to reveal to him the commission entrusted to you by me . . .'. Meanwhile, to assist in achieving his goals Baranov advised Schäffer to establish friendly relations with Billy Pitt, a nickname for one of the Hawaiian chiefs, 'this clever member of the court', and also with the wives of Kamehameha, who, 'as in Europe, direct the king's wishes according to their own plans and intentions'. In relation to other foreigners residing in Hawaii, Baranov tells Schäffer that 'I shall rely upon your good sense and ability not to miss any opportunity to advance the interests of the Company and the fatherland . . .'.

Schäffer was to present himself initially as a naturalist, until the king's trust had been won. When two more company ships, *Otkrytie* and *Kadiak*, then suddenly arrived as reinforcements, he was to reveal to Kamehameha his true mission, namely to help in recovering the cargo of the *Bering* from Kaumualii. The letter that Baranov intended Schäffer to present to Kamehameha at this moment is intriguing. In the letter, Baranov addressed his old adversary as a 'most enlightened King' and the 'nearest neighbour of the Russian settlements'. The tone is very polite, but also direct. 'Violence and insult were offered to the Russian nation', Baranov declared, regarding the theft of the *Bering*. '. . . if a satisfactory compensation for the above-mentioned injury is not forthcoming, I shall consider it my duty to report to the Emperor'.

At the same time, Baranov was keen to present Kamehameha with plenty of persuasive reasons for granting the Russians special trading privileges. 'We are the closest neighbours because all other nations are separated from you by a great expanse of sea', he wrote; 'it is most appropriate that we, rather than anyone else, should establish with you friendly and mutually advantageous relations . . .'. The letter went on to request that Schäffer be permitted to continue his 'scientific work', while also acting as Baranov's agent in recovering the property that had been so 'insolently seized'.

Finally, a rather less friendly edge can be detected. If Kamehameha did not help the Russians in this way, declared Baranov, 'I shall know that you have no authority over this ruler [Kaumualii] and that you have no means of curtailing his insolence . . .'. If Kaumualii then did not satisfy Baranov's 'just demands', 'I shall be obliged to take measures myself in order to obtain just satisfaction and, with your permission, I shall treat him as an enemy'.

With this letter in his pocket, Schäffer sailed for Hawaii in October 1815. He travelled on the *Isabella* under Captain Tyler, with two Creole boys, including Baranov's own son Antipatr.

From the very first moment of Schäffer's arrival in Hawaii, a note of paranoia began to creep into his journal. Before even landing, he wrote of how 'everyone' went ashore in the *Isabella*'s whaleboat to visit 'old John Young', leaving him behind to find transport 'in an Indian boat'. His sense of personal enmity with the Americans who had travelled with him on the *Isabella* was intense. He believed they had gone ashore ahead of the Russians, in order to gain exclusive access to Kamehameha's ear, to tell him 'God knows what sort of tales about the Russians'. Of Captain James Bennett in particular, he wrote bitterly of 'his intrigues and malicious slanders against the Russians'.

Schäffer seems to have been the kind of person whose fear of rejection is so intense that he reacts aggressively to people in advance. It is hard to imagine that such behaviour would not have aroused a degree of suspicion. Perhaps in consequence of this, as Schäffer subsequently complained, 'the King went through all my clothes and the cargo entrusted to me . . .'. Fortunately Kamehameha was not the type to engage in sulky standoffs, even with the Schäffers of this world. Despite initial doubts, a kind of rapport seems to have been established between the two men over the coming weeks. Schäffer presented the king with a medal and official certificates from the tsar. Kamehameha, in response, according to Schäffer 'showed the greatest respect for both of these things . . . and he exclaimed that of course the Russians had more friendship for him than the English did; for Captain Vancouver had already promised a long time ago that the King of England would send him a letter, but up to that time he had received nothing'. Soothed by such reassurances, Schäffer's mood gradually improved. Before the end of the year we hear from his journal that the king was singling him out for special attention. Kamehameha apparently 'walked around' the island with him, inviting him to choose the location in which he desired to live. The king then even devoted time to supervising the construction of Schäffer's house. Later, when Kamehameha fell sick with a cold and a fever, Schäffer was able to give him medicine, whereupon 'he got well in a short time'.

The Queen Kaahumanu granted Schäffer a few miles of 'fishing grounds along the seashore', as well as 'ten sheep and forty goats'. The queen's brother Kuakini (known to the foreigners as 'John Adams') also chipped in with some assistance. In short, things were looking good for the Russians.

Schäffer's sycophantic letter to the main office of the Company, written in January 1816, is bright and optimistic. He was confident, he wrote, that he would soon recover the cargo of the *Bering* 'worth about 20,000 piastres'. He also declared that he had the confidence of Kamehameha whom he was 'treating for heart trouble' (having also 'succeeded in curing his favourite wife, Queen Kaahumanu, of Yellow Fever'). Although he had arrived just four weeks ago, he had in this short time managed to offset the effect of malicious information spread here by William Hunt and other Americans. He hoped soon 'to acquire the trade monopoly in sandalwood for the Company'.

Independent testimony to these claims exists. Early in 1816 a travelling American, Charles Barnard, wrote that Schäffer 'had succeeded in removing the prejudices of the King, had acquired his favour, and stood high in his good graces; he was at this time attending one of his queens, who was indisposed, as her physician. The King had caused a house to be built for him in the centre of a breadfruit grove, where the doctor could pursue his botanical researches without interruption. I visited him there and passed some hours with him'.

In the doctor's own view, too, relations with the king promised to be free of difficulties, were it not for one thing: the interference of troublesome seafarers from the United States. The Americans, in other words, could see through his flimsy guise of 'naturalist'. John Young, it seems, had already been suspicious of Schäffer. Now, on the arrival of Captain Ebbets, master of Astor's ship *Enterprise* (coming from New York) and William Hunt on the *Pedlar*, *en route* to Canton, in December 1815, we learn from Schäffer of how 'abuse and slander' about the Russians once again began to spread. The doctor, it seems, was not hiding his secret imperial designs at all well. To judge by what the Americans were evidently telling Kamehameha, his plans seem to have been nakedly transparent. Not that Schäffer could understand this. 'After Ebbets and Hunt had left', he complained, 'the King became more fearful, constantly changing his place of residence', and asking suspiciously, '"Will the Russians come to fight? Will they take the island?" No reply would satisfy him'.

He seems to have been unconscious of how sinister his own position must have looked. But Kamehameha, hearing of the predatory intentions of the Russians, found himself with no choice but to circumscribe his movements. Some of the king's advisors (Schäffer later claimed) were even urging that he be killed. Alarmed by rumours to this effect, Schäffer decided to move his operations to the neighbouring island of Oahu. Kamehameha, it seems, was still willing to assign one of his warehouses to Schäffer, for use as a factory, at Honolulu.

Meanwhile, the reinforcements for which Schäffer was waiting were slowly on their way. The *Kadiak* was not yet ready to be sent, but in the meantime Baranov had decided to send the *Otkrytie* by herself, apparently fearful that the Bostonians might take advantage of any further delay by renewing their sandalwood deals with Kamehameha. So in April 1816 the *Otkrytie* reached Hawaii under the captaincy of Lieutenant Iakov Anikievich Podushkin. On board, as well as a few Russians, was a troop of Aleuts, whom Baranov intended to be used not only as standby soldiers, but for offering folkloric Aleutian entertainments to the Hawaiians.

Podushkin was also bringing more letters from Baranov, written for himself and for Schäffer. Baranov's latest instructions were clear. If Schäffer had not yet resolved everything through diplomacy with Kamehameha, he and Podushkin were to go together to Kauai to ask for 'satisfaction' for the 'outrageous seizure of the company's property and the insult to the flag of the Russian nation'. At first they were to attempt this peacefully: the ideal solution, it seemed, would be to shame Kaumualii and King Kamehameha between them into offering the Russians an exclusive sandalwood deal by way of compensation along the lines of the agreements made formerly with the Winships. In which case, Schäffer could start negotiations for 'a contract for the next few years for the delivery of wood to be sold in China and Manila'. But if, on the other hand, Kaumualii failed to offer any such satisfaction, Baranov's message for him was stark. In that case, he told Schäffer, in a sudden outbreak of bluntness 'it might be necessary to give him a lesson in the form of military chastisement . . . in such an event, the whole island of Kauai should be taken in the name of our sovereign Emperor of all the Russians and become a part of his possessions'. In addition to this, if specific permission could be obtained, a factory was to be established on the island of Oahu 'where the Americans, the Winship brothers, used to have one'.

In giving these instructions to Schäffer, above all the threat that Kauai should simply be seized by Russia in the absence of satisfaction of its claims, Baranov seems to have been overlooking the crucial fact that Kaumualii had accepted the overlordship of Kamehameha over all the islands of Hawaii. And Kamehameha was not a man to overlook his claims to any of these islands. It was this that seemed to lie at the root of Kaumualii's constant hesitations and vacillations in his relations with the Russians at this time, and to Schäffer's belief that once Kaumualii had signed up to the terms demanded by the Russians, all his difficulties would be over. Ultimately, it was Schäffer's failure to take account of Kamehameha's claims that led to his ignominious expulsion from the islands of Hawaii, and the total collapse of his mission.

But for the moment Baranov was assuming that Kamehameha could be pacified by negotiations with the Russians, and he was blandly assuring Schäffer that the *Kodiak* would soon be on her way, to pick up the *Bering*'s cargo (or a compensatory supply of sandalwood) and take it to sell in Macao. Baranov also mentioned another Russian ship currently on its way to Hawaii, to which Schäffer might turn for assistance. The ship he referred to was the round-the-world *Rurik*, under the command of Otto von Kotzebue, which had left St Petersburg in July 1815.

From Podushkin's own journal we can follow the progress of his mission. In April, as has been said, he arrived in the *Otkrytie* on the island of Hawaii, only to find that Schäffer had already left for Oahu. Nonetheless, Podushkin obtained an audience with Kamehameha. He and his six oarsmen (he claims) then 'made a great impression' on the King who 'liked my uniform so much that he shamelessly asked for it'.

Kamehameha had evidently heard some worrying things either from Schäffer or someone in his entourage, and he was not one to hold back from expressing the matters that were on his mind. Podushkin was clearly surprised when he 'frankly stated that he had heard that Russian ships would arrive soon to take over his possessions. I reassured him in this respect as far as I could, but in the end he was still in doubt'.

Podushkin entertained the king and an 'enormous crowd' with the Aleut dances. The king began to get more and more cordial, insisting that they stay. He tried to buy their howitzer, which they would not sell. Podushkin told him he would return as soon as possible, and 'the King told me that he would wait for me and promised to abstain from trading with anyone else until my return'. They said goodbye, exchanging kisses 'in the Russian manner'.

Podushkin also seems to have overlooked Kamehameha's claims to overlordship of all the islands, and was convinced that 'if the Americans could be driven out [of Kauai], this island would become ours. The Americans are liars and calumniators. The captains of their ships flatter the chief manager of Novo-Arkhangelsk [ie Baranov] when they see him, but behind his back spread tales about him as well as about the Russians in general. These tales are so vile that one cannot listen without revulsion to what they have said on the Sandwich Islands about my countrymen'. He reminded himself of the proverb: 'Be patient, Cossack, and you will become an ataman'.

At some point in May, relations with Kaumualii became a touchy business. On 21 May, the tsar's birthday, Podushkin invited the king to celebrate. He accepted but at the last minute cried off, apologetically 'as a result of intrigues on the part of the Americans'. This was 'an insult' to the Russian flag and force was now threatened against him. Kaumualii, in consequence, finally showed up, claiming that he had 'been seeking our friendship for a long time'. Schäffer then gave him his uniform. Kaumualii announced to the whole crew of the ship *Otkrytie* his decision to become a subject of the Russian Crown. He took the flag from the *Otkrytie*, and on his way home that evening, amid various salutes 'he raised the Russian flag on the spot. The people with him greeted it with hurrahs'.

The next day, the exact story of how the deal was reached was recorded by Podushkin. 'The King and his wives met me under the trees, where the King seated me in an armchair near to himself. The square where the meal was served was covered with grasses and flowers. Thirty men of the King's guard, somewhat resembling soldiers, stood in orderly formation in front of the King's residence. The crowd grew gradually until there were a thousand people or more standing at a distance of thirty feet from us. At one o'clock we were seated at the table which was similar to an officers' table . . . the King himself offered a toast to our Imperial Majesty while cannon were fired and his guard shouted "hurrah". After that we drank the King's health. Three Sandwich men performed a rifle drill, the Aleuts sang songs and danced, and one man gave an exhibition of horsemanship . . . thus a whole day passed and apparently a full accord was reached with Kaumualii who agreed to all of the doctor's demands and gave his consent for the opening of a good trading branch by the company and for the establishment of a colony in this rich land and wonderful climate'.

The king was greatly excited on taking possession of the cannon, now delivered by Podushkin. All the islanders participated in getting it from the longboat to the shore, and then to the King's palace. 'Sand and rocks were no obstacle. One man got under the wheel and lost a leg'. Then Podushkin went ashore and fired a grenade 'which exploded with great noise'. The king was so pleased with it 'that the doctor might have bartered it for almost a full cargo of fragrant wood'.

Just eight days later—this was now May 1816—another Russian ship, the *Il'mena* unexpectedly arrived from California, after an adventurous voyage.

Il'mena had been bought late in 1813, and sent early in 1814 to Fort Ross with supplies. Aboard was a party of Aleuts, led by Timofei Tarakanov and John Elliot de Castro, former physician to Kamehameha (who had gone to Alaska and there been employed by Baranov because of his knowledge of Spanish). *Il'mena* had poached off the California coast; but in 1814 Tarakanov and eleven Aleuts were seized near San Pedro by the Spanish. Eventually, Tarakanov and some of the Aleuts were freed to rejoin the ship, but the ship itself suffered damage while attempting to sail from Bodega to Sitka at the end of 1815; the captain, Wadsworth, decided to stay for the winter, and sailed in April 1816. The ship now sprang a leak, and Wadsworth detoured to Hawaii for repairs, arriving in May 1816.

Schäffer now 'ordered' Wadsworth to remain at Honolulu, leaving the factory in charge of a *promyshlennik* named Kicherev. Schäffer himself went to Hawaii for a cargo and to get an order from Kamehameha, to give to Kaumualii. He didn't get it. Once again there is a hint of disputes, of which no details are available, and once again it is possible that these disputes concerned Kamehameha's anxieties over Russian claims to Kauai.

Schäffer now went to Kauai and anchored in Waimea Bay. Here conditions were good. In fact Kaumualii was already having anxieties about having appropriated the cargo of the *Bering*. Back in February 1816, he had written to Baranov saying that he was sending furs with Ebbets on *Enterprise*, which had stopped *en route* for the northwest coast, and would deliver other Russian property, or compensation, if a ship was sent. And indeed, Podushkin collected some of the furs from the *Bering*, and loaded them on the *Okrytie*.

Kaumualii, on seeing Schäffer, now became tearful again (a habit of his, it seems), complaining of Kamehameha, and asking for an alliance with Russia; he was even wanting to get back all the other islands. He did not mention the small matter of the peace he had made in 1810 with Kamehameha, and the fact that he had agreed to pay tribute to him and acknowledge his overlordship.

Schäffer was now very excited. Vancouver had claimed the islands of Hawaii in 1794, but Britain had taken it no further. So Schäffer assumed the islands were open to the first claimants. And here was a personal invitation from someone claiming to be the rightful ruler. Schäffer had the chance to take the initiative. By June 1816, Schäffer had, on paper at least, achieved all his objectives and more. Kaumualii had agreed to restore what remained of *Bering*'s cargo, and (dressed all the while in Podushkin's uniform with epaulets, hat and cutlass) he had pledged allegiance to Alexander I in a formal ceremony witnessed by Schäffer himself and also by Podushkin. He also promised to trade exclusively with RAC for sandalwood, to allow factories anywhere in its domains to supply men to erect company buildings and plantations, and furnish a cargo of sandalwood when it was ready. Schäffer gave him a silver medal and made him a line staff officer in the Russian navy, to be honoured as such on all formal occasions.

Perhaps to celebrate, Schäffer now began building a house at Waimea, and establishing a trading post in a stone building given to the RAC by Kaumualii. On 11 June, leaving two Russians and some Aleuts, he sailed for Oahu on *Otkrytie*. Schäffer says his intention was to sort out trade affairs on Oahu, and there await the company ship *Kadiak*. Instead, *Otkrytie* ran into a severe storm, lost two masts, and was obliged to take shelter on Niihau; eventually, after repairs, Podushkin was able to take her to Alaska.

So Schäffer went back to Waimea with a baidarka and one Aleut. By July 1816 Schäffer seemed to be suffering from delusions of grandeur and, calling himself von Sheffer, he and the king exchanged still wider commitments in a secret treaty. Kaumualii agreed to send an army of 500 men, under Schäffer, to conquer islands held by Kamehameha and help build a Russian fort on each of them. The king agreed to give the RAC half of Oahu, plus all its sandalwood, plus strips of land on other islands, and 'to refuse to trade with citizens of the USA'. Schäffer agreed to provide necessary ships and ammunition, to supply the king with fish and timber from the mainland, and 'to introduce a better economy, which will make the natives educated and prosperous'. As a token of esteem, Kaumualii put his mark on a paper making Baranov a chief of the Sandwich Islands, in recognition of all he had done for the islanders. This deal looked like a tremendous *coup* for Schäffer which would have given Baranov and the RAC everything they could have hoped for, but the fact was that Kamehameha and not Kaumalii was generally recognised as the overall chief or king of the Hawaii Islands. Ignoring this point, Schäffer reported to the main office of the RAC that he had 'finished his business in twenty-four hours and saved the company 20,000 piastres'.

Soon after, the American schooner *Lydia*, under Henry Gyzelaar, arrived from Oahu with messages from the Russians there. *Il'mena* was still at Honolulu (as requested) and now *Kadiak* had arrived, under its American captain George Young. *Kadiak* was leaking, but the arrival of its crew was useful. Gyzelaar brought an offer from Ebbets, to sell the *Lydia* to Kaumualii. The king was keen to accept the offer, and Schäffer, to keep his word, felt obliged to buy it for him. He sailed to Oahu on the *Lydia* to make the arrangements.

In Honolulu at the beginning of September, in the presence of John and Richard Ebbets, Nathan Winship, Gyzelaar, George Young (who was loyal to Baranov) and Wadsworth and others, Schäffer purchased the *Lydia*, giving a promise of payment by the RAC. He then invited all the party to dinner at the Russian factory, but the affair broke up in a quarrel with John Young (who was no friend of the Russians), angry at the presence of two armed Russian guards at the factory. He saw this as a breach of Hawaiian sovereignty, perhaps rightly recognising the implications.

Sending his three ships off to Waimea, Schäffer now sailed on another American ship the *Avon* (Captain Isaac Whittemore) for the bay of Hanalei on the north side of Kauai. He liked this place, and later gave the *Lydia* to Kaumualii in exchange for the port and valley of Hanalei, in a convention witnessed by captains Whittemore, William Smith and Gyzelaar. Then he bought the *Avon* from Whittemore for 200,000 piastres, payable by the RAC in Sitka. In thanks, and for added security, Kaumualii also contributed three cargoes of sandalwood for this. By September Whittemore was sailing for Sitka in the *Avon*, to claim the money, with Antipatr aboard.

Schäffer now began the construction of a stronghold of lava blocks, called Fort Elizabeth, after the consort of Alexander I. He also sent Gyzelaar to Honolulu on *Lydia* to see how the company post there was faring. Ten days later, it returned bringing some men from the factory, with news that natives, egged on by John Young and 'the American hotheads' had burned it. What was more, Chief Kalanimoku ('Billy Pitt') in consultation with George Young, had then begun to build another fort there to forestall a future Russian incursion.

Shortly after this the ship *O'Cain* (Captain Robert McNeil) arrived at Waimea with passengers captains Nathan Winship, William Smith, Richard Ebbets, Henry Gyzelaar and others. These came ashore and tried hauling down the Russian flag, but Kaumualii's guards stopped them. It was all the same an ominous portent of worse to come. But for the moment matters still looked hopeful for the Russians. Schäffer went to Hanalei to raise the Russian flag in a formal ceremony. Kaumualii had asked him to give Russian names to the place, and to the chiefs there. This resulted in the valley becoming 'Schäfferthal', while the local chief Taera became 'Vorontsov'. Two forts overlooking the river mouth became Alexander and Barclay, named after the tsar and Barclay de Tolly. Also, the Hanapepe River became the River Don, on the left bank of which Tarakanov got a village with eleven families.

Returning to Waimea on 8 October, Schäffer was given a seven-gun salute. Other notables of the island proclaimed their devotion by deeding land for gifts. The local chiefs were now keen to ingratiate themselves with Schäffer; one declaration from Kamahalolani exists, declaring his eternal love for Russians and the Russian-American Company. 'From the Russians' he said, 'we never heard anything that was not good. From the Americans we have heard a great deal of evil'.

Schäffer was now very optimistic: 'In five days I expect the Russian ship which is now in Oahu', that is, Kotzebue's. Schäffer even presumes to inform Baranov about it, telling him that Kotzebue will visit him next year. By early December 1816 came word of the arrival at Honolulu of the Russian brig *Rurik* under Kotzebue. Schäffer thought this spelt the end of his difficulties, and was expecting the *Rurik* to come to his aid. But it didn't, and far from being the end of his difficulties, Schäffer's troubles were about to become far more serious. Captain Wadsworth of the *Il'mena* told Kaumualii that Schäffer intended to arrest him and his chiefs. Schäffer retaliated by ordering Wadsworth's arrest and confinement on board the ship. In Wadsworth's place, he was obliged to appoint another American, Voroll Madson. Then came news of trouble at Hanalei, where natives had killed an Aleut and burned the Russian distillery.

In January 1817 word finally came from Baranov, in a message brought by the *Cossack* (Captain Brown). Whittemore had arrived in Sitka on the *Avon* expecting payment for it. Instead, Baranov had repudiated the transaction and Whittemore had then gone to California and Hawaii, keeping the ship as his own. There is no record of Baranov's reaction to the news of what Schäffer had been doing because his letter has not survived, but he is quoted as forbidding further speculation and demanding the return of the *Kadiak* and the *Il'mena*, their crews, and the capital entrusted to Schäffer. Evidently Baranov was losing patience, if not all confidence in Schäffer.

Schäffer, it seems, was still banking on Kotzebue, his fellow German; Kotzebue's *Travels* tell us what he had been doing. *Rurik* had picked up Kotzebue's friend, Elliot de Casrto, in California and on the way to

Hawaii he had turned out to be very agreeable company. But on arrival in Hawaii, they had been struck by the 'reserved and suspicious' manner of the first native they met. 'Elliot was of the opinion that some disagreeable circumstance had occurred on the island, which required the greatest precaution'.

Elliot went ashore to find out. He was told that two Russian ships had stopped there five months earlier, and that there had been 'disputes'. When the ships left, their officers had threatened to return soon with strong force and a ship of war. Kamehameha told Elliot that Schäffer had come to botanise, but had gone to Oahu, profaned the sanctuary, and persuaded Kaumualii to rebel.

Kotzebue was grateful to Elliot, without whose help "we should probably have fallen victims to the faults of others'. He told Kamehameha that he wanted nothing to do with Schäffer's enterprise. He went on to Honolulu where he heard more complaints, this time from Billy Pitt. 'I assured him', wrote Kotzebue 'that everything done by Schäffer had been contrary to the will of the Emperor, and tried to make him easy respecting the future'. The Russians were clearly now trying to dissociate themselves from some of Schäffer's activities. Kotzebue found many new signs of insensitive behaviour by Schäffer, such as putting up flags as markers while surveying the harbour; and wanting to inspect the new fort, which he had been told was 'taboo'.

Kotzebue summed up the situation as he saw it in his *Travels*: 'the Sandwich Islands will remain what they are—the free port and staple of all the navigators of the seas. But should any foreign power conceive the foolish idea of taking possession of them the jealous vigilance of the Americans, who possess the almost exclusive commerce of these seas, and the secure protection of England, would not be wanting to frustrate the undertaking'. He had left Honolulu in December 1816, not bothering to go to Kauai himself.

Opposition to Schäffer and his activities was now growing, and there were signs of official disapproval by Baranov and also by the RAC main office. Moreover, Kamehameha was also increasingly unhappy at Kaumualii's association with the Russians. According to Osipov's report, Kamehameha had told Kaumualii that he had to expel the Russians, or he would be in serious trouble.

Schäffer got back to Waimea on 9 April 1817, after a prolonged stay at Hanalei. There he found that Adams, *en route* to Canton, delivering orders to Kaumualii from Kamehameha, had stopped by and tried to destroy the Russian flag, though he was prevented from doing so. Adams' own log records this on 12 March: 'gave the King our ensign to hoist in lieu of the Russians, who said it was on account of his having no other'.

When Schäffer got to Waimea, he was received by the king normally, except that as he noted, the king did not raise the Russian flag or salute. He also saw that the king had been taking too many goods from the company warehouse. Psychological warfare now began against Schäffer. On 16 April the *Columbia* (Captain Jennings) called at Waimea; Schäffer was misinformed by Jennings that Russia and the United States were falling out, indeed that the Russian ambassador had left America. A group of formidable Americans were in Hawaii about this time; it seems they had decided that Schäffer had to go. Captain Ebbets on *Enterprise*, Caleb Brintnell (*Zephyr*), Dixey Wildes (*Paragon*), Isaac Whittemore (*Avon*) and William Heath Davis (*Eagle*) were all warning Kamehameha about Schäffer.

But Kaumualii was still co-operative. In April Jennings told Schäffer that an agreement he had made with Kaumualii to exchange the *Columbia* for sandalwood was not being acted upon. Schäffer chided the king about this breach of agreement, and asked him to load Russian ships so they could be sent to Sitka. The king agreed, and on 23 April reaffirmed his previous agreement.

On 7 May Schäffer heard rumours of boats arriving from Oahu and 'news of war'. He hurried back to Waimea to see the king. He found him at a gathering of ministers, surrounded by a thousand men. Schäffer again demanded that Russian ships be loaded. As he turned to walk to his factory he was seized by a native and 'six American seamen' and told to leave Kauai at once. Over his protests he was put in a leaky boat (according to Tarakanov the Natives had drilled holes in it, to try and kill him) and forced to paddle to *Kadiak*. From there, he heard cannon shots, and saw a 'pirate' flag being raised.

Schäffer and his men now sailed the *Kadiak* and *Il'mena* round to Hanalei, to collect some property, and perhaps hoping to make a stand at Fort Alexander. On the way Schäffer wrote to Kaumualii, scolding him and warning him. But by now, Kaumualii had already written to Baranov, explaining why he was expelling Schäffer 'I mean to have free trade as I used to before', he wrote, evidently meaning that he was claiming the right to trade with the ships of any nation.

At Fort Alexander Schäffer made a formal claim to the whole island of Kauai. The Russian flag was raised, and the men were persuaded to sign a compact, to make a stand. Schäffer was still optimistic that with Russian reinforcements expected from Sitka, he was capable of crushing the 'Indian bandits' as he called them.

Kadiak, under the loyal Captain George Young was not seaworthy, so Schäffer put Young in charge of *Il'mena* and sent a report to Baranov of his expulsion. By now Schäffer was becoming almost incoherent in his reports. This letter to Baranov in particular was rambling, slightly evasive and even chaotic. But it does throw some light on the reasons which underlay his seizure and arrest of Wadsworth, namely that Wadsworth had been openly critical of, and even hostile to what the Russians had been doing. He had said that he wanted to help the King drive the Russians from Kauai.

Schäffer's relations with Kaumualii were about to disintegrate totally. In his letter to Baranov, Schäffer complained that he had sent a letter to Kaumualii 'and the barbarian sent back an answer without his royal signature'. All the same, he was still hopeful that with reinforcements the Russians would soon 'be on top again' and the Sandwich Islands would be Russian.

But Schäffer's game was finally up. In another brief letter to Baranov, Schäffer describes the dangerous situation he and his men were now in, and stressed the need to get away. '[T]oday the whole crew refused to stay here any longer and . . . we decided to go to the island Oahu, there to repair our ships as well as possible and to await your decisions'. Schäffer himself went in the leaky *Kadiak* to Honolulu with some Russians, including Tarakanov, and more than forty Aleuts. He had hoped to stay there and wait for reinforcements, but when these unwelcome Russian guests arrived at Honolulu, there was uncertainty what to do with them. They were kept outside the harbour for eight days in their leaking ship. At one moment they were told that Schäffer had to be handed over in irons. Tarakanov refused to do this, despite being told by one American, 'it is better that one man should die than sixty-six'. Schäffer insisted on hanging his flag upside down, to indicate his vessel was in distress, but the sight of an upside-down flag annoyed all the American ships in the harbour on 4 July. Finally an American brig, *Panther*, under Captain Isaiah Lewis, who was already familiar with Schäffer, offered him passage to Canton, leaving the remaining Russians, headed by Tarakanov, behind with *Kadiak*. The other Russians agreed with this plan; by now they probably wanted to get rid of Schäffer who finally left on 7 July. With Schäffer went any chance of reviving the whole Russian Hawaiian enterprise.

Schäffer's failed escapades had come at a high price. Hawaii was a great prize in Russian eyes; indeed it had offered the key to mastery of the whole ocean. With Hawaii now gone, Russia's other American possessions suddenly looked fragile and illusory.

In January 1818, Lieutenant Ludwig von Hagemeister broke the news to an old and exhausted Alexander Baranov that he was replacing him as chief manager of the colonies. The urbane Hagemeister, who had worked under the British Lord Nelson and spoke six languages, represented the new, aristocratic—if unambitious—face of Russian America. 'The south is not so benevolent' he later admitted, 'the Sandwich Islands have refused us, and in Ross there are no sea otters . . .'.

The Russian retreat to fortress Siberia had commenced.

What was now left for Baranov? 'At times' wrote one contemporary, 'he considered moving to the Sandwich Islands and ending his days in those charming valleys . . . presented him by his old friend King Kamehameha, and which even after the Schäffer episode, were considered part of Baranov's property . . .'. But in the end, Lieutenant Hagemeister made it clear that Baranov was being recalled to Russia, to 'render account' for his long years in America. He was suspected, in St Petersburg, of having fiddled the books. Thus did the old man depart from New Archangel on 27 November 1818, bound for a Russia he had left over 28 years earlier.

He was not destined to reach it. After a stopover in Batavia (today's Java), Baranov, now aged 72, fell victim to the tropical airs, and died. Across the Pacific, Kamehameha would follow his great counterpart to the grave within a month. The deaths of these two old-fashioned heroes would foreshadow not only the end of Russian America, but the end of an independent Hawaii. The seeds of the forty-ninth and fiftieth states had been planted, and the rise of the United States as a global superpower had become certain.

BIBLIOGRAPHY

Alekseev, AI (1990) *The Destiny of Russian America 1741–1867* (Fairbanks, Alaska and Kingston, Ontario, Limestone Press).

Bancroft, H (1886) *History of Alaska 1730–1835, Works, vol 33* (San Francisco, AL Bancroft).

Barratt, G (1981) *Russia in Pacific Waters 1715–1825*. Includes notes on whereabouts of Billings' diary (Vancouver, University of British Columbia Press).

—— (1983) *Russian Shadows on the British Northwest Coast of North America 1810–1890* (Vancouver, University of British Columbia Press).

—— (1987) *The Russian Discovery of Hawaii* (Editions Limited).

Beaglehole, JC (ed) (1967) *The Journals of Captain James Cook, Vol III, The Voyage of the Resolution and Discovery 1776–1780* (Hakluyt Society, Cambridge University Press).

—— (1973) *Cook and the Russians* (Addendum).

Bolkhovitinov, N (1966) (tr E Levin 1975) *The Beginnings of Russian-American Relations 1775–1815* (Cambridge, Mass, Harvard University Press).

Burney, J (1817) *A Memoir on the Geography of the North-Eastern Part of Asia, and on the Question whether Asia and America are Contiguous, or are Separated by the Sea* (London, Royal Society of London Proceedings).

Busch, BC and Gough, BM (eds) (1997) *Fur Traders from New England, The Boston Men in the North Pacific 1787–1800* (Arthur H Clark).

Campbell, A (1816) *A Voyage Round the World, from 1806 to 1812* (Edinburgh, Archibald Constable and Company).

Chamisso, A (ed Winkler) (1975) *Sämtliche Werke, Band II, Reise um die Welt* (Verlag, Munchen). No English translation exists.

Chevigny, H (1946) *Lord of Alaska. Baranov and the Russian Adventure* (New York, Viking Press).

—— (1966) *Russian America, The Great Alaskan Venture 1741–1867* (New York, Viking Press).

Christie, I (1993) *The Benthams in Russia 1780–1791* (Oxford, Berg Publishers).

Cochrane, J (1830) *Narrative of a Pedestrian Journey* (London, Henry Colburn).

Corney, P (1896) *Voyages in the Northern Pacific 1813–1818* (Honolulu, Thos. G. Thrum).

Coxe, W (1780) *Account of the Russian Discoveries between Asia and America* (London, Cadell).

Cross, A (2001) *Catherine the Great and the British* (Nottingham, Astra Press).

Davydov, GI (tr C Bearne 1977) *Two Voyages to Russian America 1802–1807* (Kingston, Ontario, Limestone Press).

Daws, G (1968) *Shoal of Time. A History of the Hawaiian Islands* (New York, Macmillan Publishing).

De Madariaga, I (1981) *Russia in the age of Catherine the Great* (New Haven, Ct, Yale University Press).

—— (1990) *Catherine the Great* (New Haven, Ct, Yale University Press).

Dietrich, W (1995) *Northwest Passage: The Great Columbia River* (New York, Simon & Schuster).

Dixon, EJ (1992) *Quest for the Origins of the First Americans* (Albuquerque, University of New Mexico Press).

Dmytryshyn, B and Crownhart-Vaughan, EAP (eds) (tr 1988) *Russian Penetration of the North Pacific Ocean 1700–1797, a Documentary Record* Vol II (Portland, Oregon, Historical Society Press).

—— (tr 1989) *The Russian-American Colonies, 1798–1867, a Documentary Record* Vol III (Portland, Oregon Historical Society Press).

Dumond, D (1987) *Eskimos and Aleuts* rev edn (New York, Thames & Hudson).

Edwards, P (ed) (1999) *The Journals of Captain Cook* (London, Penguin Classics).

Essig, EO *et al* (1991) *Fort Ross, California Outpost of Russian Alaska 1812–1841* (Fairbanks, Alaska, Limestone Press).

Gibson, JR (1992) *Otter Skins, Boston Ships and China Goods: The Maritime Fur Ttrade of the Northwest Coast 1785–1841* (Seattle, University of Washington Press).

Gideon, H (ed R Pierce) (1979) *The Round the World Voyage of the Hieromonk Gideon 1803–1809* (Kingston, Ontario, Limestone Press).

Golovin, PN (1862) (tr Dmytryshyn and Crownhart-Vaughan 1979) *The End of Russian America,* Final government report on state of colonies (Portland, Oregon Historical Society).

—— (1863) (tr Dmytryshyn and Crownhart-Vaughan 1983).

Civil and Savage Encounters 1860–1861 (Portland, Oregon Historical Society).

Gough, BM (1992) *The Northwest Coast* (University of British Columbia Press).

Gowen, H (1919) *The Napoleon of the Pacific. Kamehameha the Great* (New York and Chicago, Fleming H Revell Co).

Henderson, D (1944) *From the Volga to the Yukon* (New York, Hastings House).

Hittell, T (1885) *History of California*, 2 vols (San Francisco, Pacific Press Publishing House).

Howay, F (ed) (1941) *Voyages of the Columbia to the Northwest Coast 1787–90 and 1790–93* (Boston, The Massachusetts Historical Society).

Hunt, WR (1975) *Arctic Passage, The Turbulent History of the Land and People of the Bering Sea 1697–1975* (New York, Scribner's Sons).

Inglis, R (ed) (1992) *Spain and the North Pacific Coast* (Montrreal and Kingston, McGill-Queen's University Press).

Irving, W (1839) *Astoria* (London, R Bentley).

Kelly, L (1981) *St Petersburg, a Travellers' Companion* (London, Constable).

Khlebnikov, KT (1835) (ed R Pierce 1973) *Life of Baranov* (Kingston, Ontario, Limestone Press).

—— (1861) (tr Dmytryshyn and Crownhart-Vaughan 1979) *Colonial Russian-America 1817–1832* (Portland, Oregon Historical Society).

Krasheninnikov (1755); reprint Richmond Publishing Co (1973) *A History of Kamchatka and the Kurilski Islands* (Richmond, Surrey, Richmond Publishing Co).

Kruzenshtern AJ (tr 1814) *Voyage Round the World* (London, J Murray).

Kushner, HI (1975) *Conflict on the Northwest Coast: American-Russian Rivalry in the Pacific Northwest, 1790–1867* (Westport, Ct, Greenwood Press).

La Pérouse, JFG (1797) *Voyage autour du Monde* (Paris, Imprimerie de la République).

Langsdorff, GH (tr 1813–14) *Voyages and Travels* (London, H Colburn).

Laughlin, WS and Harper, A (eds) (1979) *The First Americans: Origins, Affinities and Adaptations* (New York, G Fischer).

Ledyard, J (ed S Watrous) (1966) *John Ledyard's Journey through Russia and Siberia 1787–88* (Madison, University of Wisconsin Press).

Lincoln, WB (1993) *Conquest of a Continent* (New York, Random House).

Lloyd, C (ed) (1959) *A Memoir of James Trevenen by C.V. Penrose* (London, Navy Records Society).

Lower, JA (1978) *Ocean of Destiny* (Vancouver, University of British Columbia Press).

Mahr, AC (1932) *The Visit of the 'Rurik' to San Francisco in 1816.* Includes translation of Chamisso's account (Stanford, Stanford University Press).

Makarova, RV (1968) (eds/trs Pierce/Donnelly 1975), *Russians on the Pacific, 1743–1799* (Kingston, Ontario, Limestone Press).

March, GP (1996) *Eastern Destiny* (Westport, Ct, Praeger).

Miller, DH (republished 1981) *The Alaska Treaty* (Kingston, Ontario, Limestone Press).

Munro, WH (1917) *Tales of an Old Sea Port.* Includes John D'Wolf's Voyage of the Juno (Princeton, Princeton University Press).

Okun, SB (tr C Ginsburg 1951) *The Russian-American Company* (Cambridge, Mass, Harvard University Press).

Owens, KN (ed) (1985) *Wreck of Sv Nikolai: Two Narratives of the First Russian Expedition to Oregon Country 1808–1810* (Portland, Oregon Historical Society).

Pierce, R (ed) (1972), *Rezanov Reconnoitres California, 1806* (San Francisco, Book Club of California).

—— (ed) (1976) *Russia's Hawaiian Adventure, 1815–1817* (Kingston, Ontario, Limestone Press).

—— (1986) *Builders of Alaska. The Russian Governors 1818–1867* (Kingston, Ontario, Limestone Press).

—— (ed) (1990) *Russian America: A Biographical Dictionary* (Fairbanks, Alaska, Limestone Press).

Porter, KW (1931, 2 vols) *John Jacob Astor, Businessman.*

Ray, DJ (1975) *The Eskimos of the Bering Strait 1650 –1898* (Seattle, University of Washington Press).

Sarychev, G (1806) *The Frozen Ocean and the Northeast Sea* (NB this is also included in: *A Collection of Modern and Contemporary Voyages and Travels* (1807) vols V and VI) (London, R Phillips).

Sauer, M (1802) *Account of a Geographical and Astronomical Expedition to the Northern Parts of Russia* (London, T Cadell).

Taylor, A and Kuykendall, R (eds) (1930) *Hawaiian Islands: Papers Read during the Captain Cook Sesquicentenial Celebration 1928.*

Tikhmenev, PA (1979) *A History of the Russian American Company* (vol 2, *Documents*) (Kingston, Ontario, Limestone Press).

—— (1863) *Historical Review of Formation of the Russian-American Company* (Washington Press).

Vancouver, G A (1984) *Voyage of Discovery to the North Pacific Ocean and Round the World 1791–95* (London, Hakluyt Society, London).

INDEX

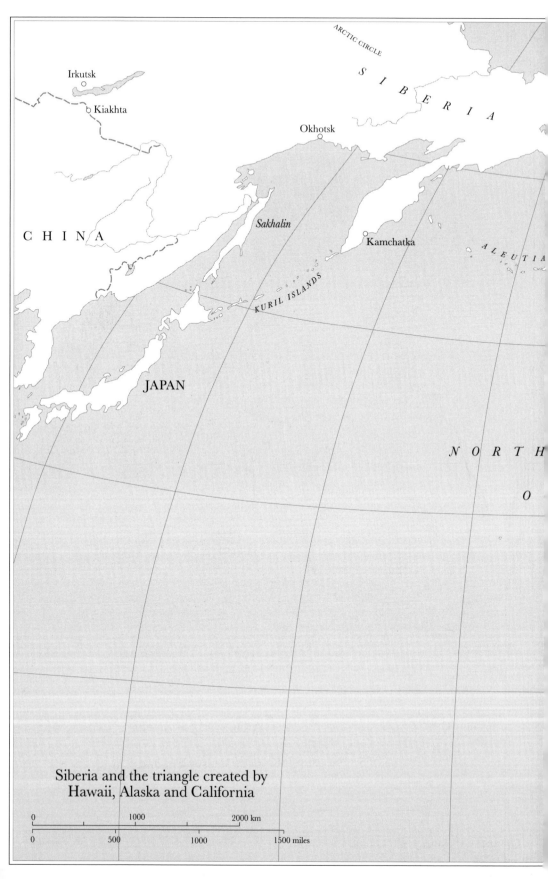

Siberia and the triangle created by
Hawaii, Alaska and California